Language in Culture

Comparative Studies of Cultures and Civilizations

Edited by

ROBERT REDFIELD *and* MILTON SINGER

Studies in Chinese Thought
ARTHUR F. WRIGHT, *Editor*

**Studies in Islamic Cultural History*
GUSTAVE E. VON GRUNEBAUM, *Editor*

Language in Culture
HARRY HOIJER, *Editor*

The Little Community
ROBERT REDFIELD

Unity and Variety in Muslim Civilization
GUSTAVE E. VON GRUNEBAUM, *Editor*

Village India
McKIM MARRIOTT, *Editor*

Chinese Thought and Institutions
JOHN K. FAIRBANK, *Editor*

*Available only as a Memoir of the American Anthropological Association

LANGUAGE IN CULTURE

Conference on the Interrelations of Language and Other Aspects of Culture

Edited by

HARRY HOIJER

Contributors

FRANKLIN FEARING — NORMAN A. McQUOWN

JOSEPH H. GREENBERG — STANLEY NEWMAN

CHARLES F. HOCKETT — C. F. VOEGELIN

HARRY HOIJER — J. F. YEGERLEHNER

FLORENCE M. ROBINETT

THE UNIVERSITY OF CHICAGO PRESS

CHICAGO & LONDON

This volume is also published as Memoir No. 79 of
The American Anthropological Association

Library of Congress Catalog Card Number: 54-11977

THE UNIVERSITY OF CHICAGO PRESS, CHICAGO & LONDON
The University of Toronto Press, Toronto 5, Canada

Published 1954. Sixth Impression 1967. Printed in the United States of America

FOREWORD

THIS series of publications expresses results of a program of intercultural studies made possible by grants from the Ford Foundation. One aspect of the program, which is represented in the two earlier publications (*Studies in Chinese Thought*, edited by Arthur F. Wright, 1953; and *Studies in Islamic Cultural History*, edited by G. E. von Grunebaum, 1954), is the encouragement and financial support of groups of specialists who undertake characterization and comparison of major civilizations. This part of the program continues: two more publications on Muslim civilization, one on social organization in Chinese civilization, and a fourth on Indian civilization as seen through village life are in preparation.

The present volume brings forward another aspect of the program: appraisal and improvement of the methodology of such characterizations and comparisons. Concepts and methods for the comparison of civilizations—indeed, for comparison of the cultures of small and simple societies—are uncertain and problematic. Consideration of these methodological problems goes forward today in many places; to the effort, the grants from the Ford Foundation have allowed us to add at the University of Chicago a series of seminars and investigations in which consideration is given to many of the questions about the intellectual structure and the procedure that need be developed if the comparisons are to become more dependable. Results of this endeavor will also appear in future publications of this series.

The nature of the relationship between a language and the culture or civilization embodied in those who speak that language is an old and a difficult problem of this kind. Here viewpoints have been exceedingly various. The study of a language, almost as "pure form," as a system of sounds and signs, is to be contrasted with the view of a language as an exposition of a unique view of the world. For many years students of particular languages and literatures, and students of that more general and widely comparative kind of study that is called "linguistics," said what they had to say about the relation of language to thought and to culture. Then interest in these problems was suddenly mobilized by the publication of that series of papers by Benjamin L. Whorf which is cited on the first page of the Preface that follows. Working especially with Hopi, Whorf found in that language a "hidden metaphysics." The very categories of the language predisposed Hopi to think about the nature of the universe in ways different from the ways consistent with speaking English or Russian. Was this true?

The discussions of the problem at the International Symposium of Anthropology held in New York in 1952 tended to the conclusion that the view of Whorf was unproved but in much need of further investigation. The reader might want to read the substance of what was there said; he will find it in a paper by Dr. Hoijer, "The Relation of Language to Culture," in *Anthropology Today: An Encyclopedic Inventory*, prepared under the direction of A. L. Kroeber (Chicago: University of Chicago Press, 1953), pages 554–73, and in *An Appraisal of Anthropology Today*, edited by Sol Tax *et al.* (Chicago: University of Chicago Press, 1953), especially pages 279–81 and 369–70.

The editors are grateful to Dr. Hoijer and his associates for undertaking that further investigation of the question, as precipitated by Whorf, in the conference that brought about this present publication. The possibilities and limitations of a comparison of cultures in terms of the "hidden metaphysics" of their languages are for the first time explored by a group of scholars drawn from several disciplines and familiar with the problem.

ROBERT REDFIELD
MILTON SINGER

CHICAGO, ILLINOIS

PREFACE

THE CONFERENCE which is reported in this volume was proposed originally by Robert Redfield, who also was instrumental in securing the financial aid to make it possible. It was Redfield's idea to bring together a small group of scholars, representative of linguistics, anthropology, psychology, philosophy, and other disciplines, who shared an interest in the problem of meaning and the relationship of language to other aspects of culture, and to have them discuss their own and others' efforts in this area of research. After some oral and written discussion of this project, Redfield and I drew up a preliminary statement of the objectives of such a conference, which may be summarized as follows.

1. To define, as clearly as possible, the problems raised by the attempt to interrelate language and other aspects of culture, particularly in reference to the hypothesis suggested in Benjamin L. Whorf's *Collected Papers on Metalinguistics* (Washington, D.C., 1952).

2. To review what has been done, and is being done, in the study and analysis of these problems.

3. To examine and discuss plans for future research, wherever possible in terms of particular projects and personnel, that may contribute to the solution of ethnolinguistic problems.

4. To provide, if possible, for the integration of the research of the scholars, whatever their academic discipline, who are working in the area.

The Conference was held in Chicago from March 23 to 27, 1953, inclusive, under the sponsorship of the Department of Anthropology, University of Chicago, and with the financial aid of the Ford Foundation. A list of participants is given below.

FRED EGGAN, Anthropology, University of Chicago.

FRANKLIN FEARING, Psychology, University of California, Los Angeles. (Chairman, Seventh Session.)

JOSEPH H. GREENBERG, Linguistics and Anthropology, Columbia University.

GUSTAVE E. VON GRUNEBAUM, Oriental Languages, University of Chicago.

ERIC HAMP, Linguistics, University of Chicago.

CHARLES F. HOCKETT, Linguistics, Cornell University.

HARRY HOIJER, Linguistics and Anthropology, University of California, Los Angeles. (Chairman.)

ABRAHAM KAPLAN, Philosophy, University of California, Los Angeles.

EDWARD A. KENNARD, Linguistics and Anthropology, Foreign Service Institute, Department of State.

ALFRED L. KROEBER, Anthropology, University of California, Berkeley.

ERIC H. LENNEBERG, Psychology and Linguistics, Massachusetts Institute of Technology.

FLOYD G. LOUNSBURY, Linguistics and Anthropology, Yale University.

NORMAN A. MCQUOWN, Linguistics and Anthropology, University of Chicago.

STANLEY NEWMAN, Linguistics and Anthropology, University of New Mexico.

ROBERT REDFIELD, Anthropology, University of Chicago.

JOHN M. ROBERTS, Anthropology, Harvard University.

MILTON SINGER, Philosophy and Anthropology, University of Chicago.

SOL TAX, Anthropology, University of Chicago.

C. F. VOEGELIN, Linguistics and Anthropology, Indiana University.

ARTHUR F. WRIGHT, History and Sinology, Stanford University.

Seven of the participants prepared papers on various phases of the subject to be discussed. Copies of these, in preliminary form, were sent to all the participants well in advance of the Conference, and served as a basis for the discussions. After the Conference, each author revised and enlarged his paper, often including in it new material suggested by the discussants, or amplifying his own data to meet criticism encountered at the Conference. The final versions of these papers make up Part I of this volume, and are printed without editorial revision or cutting.

The discussions were recorded both by stenotypy and on tape, and a typewritten transcript of 919 pages was prepared. This has been reduced to its present size by the editor and is presented as Part II of this volume. In preparing the transcript for publication, it was necessary (1) so to revise the material as to put it into standard written, as opposed to spoken, English form; (2) to eliminate repetitions which, however useful in oral discussion, are unnecessary to the written report; (3) to reduce severely or eliminate altogether material which in the light of the general trend of the discussion as a whole proved to be trivial or wholly irrelevant; and (4) to eliminate material presented orally but later incorporated into the revised papers. In some cases too, though these were very few, speeches were so poorly recorded as to be almost incomprehensible. These were rewritten by the editor when the sense intended could be determined; otherwise the material was eliminated. These cuts and revisions are not specifically indicated in the printed transcript.

It is too much to say that the Conference succeeded in all its objectives. As it turned out, the bulk of our time was devoted to the Whorf hypothesis and the many questions it raises; we did too little in the definition of particular research projects or in providing a strategy of research. There is little doubt in my mind, however, that all of us gained a new and better understanding of the Whorf hypothesis and its problems. As is clear from both papers and discussions, there was little agreement among the members of the Conference on what Whorf actually said, and there were many who severely criticized his findings. But the critical tone of the Conference was in no sense negative or destructive. Rather, the Conference directed its energies in the main to a better definition of the problems inherent in the interrelations of language and the rest of culture; we strove not so much to dismiss these problems as trivial or unimportant as to restate them and examine their implications. The record of our discussions certainly solves no problems; indeed, it raises a great many new ones. The record is, however, provocative, and it should serve as a stimulus, and perhaps even as a directive, to future and more productive research.

Speaking in the name of all the participants, I wish to record our thanks to Robert Redfield for his initiative in organizing the Conference; to Sol Tax, editor, American Anthropological Association, for his aid in publishing the proceedings; to the Department of Anthropology, University of Chicago, for its sponsorship and hospitality; to the Ford Foundation for financing the Conference; and to the court reporters, of Leon M. Golding and Associates, Chicago, for their excellent transcript. As editor, I am indebted as well to the authors of the papers included herein, for their co-operation in bringing this volume together, and to Anna M. Pikelis, editorial assistant, who helped enormously in the time-consuming task of preparing the manuscript for the press.

HARRY HOIJER

UNIVERSITY OF CALIFORNIA, LOS ANGELES

TABLE OF CONTENTS

PART I. THE PAPERS

PART II. THE DISCUSSIONS

INDEX

PART I

THE PAPERS

CONCERNING INFERENCES FROM LINGUISTIC TO NONLINGUISTIC DATA

JOSEPH H. GREENBERG

I. INTRODUCTION

IT IS THE great merit of Benjamin Whorf that by the enthusiasm and persuasiveness with which he presented his point of view he has become a major factor in arousing a widespread and growing interest in some of the most significant problems in the relation between linguistic and nonlinguistic phenomena. The present discussion is intended merely as a brief review of some of the basic issues raised by his writings. Occasional reference will be made also to similarly oriented approaches of both American and European writers. It seemed especially worth while to call attention to some of this latter work, since it can lend additional perspective to our understanding of the problems and since these contributions are apparently not as well known as might be expected in view of their inherent interest and their relevance to issues now being discussed in the United States.

There is a European tradition, particularly strong in the German-speaking world, which can be traced back at least as far as Herder in the latter part of the eighteenth century, but which first assumed central importance in the writings of Von Humboldt. The influence, direct and indirect, of Von Humboldt on the Continent has been a profound and continuing one, and may be seen in contemporaries or near-contemporaries such as Ernst Cassirer in philosophy and Johann Leo Weisgerber and Jost Trier in linguistics. A few citations may serve to illustrate the general resemblance of the approaches of these writers to that of Whorf. Thus Cassirer, himself a prominent exponent of this point of view, sums up the position of Von Humboldt in the following words: "The difference between languages derives, in his view, less from differences in sounds and signs than from differences of world-view" (1933: 20). Weisgerber writes concerning language: "As an intermediate psychic realm, it is clearly distinct from the area of 'objective meanings,' particularly in the sense that it is not a simple reflection of the world of objects, but rather embodies the result of an intellectual remolding of this world" (1949: 13).

Inasmuch as these resemblances in approach extend beyond such generalities to specific details, reference is made to them whenever relevant in the course of this exposition. One characteristic difference between European and American approaches, which lies in the sphere of value judgments, may be pointed out; European writers have, with some exceptions, taken a view of primitive mentality similar to that of Lévy-Bruhl. The world perspective stated to be revealed shows the primitive at an early prelogical stage of development. In the United States an equality of valuation is maintained, the scale, if anything, tending to weigh in favor of the primitive. (See, e.g., Whorf 1952: 31, and Lee 1940.)

The present paper is primarily analytic in scope. It is an attempt to classify the extremely varied assertions which have been made connecting linguistic and nonlinguistic behavior and, in regard to each class, to raise the question as to what types of evidence are relevant in establishing and verifying hypotheses.

In any specific attempt to connect linguistic with nonlinguistic phenomena, we may ask three kinds of questions: (1) What kinds of linguistic facts are being adduced in evidence? (2) With what other phenomena is a connection being made? (3) What is the nature of this connection? Under the first of these rubrics we ask whether the linguistic facts pertain to phonology, to grammar or to semantics. If, for example, they pertain to semantics, we may further inquire whether they are based on the meanings of some particular morpheme, of a morpheme class, of a construction, etc. Under the second heading come such questions as the following: Are the linguistic phenomena cited to be associated with facts of sense perception, logic, individual behavior, or cultural behavior? The third category involves the nature of the asserted connection. Is it a causal relation and, if so, which is the causal factor, the linguistic or the nonlinguistic? Or is it neither, the connection between the two being the result of a third factor? This is perhaps what is intended by some who do not view either the nonlinguistic or linguistic phenomena as primary but consider both the resultant of a third element, a "world view." Moreover, causality should not be confused with predictability. Perhaps only a predictability relation is discerned in some cases, without any claim to knowledge of the causal factors involved. Or it may be that the connection is merely a statistical probability of more than chance correlation between some aspects of language and extralinguistic phenomena.

The present paper is ordered about the first of these questions, the nature of the linguistic unit involved, since it seemed to provide the clearest focus of discussion. In what follows, no complete review of all possible or actual hypotheses is attempted. Attention is concentrated on those types of inference which have been most prominent in the literature.

II. INFERENCES FROM PHONOLOGY

Phonology has exercised a twin attraction and repulsion on those seeking to establish connections between linguistic and extralinguistic phenomena. On the one hand, this has been the area of dominant interest and greatest achievement for modern structural linguistics, thus providing linguistic data whose rigorous formulation furnishes excellent systematic material for further comparison with other classes of data. On the other hand, concrete and plausible theories are difficult to formulate because phonology is that aspect of language which appears to be the most autonomous and self-contained in its functioning and hence the most difficult to relate to other phenomena. With what cultural or other facts would one connect a contrast between aspirated and nonaspirated consonants in a given language? Where is the *tertium comparationis?*

Two approaches seem possible, the direct and the indirect. In the former, phonological phenomena are compared directly with extralinguistic events. In the latter, the comparison is mediated by first seeking correspondence between phonological and nonphonologic aspects of language and then connecting the latter with extralinguistic data.

The direct approach might well be based on something like Jakobson, Fant and Halle's over-all analysis of principles of phonemic contrast in terms of a small number of basic oppositions (1952). One might then proceed inductively and cross-culturally investigating whether certain principles of contrast show significant correlations with certain social or cultural features. Beyond the methodological difficulties inherent in all cross-cultural attempts, there remains the fact that favorable results would seem difficult to interpret by any plausible theories of interaction.

The indirect approach is exemplified in the ingenious scheme of Bally (1944) by which, in conformity with a widely held view regarding French and German national character, he seeks to characterize the French language as analytic and abstract as against the synthetic, phenomenalistic tendencies of German. The typical French word order, modified-modifier, as opposed to the German order, modifier-modified, is correlated with a tendency toward final stress in French as against initial stress in German (e.g., French *chapeau gris* vs. German *grauer Hut*). This, in turn, is brought into connection with the French preference for open syllables, the absence of complex phonemes (e.g., affricates) and of falling diphthongs. The opposite characteristics are found in German. We have, then, a proposed correlation between certain prevalent types of construction in morphology and certain phonological traits.

The question as to whether these morphological-phonological correlations are valid—a matter which might be tested by cross-linguistic comparisons—is clearly independent of the problem of the demonstrative values of these element-orders as marks of two types of mentality and cultural expression. One might well be valid without the other. Any attempt to show agreement between grammar and phonology, as, for example, Jakobson's systematic discussion of the matter (1948), would give indirect relevance to phonology, once hypotheses linking morphology and cultural features are advanced. The cumulative influence, in turn, of foreign patterns through the medium of loan words on the phonological structure of a language is emphasized by Hoijer in his discussion of linguistic and cultural change (1948).

In an area other than one of cultural behavior, that of sound-perception, the connection between phonological structure and external phenomena is obvious. That the phonological structure of one's own language in respect both of constituent phonemes and of permitted combinations, cited by Whorf as a linguistic pattern phenomenon par excellence, is a factor in the perception of unfamiliar sounds is clear from gross observation of foreign-language learning, the teaching of general phonetics, and similar experiences. Bloomfield has suggested a number of phenomena of perception and articulation in this area which, though plausible, are evidently not the result of observation under scientifically controlled conditions (1933: 80–84). These hypotheses might well be made the subject of co-operative experimental investigation by psychologists and linguists. Besides such psychological experimentation, there is available a considerable amount of data from historical linguistics regarding the systematic treatment of foreign sounds in loan words by various linguistic communities, which are relevant for the same problem.

III. INFERENCES FROM SEMANTICS

A. TERMINOLOGY

The great majority of inferences from language has been drawn from semantics, for the obvious reason that, outside of linguistic meanings (discussed below), the referents involved in the meaning relation are nonlinguistic events. Before approaching this complex field, it will be useful to specify a few definitions distinguishing different kinds of meanings. Some of these were first used by Bloomfield in his well-known book (1933), others by Nida (1951). In a few cases I have reluctantly added terms of my own.

1. A sememe is the meaning of a morpheme (e.g., of "hand," "-ing").

2. An episememe is the meaning of a construction (e.g., possession, actor-action).

3. A macrosememe is the meaning of an idiom. It applies in those cases where the meaning of a complex whole cannot be predicted from the constituent sememes and episememes (e.g., of "I'm from Missouri" in the meaning "I am skeptical").

4. An ethnosememe is a meaning whose referent involves the nonlinguistic aspects of a situation (e.g., of "house").

5. A linguisememe is a meaning whose referent involves the linguistic aspects of a situation (e.g., of "to" with the infinitive). The division into ethnosememes and linguisememes involves a separate basis of classification and cuts across the distinction of sememe, episememe, and macrosememe.

6. Elementary meaning unit (E.M.U.). This is a cover term for sememes, episememes, and macrosememes, the elementary units which in combination make up more complex linguistic forms up to sentence.

7. Complex meaning unit (C.M.U.). The meaning of a structural complex containing more than one E.M.U. (e.g., the meaning of a phrase).

8. Sentential meaning. The meaning of a maximal linguistic structure (i.e., of a sentence). It is a special case of complex meaning unit (C.M.U.).

9. Generic meaning. The meaning common to a specified group of E.M.U.'s, e.g., "male" in English as a common meaning in the following kinship terms: father, son, brother, uncle, nephew, grandfather, grandson.

Corresponding to the terms sememe, episememe, and macrosememe we have seme, episeme, and macroseme. These latter are subvariants of the respective units. Seme : sememe : : phone : phoneme. For example, the sememe or total meaning of the morpheme "table" would include as individual semes the meaning in "statistical table," in "table of contents," and the meaning of "table" when it refers to a four-legged flat-topped object.

The following discussion is based on the distinction that can be made between two types of inferences from semantic data, inferences of discrimination and inferences of similarity. In the former we connect a difference in linguistic reaction with a difference in extralinguistic reaction. In the latter we assume that situations similarly responded to linguistically are treated similarly from some other point of view.

B. HYPOTHESES OF DISCRIMINATION

The most evident and frequently employed basis for drawing conclusions in this area is given by the fact that E.M.U.'s differ from language to language—indeed, are probably never identical in any two languages. It follows that different languages provide different defining characteristics for their elementary units in terms of the nonlinguistic environment. An extreme conclusion that is sometimes drawn from this fact is that the speakers of a language are aware only of those distinctions which are provided by differences of meaning in E.M.U.'s. This was assumed, for instance, by some of the participants in the celebrated controversy regarding ancient Greek color perception, in which the absence of elementary terms for certain colors led to the conclusion that the Greeks were color-blind in these areas. An allied but opposite conclusion is that the presence of discrimination furnished by two or more different E.M.U.'s prevents the speaker from noting their similarities or common features, unless a general term exists in addition. Lévy-Bruhl constantly draws conclusions of this type from the languages of primitive peoples. For example, the Bororo of Brazil are said to be incapable of noting the features common to all parrots because they have names for individual species of parrots but no term for parrots in general. American writers have usually repudiated this extreme form of determinism (e.g., Hoijer 1953: 560–61).

The possibilities of correlation with E.M.U. distinctions would seem to be in the area rather of cultural behavior than of perception. The type of hypothesis which we are justified in proposing here takes the form of significantly more than chance correlation between the frequency of response to those stimuli in a situation which are defined by elementary meaning units, except linguisemes. In this formulation the emphasis is on frequency of the response, which implies habits common to a large number or all speakers of a language. Hence this can be said to constitute a correlation with cultural behavior. By stating such hypotheses in terms of frequency, we also avoid the assumption of total uniformity which leads to the type of linguistic determinism rejected above. Moreover, this is simply a rule for forming hypotheses. We do not state that such hypotheses are always, or even in general, true, although they may well turn out to be so. The classical area of investigation of hypotheses of this type in ethnology has been that of kinship. I believe that the general conclusion can be drawn from these studies that significantly better than chance correlation does exist in this particular instance.

Where such correlations hold, on a synchronic plane we note the congruence between linguistic and nonlinguistic behavior. The attempt to establish priority of the verbal or nonverbal aspect seems to resemble the proverbial situation of the chicken and the egg. If we phrase the correspondence in terms of linguistic priority, we say that reactions are directed with more than chance frequency into certain habitual channels by language. Viewed historically, however, there is a greater plausibility in the notion that the stock of E.M.U.'s tends to adapt to nonlinguistic changes rather than that nonlinguistic aspects are adjustments to linguistic shifts. This is certainly true in technology, but even in philosophy, science, and religion it seems likely that the appearance of new E.M.U.'s is chiefly a response to needs which have arisen at the particular point of development of the subject matter itself. (See Boas 1911.) The phrase "tends to adapt" was employed above because there is sometimes a time-lag (in which case the linguistic survival aids us in historical reconstruction) or sometimes no adjustment takes place, the new situation being handled somewhat clumsily by a complex rather than elementary meaning unit (i.e., by a phrase, or the like).

A further fact is to be noted in regard to such correspondences. The existence of distinct E.M.U's makes us suspect a difference in response to the situations designated by the terms. It does not, in general, tell us the nature of this difference in response. For example, the existence of separate unanalyzable terms for father's brother and mother's brother makes us posit a difference in reaction to these relatives. It does not tell us wherein the difference consists, whether, for example, the first is treated with deference but the second with familiarity. To discover this, we must observe behavior, both verbal and nonverbal, that is, what things are habitually said and done with reference to the father's brother and the mother's brother.

At this point it seems essential to point out a difference expressed here in the distinction between language and verbal behavior. It is parallel to the contrasts langue : parole (De Saussure), syntactic and semantic : pragmatic (Morris, Carnap), and code : message (information theorists), and seems to embody a necessary distinction. A complete knowledge of the language system, including the phonology, the semantics, and the grammar, cannot tell us a priori which of the indefinitely large number of possible sentences which can be constructed in accordance with the rules will actually be employed. This latter is verbal behavior.

If, however, a macroseme (i.e., an idiom) is employed, an attitude or value may sometimes be inferred. The conditions for drawing valid conclusions in these instances are discussed below in connection with inferences of similarity. An example is the macroseme cited by Hoijer as used in Apache by a man to designate his wife's relatives: kàˀìšxéhé *those for whom I carry burdens* (1948: 337).

There are some instances in which hypotheses of connection between E.M.U. differences and differences of cultural behavior are particularly plausible. One example is where generic meanings, defined above as the meaning common to a specific group of E.M.U.'s, are involved. Here we often have to do with whole groups of terms in areas like numerals, kinship terms, etc., which involve a small number of generic meanings in varied combinations. In such cases, the probabilities of significant correlation with behavior increase because we have to do with meaning distinctions found in a whole group of terms. (See, e.g., Trier 1932.)

So-called compulsory categories are another case in point. These are instances where the rules of the language force us to choose one of a set of alternative meaning units. Actually there are degrees of compulsion. One extreme is that of compulsory morpheme classes which must appear in all or nearly all types of sentences (e.g., number in English, which is, however, not specified if the construction consists of a verb imperative without an object: "Sit quietly!"). On the other hand, a lesser degree of compulsion exists where a general term is absent and the meanings which refer to it are classified on one or more general bases. Thus, in Navaho, one cannot state motion in general but must choose among a number of terms specifying the vehicle involved and other aspects of the motion. Such a choice is less often required of us than in the case of number in English, since it only comes into play when we wish to describe motion. Instances of compulsion necessarily refer to choice among morphemes belonging to the same morpheme class, i.e., which are mutually substitutable. Where this holds, the hypothesis of correlation with cultural conduct becomes particularly plausible, as, e.g., in the case of Eskimo words for "snow" and Arabic words for "camel."

However, the frequency aspect of our hypothesis still holds. There may well be particular instances where linguistically required bases of distinction are not relevant to the speaker's reaction. In the English sentence, "Anyone who owns a home must pay real estate taxes," as usually interpreted, number would be irrelevant, as is evident if we replace it with "Homeowners must pay real estate taxes," where the number of homes owned by each person is not specified. On the other hand, any aspect which receives compulsory expression in a language is likely to be one which is important in a large number of situations. It cannot be said, however, that these E.M.U.'s more than any other determine aspects of the speaker's conduct, since they can certainly be disregarded when not relevant to the situation, even where linguistically required. This linguistic requirement is sometimes phrased in a way that suggests determination of the speaker's conceptualization. This is a legitimate manner of speaking, if we realize that we are merely restating our linguistic facts in different terminology, since by concepts are meant the definitions of E.M.U.'s. If we then ask for evidence of these conceptualizations, we are led back in circular fashion to the linguistic facts as sole evidence.

The exclusion of linguisemes and linguisememes (linguistic meanings) from all hypotheses of discrimination, as stated in our definition, applies also to hypotheses of similarity. It will, therefore, receive separate discussion later.

C. HYPOTHESES OF SIMILARITY

In certain cases, language groups a number of meaning elements together, and we are therefore led to hypotheses connecting such facts with similarities in nonlinguistic behavior. These arise chiefly from two sets of linguistic phenomena, the relation of a sememe to its member semes and that of a macrosememe to its constituent sememes and episememes. An example of the former is the instance cited by Whorf where a watchman reacted carelessly in the presence of "empty" gas drums presumably because the sememe of "empty" in English has at least two semes, one being synonymous with "void" and the other with "not dangerous" (1952: 27). The macrosememe, by definition a construction in which the meaning of the constituents is not sufficient to predict the meaning of the whole, gives us two meanings, a literal and an idiomatic, which can lead to a hypothesis of similar reactions in the two situations. For example, a Hausa construction has the literal meaning "companion in play" and the macrosememe "cross-cousin." From the equation of these two meanings one can arrive at the hypothesis that one plays with one's cross-cousin (i.e., has a "joking" relationship in the sense employed in the literature on social organization). This turns out to be correct.

Interpretations of similarity usually assume one meaning as basic and the other or others as metaphorical extension. It is then stated that the latter is evaluated or reacted to in terms of the former. For sememes the basic seme is usually selected on one or a combination of the following grounds: historical priority, frequency of use, closeness in meaning to that of an accepted grammatical term (e.g., Whorf 1952: 34), translation equivalence in the writer's own language, or centrality. A seme is said to exhibit centrality when most or all of the other semes of the same sememe can be derived from it by specialization or other metaphorical shifts. For the macrosememe, the literal meaning is always taken as basic.

Here again, as for the hypotheses of discrimination, what the linguist's material furnishes is hypotheses leading to the equation of certain situations. To discover whether they are responded to in similar fashion or identically, we must observe verbal and nonverbal behavior. For example, in the case of the Hausa phrase we must observe how such people behave to each other in word and in deed. Without such corroborative evidence, the conceptual equation becomes a mere tautologic restatement of the linguistic fact.

The study of behavior in reference to situations thus equated linguistically opens up the whole field of false beliefs which employ the facts of particular languages as premises, pointed to by the general semanticists. The extent to which such equations in behavior are made, even where inappropriate or definitely harmful, varies from society to society. At one extreme, semantic sophistication leads to their avoidance though perhaps never with complete success and under all circumstances. At the other end of the scale, certain societies with systematic doctrines of word magic have sought to draw as many such conclusions as possible and make them the object of belief. In investigation of all cases, however, the observation of behavior, both verbal and nonverbal, is necessary.

The situations discussed in this section arise historically in two ways, through metaphorical extension and accidental homonymy. Metaphorical extension results when someone sees a resemblance between one situation and another and this resemblance is generalized among the speakers of the language. For example, the "leg" of a table resembles that of a human being sufficiently in some respects so that a metaphorical extension was induced among speakers of English. False belief stems from metaphors or homonyms when propositions are believed in which one meaning (seme) is inappropriately substituted for the other. Nothing compels me to entertain such beliefs, but, when I do, the form which they take depends on the particular meanings in the language I speak. The case cited above of the watchman who behaved carelessly around "empty" cans may serve as an illustration. By equating two of the semes of "empty," he falsely entertained the proposition, "All void things are harmless." If he survived the explosion, he presumably ceased to believe this proposition.

The effects on behavior of such semantic equations may be viewed as varying along a continuum. As in the above example, they may constitute grounds for belief powerful enough to produce overt nonverbal behavior. At the other extreme, they may be quite ineffective or function merely as a suggestive stimulus to imagery not necessarily more vivid or more frequent than that which is unsupported by linguistic analogy. Indeed a faded metaphor of little vitality and without influence on the behavior of the speaker may appear very striking to the outside observer and be vested with undue significance. It is instructive, for example, that Weisgerber, who is, as we have seen, a prominent European exponent of the "linguistic Weltanschauung" point of view when it is a question of German, his own language, criticizes Bally for attaching too great an importance to certain idioms: "Mag Bally in dieser Hinsicht in manche dieser Beobachtungen vielleicht mehr hineinlegen als durchweg darin dem Sprachbewusstsein lebendig ist, . . ." (1950: 209). Because the sergeant barks at his men it does not follow that we feed him dog biscuits.

One of the grounds for selecting basic meaning enumerated above, translation meaning, deserves particular mention for its bearing on the problems discussed here. What is meant is the choice of an equivalent from another language, normally that of the writer, as a basic seme for inferences of similarity. This is the process which underlies the uncritical use of literal translation frequently encountered in the literature. It can be seen that this procedure is quite arbitrary inasmuch as interpretation of the same data will differ, depending on the particular language employed for translation. We may take as an example Whorf's reasoning regarding the Hopi use of cardinal and ordinal numbers. Finding two sets of numerals in Hopi and two in English, Whorf equates one Hopi set with the English cardinals and the other with the English ordinals, making, it may be added, a justifiable choice on the basis of frequency of meaning correspondence. In those instances where Hopi employs the set which has been equated by translation to English ordinals for situations in which we use cardinals, the Hopi is said to view the situation ordinally, that is, in terms of our ordinals. Hence the use of the Hopi "ordinal" in phrases stating the number of days of duration leads Whorf to the conclusion that:

> The count is by ordinals. This is not the pattern of counting a number of men or things, even though they appear successively, for even then they could gather into an assemblage. It is the pattern of counting successive appearances of the same man or thing, incapable of forming an assemblage. The analogy is not to behave about day-cyclicity as to several men ("several days"), which is what we tend to do, but to behave as to the successive visits of the same man [1952: 37].

Employing the same reasoning, a Frenchman who calls his kings Henri quatre (*Henry four*) and Louis treize (*Louis thirteen*) might draw the conclusion that English speakers who use the phrases "Henry the fourth" and "Louis the thirteenth" view each king of the same name as the same man appearing anew. He might even conjecture a belief in reincarnation of like-named kings. Further, a French observer might even be moved to conclusions similar to those entertained by Whorf for Hopi regarding the English conceptualization of time periods, by contrasting the French Juillet quatorze (*July fourteen*) with English "July fourteenth." On the other hand, the German metalinguist accustomed to Heinrich der vierte (*Henry the fourth*) and der vierzehnte Juli (*the fourteenth July*) would not have a basis for drawing conclusions similar to that of the French scientist concerning the English-speaking community.

D. LINGUISTIC MEANING

It would now be generally agreed that meaning is to be understood functionally, i.e., that meaning is to be described in terms of a rule of use stated in terms of the environment. This environment is twofold, ethnic and linguistic. All meaningful elements can be defined in terms of linguistic contexts, this being the basis of the "content-analysis" approach of Zellig Harris. Most meanings can also be described by reference to the nonlinguistic environment, but, for a few sememes, some or all semes are solely linguistic in function (linguisemes). By definition, such terms are not susceptible of semantic interpretation in terms of nonlinguistic environment. For example, if we wish to set up rules for the use of the morphemes marking the various noun-classes of the Bantu language, we operate for the most part in terms of linguistic context; i.e., most of them can be defined only by reference to an arbitrary subclass of noun root-morphemes, a class which shows grammatical significance in terms of adjective and pronominal agreement. Such linguisemes have been excluded from the definitions of the previous sections for the simple reason that, if correlations with nonlinguistic phenomena could have been found, then it would not have been necessary to define the seme purely in terms of linguistic context. If correlations had been found, the semes would already have figured in our linguistic analyses as ethnosemes. The problem, then, is to discover under what circumstances ethnosemes, as opposed to linguisemes, can be defined in linguistic investigation. We cannot a priori decide that situations which in our culture are marked by no common denominator of behavior might not have one in some other culture. Our evidence then must come from ethnographic observation of the conduct of the speakers to see if such elements can be defined in terms of behavior of the speakers.

Let us take as an example the Central Algonquian division of nouns into two classes which we will call, neutrally, I and II. Class I has singular *-a*, plural *-aki* (Bloomfield 1946: 94). Class II has singular *-i*, plural *-ali*, and there are other differences relating to pronominal reference. If we wish to specify the total meaning of the morphemes *-a*, *-aki* (outside of the ethnosemes of number), we must take the following facts into consideration. Members of Class I include persons, animals, spirits and large trees, tobacco, maize, apple, raspberry (but not strawberry), calf of the leg (but not the thigh), stomach, spittle, feather, bird's tail, horn, kettle, pipe for smoking, snowshoe, and a few others. The classification "animate" covers a large part of this class, but what of the rest? Unless the actual behavior of Algonquian speakers shows some mode of conduct common to all these instances such that, given this information, we could predict the membership of Class I, we must resort to purely linguistic characterization. If it turned out, for example, that speakers of Algonquian have a shrine to the raspberry and treat it like a spirit, while the strawberry is in the sphere of the profane, and if similar facts could be adduced regarding the other terms, then a definition of Class I affixes would be possible by reference to the nonlinguistic behavior of Algonquian speakers. I do not believe that the ethnographic facts about these peoples will allow of such a definition. Since all persons and animals are in Class I, we have at least one ethnoseme, but most of the other meanings can be defined only by a linguiseme.

Tautologic statements of similarity based on a valid ethnoseme, usually described by a grammatical label, are sometimes made. If, for example, we call I "animate" and II "inanimate," then the statement that the Central Algonquians conceive of kettles as animate is merely a tautologic statement of the grammatical fact.

IV. INFERENCES FROM STRUCTURE

By structure is meant here facts about a language stated as an abstract calculus without reference to meaning. If, for example, it is stated in regard to a particular language that no morpheme contains more than six phonemes, this is a structural fact. Inferences from structure like those from phonology, the other nonsemantic aspect of language, are of two kinds, mediated and unmediated. The linguistic typologies popular in the nineteenth century, isolating—agglutinative—inflective and the like, involved chiefly structural criteria, for example, the degree of morphemic complexity of the word. The application was mediated through a supposed connection with the evolution of thought from lower unorganized (isolating) forms to higher synthesized (inflective) forms. M. Mueller even connected these at one time with economic stages of development. For a recent example of purely structural criteria, applied in unmediated form, we may cite those adduced by Lévi-Strauss in correlation with social structure. Regarding Indo-European languages he says, "The languages have simple structures utilizing numerous elements. The opposition between the simplicity of the structure and multiplicity of elements is expressed by the fact that several elements compete to occupy the same position in the structure" (1951: 161). I am not quite certain how to interpret this, but it is certainly a structural statement. Many apparently structural criteria turn out to be actually semantic when more closely investigated. A favorite type of inference from structure is interpretation by similarity involving the constituent episemes of an episememe (meaning of a construction), for example, statements that a certain situation is viewed actively rather than passively on the assumption of a basic actor-action episeme.

V. CONCLUSION

The object of this paper has been to analyze the conditions under which, in the author's opinion, inferences from linguistic to nonlinguistic data can be legitimately made. It has not been within its scope to analyze attempts such as those of Whorf (Hopi), Hoijer, Astrov, Kluckhohn (Navaho), Lee (Wintun, Trobriands), Jespersen (English), Bally (French and German), and Weisgerber (German) to isolate large-scale linguistic patterns and relate them to dominant modes of behavior and thought. While no such analysis is, therefore, attempted, the implications of certain of the conclusions of the present paper for these wider problems may be pointed out.

It is apparent that the conditions of valid inference described in the present paper allow no more than a better than chance predictability from certain semantic facts to certain particular judgments of similar and differential reactions to situations. Such scattered beliefs and behavior differentials can hardly be expected to add up to anything as coherent as a world view. Is it possible, then, to justify statements such as the following of Whorf that "the Hopi language and culture conceal a METAPHYSICS such as our so-called naive view of space and time does, or the relativity theory does, yet a different metaphysic from either" (1952: 47)?

A basic difficulty stems from the fact that in ordinary use the term "metaphysics" refers to a set of beliefs which take sentential form. But language only gives us the meanings of elementary units together with the rules of construction for making sentences from them. From the finite set of elements and rules it is impossible to predict which of an infinitude of sentences will actually be used by the members of a speech community. It is not easy to see, therefore, how we can infer any such formulations of belief.

In view of this difficulty we might wish to limit our metaphysics to one of terms, rather than one of propositions, and state that a particular manner of viewing the universe is implicit in the organization of the individual meaning elements of a language—what might be termed its semantic structure. Though this is a possible procedure, it requires an ascetic regimen to which none of the writers on this subject has, in fact, conformed. Given the difficulties already mentioned in the way of using phonological and structural criteria, the enterprise resolves itself into the attempt to find semantic orderings, particularly generic meanings or similar meanings in diverse morpheme and constructional classes. What we do find in languages are partial orderings in certain areas where the data themselves demand such systematization in order to be dealt with by the speakers. Typical instances are kinship systems, numeral systems, color terms and directional-spatial terms. But these are so different in subject matter that attempts at finding common denominators for such diverse semantic aspects are likely to seem vague and arbitrary. Thus Whorf assimilates under a common rubric of "objective world-view" the English verb tenses and the meaning of the container formula in such phrases as "two pounds of butter," but it is difficult to see on the basis of any of the various uses of the term "objective" (e.g., existing independent of the observer, outside the organism, intersubjective) how the two sets of meanings can be linked. Why, for example, are tenses more objective than aspects? It is interesting to note in this connection that Speiser takes the opposite point of view in regard to Semitic. "The Akkadian system is objective and impersonal, the verb thus assuming a stative character. . . . The West Semitic system, on the other hand, bears a personal and subjective character which imparts to the verb a temporal orientation" (1938:198).

These difficulties are, I believe, not accidental but inherent in the problem. Since natural language is not devised by philosophers but develops as a living instrument of a community in its adjustment to a variety of changing needs, one would not expect and, in my experience at least, one does not find any underlying semantic patterns such as would be required for the semantic system of a language to reflect some over-all world view of a metaphysical nature.

The subject seems to me by all means worthy of further investigation, but, if the points raised in this paper are valid, numerous methodological obstacles remain to be overcome. Should such attempts prove in the long run not to be feasible, the more modest specific correlations between linguistic and nonlinguistic cultural behavior which remain are still of immense value toward the understanding of the past and present life of a people.

REFERENCES CITED

Bally, Charles

1944 *Linguistique générale et linguistique française*. 2d ed. Berne, A. Francke.

Bloomfield, Leonard

1933 *Language*. New York, Holt.

1946 "Algonquian." In: *Linguistic Structures of Native America*, pp. 85–129. Viking Fund Publications in Anthropology, No. 6.

Boas, Franz (ed.)

1911 "Introduction." In: *Handbook of American Indian Languages*, Part 1. Washington, D.C.

CASSIRER, ERNST
1933 "La Langue et la construction du monde des objets," *Journal de psychologie normale et de pathologie* **30**:18–44.

HOIJER, HARRY
1948 "Linguistic and Cultural Change," *Language* **24**:335–45.
1953 "The Relation of Language to Culture." In: *Anthropology Today* (by A. L. Kroeber and others), pp. 554–73. Chicago, University of Chicago Press.

JAKOBSON, ROMAN
1948 "The Phonemic and Grammatical Aspects of Language in Their Interrelations," *Actes du 6e Congrès International des Linguistes*, pp. 5–18. Paris.

JAKOBSON, ROMAN, C. G. M. FANT and M. HALLE
1952 *Preliminaries to Speech Analysis. Technical Report*. Massachusetts Institute of Technology.

LEE, DOROTHY D.
1940 "A Primitive System of Values," *Philosophy of Science* **7**:355–79.

LÉVI-STRAUSS, CLAUDE
1951 "Language and the Analysis of Social Laws," *American Anthropologist* **53**:155–63.

NIDA, EUGENE A.
1951 "A System for the Description of Semantic Elements," *Word* **7**:1–14.

SPEISER, S.
1938 "The Pitfalls of Polarity," *Language* **14**:187–202.

TRIER, JOST
1932 "Sprachliche Felder," *Zeitschrift für die Bedeutungslehre* **8**:417–27.

WEISGERBER, JOHANN LEO
1949 *Die Sprache unter den Kräften des menschlichen Daseins*. Düsseldorf, Schwann.
1950 *Vom Weltbild der deutschen Sprache*. Düsseldorf, Schwann.

WHORF, BENJAMIN L.
1952 *Collected Papers on Metalinguistics*. Washington, D.C., Foreign Service Institute, Department of State.

ANALYSIS OF THE CULTURAL CONTENT OF LANGUAGE MATERIALS

NORMAN A. MCQUOWN

I

ALL CULTURAL behavior is patterned.

All such behavior manifests its patterns through distinctions made in a medium.

Such media are of varying degrees of complexity, ranging from the more tangible physical and physiological aspects of behavior to the least tangible and most subtle arrangements of the patterned products of this behavior.

For the study of cultural behavior, as it manifests itself through these diverse media, the first requirement is a device for the preliminary segmentation of the medium. Such a device must consist of a generalized descriptive frame, adapted both to the particular medium and to the variety of cultural distinctions which adequate experience and knowledge of the limitations of the medium show to be likely to manifest themselves in that medium.

The second requirement is a generalized analytic frame which provides (*a*) a set of principles which experience has shown to reflect the nature of the structure of cultural behavior and (*b*) a hierarchy of operations which knowledge of a number of diverse cultures has shown to be fruitfully applicable to the discovery of the structure of such behavior.

In accord with such principles, the operations are performed on the preliminary segments provided by the generalized descriptive frame, extending that frame where necessary, for the purpose of discovering the particular patterning immanent in particular cultural behavior. If the preliminary frame is adequate, and if the principles are carefully adhered to, as the ordered operations are performed on the preliminarily segmented cultural behavior of a variety of communities, the result will be the uncovering of a series of differently structured cultural activities. If the analysis cuts fine enough, ultimately as many different structures will be found as there are individuals in the series of communities under investigation. Subsequent comparison of these individual structures will reveal for the analyst patterns which have validity for ever increasing numbers and ever widening varieties of groups of individuals. Such patterns may be said to be characteristic of the particular groups which share them. As a result of such step-by-step procedure, the analyst will ultimately discover patterns characteristic of whole ways of life of communities, nations, and civilizations. A certain residue of patterns will be uncovered, when the procedure has been completed, which will be shared by all human beings, and may be said to be characteristic of human nature.

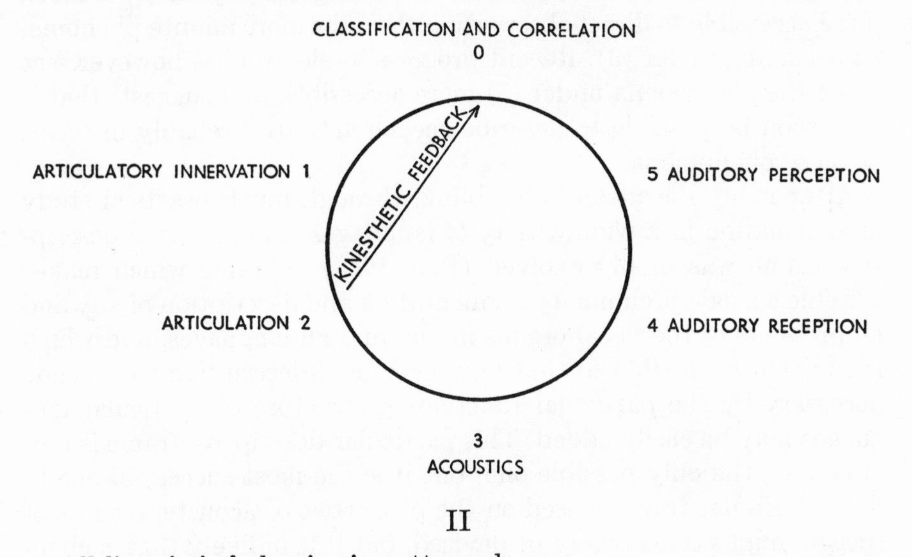

II

All linguistic behavior is patterned.

All linguistic behavior manifests its patterns through distinctions made in the various aspects of a complex continuous chain of activities, ranging from (1) the articulatory innervation of the organs of speech, through (2) the actual articulations performed by the organs, through (3) the ensuing variations in air pressure in the external medium for sound transmission, through (4) the consequent variations in water pressure and their effect on the hair follicles within the inner ear, through (5) the resulting variations in nerve activity within the auditory portions of the brain, through (0) the classificatory and correlational activity of the brain, and back again to (1) the articulatory innervation of the organs of speech. This six-stage chain (see Fig. 1; also Joos 1948: 98–99) constitutes the medium for the manifestation of linguistic patterns. At present, the only directly accessible portions of this chain are (2) and (3), although some experimental work has been done on (4). The field of study which covers the activities in (2) and (3) is the field of phonetics, although in practical work the phonetician does make use of his own feeling for (1) and (5). A part of the training of the practical phonetician involves a process of generalization of the classificatory and correlational activities under (0) so as to reduce cultural bias. Most successful to date has been the work on the activity under (2) combined with the impressions conveyed by (5) and with feed-back from (2). The reason is not far to seek. The gross physiology is much more accessible to direct observation than the more minute phenomena occurring under (3). Recent progress in electronics, however, has made the phenomena under (3) more accessible, and suggests that it may soon be possible to describe speech activities reliably in terms of these phenomena.

After many decades of stumbling, through much practical study of articulation in a wide variety of languages, a generalized descriptive frame was finally evolved (Pike 1943), a frame which makes possible a single preliminary segmentation and description of any and all products of the vocal organs in any and all languages, and which is sufficiently flexible so that any additional descriptive facts made necessary by the particular functioning structure of particular languages may be easily added. This particular descriptive frame is not, of course, the only possible one, but it is the most successful one to date. A similar frame, based on the properties of acoustic records of speech, might conceivably be devised, but it is unlikely that such an acoustic frame could ever completely replace the articulatory-kinesthetic-audioperceptual one now in use. Indeed, all such preliminary frames would necessarily complement one another, each succeeding frame making accessible to controlled observation additional aspects of the whole language act.

During the last two decades, a generalized analytic frame (Harris 1951) for the revelation of the structure of speech has matured. The first part of the frame to mature was that part which concerns itself with the lowest level of patterning in the speech act, that which redistributes the preliminary phonetic segments according to their functional properties and interrelationships. The field of study which covers this level of activity is the field of phonemics. The second part of the frame to mature was that part which concerns itself with the functional properties and interrelationships of conventional sequences of phonemes, of classes of such sequences, and of classes of such classes, through several layers of structure. The study of this level of activity is covered by the field of morphemics. The general principles which are found to characterize the functional properties and interrelationships of units on all levels, both phonemic and morphemic, are those of contrast, complementation, free variation, pattern congruence, and elegance. The particular hierarchy of operations for each level and sublevel is fairly complex. The operations are so ordered as to define units, properties, and interrelationships on each level in terms appropriate to that level, and are so carried out as to pigeonhole, without residue, all raw material from a lower level in the compartments of the next higher one. There is no phonetic material among the preliminary segments which is not somewhere accommodated among phonemic units, no phonemic units which do not fit into some morpheme or other, and no morphemes or orderings of morphemes which do not fit into some higher-level structural unit. For any phonetic material produced by the vocal organs which does not fit comfortably into established phonemic structures, a berth is sought in parallel systems of vocal modifiers (Smith 1952:II.1.b), or vocal gestures. For any morphemic material whose arrangement does not correlate elegantly with broad linguistic patterns, a berth is sought in extralinguistic cultural patterns which exploit such linguistically nonsignificant selection and grouping of linguistic forms as a medium for their own manifestation.

In the course of carrying out these operations, extensions of the descriptive frame are sometimes made necessary, and in the process of uncovering a particular linguistic structure, closely associated extralinguistic structures (Birdwhistell 1952) are sometimes revealed. The end result is the laying-bare of the whole linguistic structure, the units and patterned recurrences of units in the speech act. Carrying out the operations in accord with the general principles reveals the structure of a particular idiolect (Bloch 1948 §1.7). Comparative study of the structures of a number of idiolects reveals the common core (Hockett 1952) of structure and points up the individual differences. Investigation in this fashion of a series of idiolects marks off linguistic groups of greater and greater generality, revealing dialects, languages, and families of languages. If a sufficient variety of languages is thus investigated, one will find, upon completion of the task, a residue of structural items which are common human linguistic property, characteristic, not of particular human beings, but of man as a linguistic animal.

III

If one were to consider these linguistic structures in their role as media for the manifestation of other cultural patterns, and look upon the various parts and arrangements of parts as raw data upon which to perform certain operations (Harris 1952*a*, 1952*b*) designed to reveal these other patterns, one might profitably suggest certain principial and methodological analogies as a guide to analytic procedure. If the phonemic structure of language is revealed by operations performed on raw phonetic data, and if the morphemic structure of language is revealed by operations performed on raw phonemic data, may not the structure of other cultural activities be revealed by operations performed on raw linguistic data? May we not look upon the segmentation and segment-classification performed on the speech continuum, in order to reveal linguistic structure, as a model for similar segmentation and segment-classification to be performed on the linguistic continuum, in order to reveal the structure of other aspects of culture? Just as the preliminary analytic frame, within which our first segmentation of the phonetic raw material is carried out, must occasionally be supplemented by parallel analytic frames, so the preliminary linguistic frame, with its own built-in segmentation, may need to be extended and supplemented by other such media. Among other such internally segmented media, we might mention those immediately contiguous to language, such as the voice qualifiers and vocal gestures; those a step removed, such as bodily gesture and stance; and those still further removed, such as writing and other manipulatory and gesticulatory arts. It might be suggested here, however, that just as articulatory phonetics turned out to be the most useful frame within which to perform a preliminary segmentation of linguistic activity, so language, with its built-in segmentation, might turn out to be the most useful frame within which to perform a preliminary segmentation of other cultural activity.

What, then, are the general characteristics of the linguistic frame? What kinds and numbers of structural segments result from the process of linguistic description? Table 1 (applicable to a wide variety of languages) may convey some idea of the nature of the linguistic frame.

Bundles of these structural segments (or, in the limiting case, single segments) may be thought of as loci for the manifestation of some aspect of extralinguistic cultural patterns. Just as the phonetic segments (as determined by our preliminary classificatory and descriptive frame) are per se without direct significance, and significant only as contrasting features (or bundles of features) on the phonemic level, just as the phonemic segments (as determined by our hierarchy of operations carried out in accordance with our general principles) are per se without direct significance, and significant only as con-

TABLE 1

Segment Type	Numbers of Segments
(1) Basic Sounds [segmental phonemes]	15–50
(2) Accents [suprasegmental phonemes]	2–15
(*a*) Junctures [transition types]	2–4
(*b*) Stresses [relative energy types]	0–4
(*c*) Tones [relative frequency types]	0–4
(*d*) Quantities [relative length types]	0–3
(*e*) Pauses [accentual pattern termini]	2–4
(3) Basic-Sound Combinations	
(*a*) Monosyllables	25,000
(*b*) Polysyllables	50,000
(*c*) Lexical Units [both simplex (lexemes) and complex]	250,000
(4) Accent Combinations	
(*a*) Stress Superfixes	0–25
(*b*) Tone Superfixes [intonations]	0–50
(5) Basic-Sound and Accent Combinations	100,000
(6) Words	25,000–500,000
(7) Constructions	50–500
(*a*) Derivations	0–250
(*b*) Inflections	0–50
(*c*) Phrases	5–25
(*d*) Clauses	5–15
(*e*) Sentences	2–12
(*f*) Utterances	0–2
(*g*) Discourse Sequences	5–75
(8) Categories [parts of speech]	2–12

trasting units (or bundles of units) on the morphemic level, so likewise are the morphemic segments (similarly determined) per se without direct significance, and significant only as contrasting units (or bundles of units) within the whole of extralinguistic cultural activity. There is, however, despite the apparent analogies so far cited, a possible important difference between lower-level units and higher-level units both within language itself and within other areas of cultural activity. As one goes from bottom to top, the superunits represent larger and larger classes of subunits, and the internal content of the classes becomes ever more varied. A corollary of this increase in generality and in internal variety of the units may well be a heightened susceptibility to internal restructuring, and a resulting greater plasticity as a medium for the manifestation of higher-level units and patterns. This factor may make the problems of content analysis increasingly more complex as one works upward from level to level, but this increased complexity does not necessarily imply any lack of validity of the general analytic principles. In order to apply the general principles, however, one may have to construct special hierarchies of operations for such higher-level content analysis.

What kinds of content are likely to manifest themselves in particular contrasting units, bundles of units, and bundles of such bundles?

The sounds [(1) and (2)] are, in general, contentless, performing only the somewhat colorless role of tags for distinguishing higher-level units one from another. In their sound-symbolic role, however, the user may make a conscious selection of them for aesthetic or other reasons.

The forms [(3)(*c*) through (8)], on the other hand, bear a wide range of content from the most specific and the most concrete to the most general and the most abstract.

The basic sounds (1) function chiefly as contrastive units, although they may, singly or in clusters, play a sound-symbolic role.

The accents (2) serve a variety of purposes. Some of them, singly or in combinations, distinguish one form made up of basic phonemes from another, thus adding substantially to the number of different forms (5). The junctures [(2)(*a*)] may aid in distinguishing one kind of morpheme combination from another, and a hierarchy of junctures from open to close may aid in placing a complex form along a continuum of increasing closeness of association. The patterns of stress [(2)(*b*)] may be used to characterize categories or construction-types. The patterns of tone [(2)(*c*)] may serve as special indicators of attitudinal content. The quantities [(2)(*d*)], like other accents, may serve to distinguish one basic phoneme from another, thus materially increasing the number of distinguishable morphemes (5). The pauses [(2)(*e*)] make clear the state of completion of an utterance, indicating the speaker's intent with respect to subsequent speech or other activity.

Particular phoneme combinations, the lexical units [(3)(*c*)], relate to our segmentation of our environment, and carry the most specific content, although even here a particular lexical unit implies a whole class of extralinguistic co-occurrences. Words (6), both simple and complex, bear meanings just as specific.

More general are the meanings borne by the constructions (7), since these incorporate, into the positions within them, whole classes of lexical units. Constructional meanings may bear on our modes of interrelating the segments of our universe.

More general, too, are the meanings attached to the categories (8) of lexical units (and of constructions equated, as wholes, category-wise, to particular classes of lexical units). These classes may bear on our segmentation of our universe.

Constructional patterns on the discourse level [(7)(*g*)] may reveal some of our most general and least conscious modes of interrelating and evaluating the aspects of our world.

The content items are, in general, of two kinds: (*a*) those obligatorily present by virtue of distinctions bound up in the linguistic form itself, and (*b*) those optionally present in the nonlinguistically determined selection and ordering of the linguistic forms. The former are revealed by the process of linguistic analysis itself; the latter, of necessity, require further analysis.

IV

We here suggest that an investigation of the patterns of the rest of culture as they are reflected in language, to the extent that they are independent of linguistic patterns, must begin with phenomena of this second type, phenomena of the nonlinguistically determined selection and ordering of linguistic forms. The limits of variability in this second type are set by the linguistic form. The atoms, too, which are selected and ordered, are the formal units of language. One can, therefore, investigate the phenomena of this second type only if one has available a complete and accurate inventory of these linguistic atoms. Given such a description of the linguistic medium, however, one should be able to perform a hierarchy of operations upon it, in accordance with a set of principles, which would have, as end result, the revelation of other cultural patterns as these are made manifest in language.

What might these principles and these operations be? We suggest that the general principles underlying linguistic analysis (contrast, complementation, free variation, pattern congruence, and elegance) should also be applicable here. The specific operations, although perhaps ultimately more complex, should be similar. We suggest, in brief outline, the following operations (for a somewhat different procedure with a not unrelated purpose, see Sebeok [1950]):

1. On the basis of a nonelicited text (preferably "rich" in cultural

content), one attempts to pull out and classify all nonlinguistically determined co-occurrences of linguistic items.

2. Given this preliminary classification, one elicits further linguistic forms within each of the classificatory frames, taking care to exclude those volunteered forms which are merely linguistically necessary, with the purpose of checking the preliminary classification to see whether it holds. If the frame is productive, that is, if many more forms fit it, it is provisionally retained.

3. Having obtained a number of such frames, one then attempts to discover some larger patterning by having them combined in larger sequences, taking care that the sequences are not merely linguistically necessary.

4. Having obtained a number of such sequences of productive frames, the sequences themselves are tested for productivity, by further eliciting, and by having them combined in still larger groupings, in order to determine over-all patterns.

5. In the course of the investigation, one will discover content ambiguities, on all levels. These ambiguities will force the investigator to observe, in crucial situations, other aspects of the behavior of his informants which resolve the cruxes. The limitations of the linguistic medium as a reflector of the larger patterns will be thus revealed, and the investigator will be led to outline other areas for similar investigation, with similar rigorous application of a hierarchy of operations in accord with general principles carefully observed.

V

The investigator will carefully check the implications of the observable linguistic syndromes against the data supplied by other approaches. As a time-saving device in his investigation, he may well allow suggestions as to likely patterns of culture, provided by these other approaches, to influence his selection of frames and of frame-sequences for testing. Such short cuts should not, however, prevent him from following up promising leads afforded by his linguistic data, since the investigation of such leads may very well force a reinterpretation of patterns obtained through other approaches. No possible source of correlative data should be overlooked. Both contemporary social anthropological and ethnographic-archeological studies with greater time depth should be fully exploited. Studies of the physical environment, including the geology, the geography, and the flora and fauna, should not be neglected. Physical anthropological as well as psychological characterizations of the speakers of the language should be drawn upon where available. If one is looking for general patterns of culture, one can afford to neglect no aspect of the human being, his behavior, or his environment. Only the correlation of the linguistic factors with all others will give us such a general view.

VI

What is the range of problems, suggested by linguistic syndromes, whose solution might be forthcoming from the application of such a combined approach? The following are typical of those which have suggested themselves to the writer in the course of his work on Middle American languages:

1. Why have the Totonacs (of east central Mexico) almost entirely replaced old root-words for body parts by (what seem to us) imaginative descriptive complex forms?
2. Why have the Totonacs elaborated an extensive series of special root-words for different categories of taste-smell?
3. Why have the Totonacs added to old root-words an elaborate system of size-markers (diminutive, neutral, augmentative) which crosscuts the entire vocabulary (nouns, verbs, and particles)?
4. Why are some Totonac animal names descriptive complex forms, others, invariant roots?
5. What can a study of Totonac place-names tell us about the earlier location, subsequent movement and contactual history of Totonac speakers?
6. Why have the Totonacs developed in their language a highly polysynthetic one-word sentence-core (verbal or nominal), containing within it references to all aspects of a state or activity, and constituting an utterance complete in itself (as compared to our normal English bipartite subject-predicate type of sentence)?
7. Why is the Totonac copula trifurcated into states of lying, sitting, and standing, and what in the rest of Totonac culture explains the assignation of particular objects to each of these three categories?
8. What extralinguistic factors might conceivably explain the differentiation in Totonac, in a handful of verbs, between general verb stems for the first and third persons and special stems for the second-person forms?
9. What internal relationships in the social structure might explain the use by Totonac women[1] of impersonal forms of the verb when referring to their[1] husbands[2] in their[2] absence?
10. What facts of culture history can explain the content of different layers of loan-forms (pre-Conquest non-Totonacan, Nahuat,

Nahuatl, sixteenth-century Spanish, later Spanish) in the Totonac vocabulary?

It will be readily apparent that the range of problems is as broad as the whole of culture, passing from oversummating world view to the minutiae of personal interaction.

VII

The techniques of analysis outlined in Section IV obviously require careful staging of the linguistic frames through which the investigator hopes to explore the range of larger cultural patterns. Informants must obviously be chosen with care, both from the point of view of their representativeness, as well as from that of their ability to talk freely. It is apparent that such stage-setting must make use of the native speech, not only for the particular frame being tested, but also for the background prodding. Attempts at translation in the frame-testing situation would inevitably introduce so many extraneous factors as to make impossible the investigator's task. It might be well to employ, in the process of gathering the data, native assistants carefully trained in the presentation of the linguistic frames and in the production of suitable prods for eliciting responses from a variety of informants. Involuntary extraneous factors in the performance of the investigator would thereby be avoided, and a freer flow of informant responses assured.

VIII

The very fact of a free flow of informant responses would make mechanical recording of interviews indispensable. Any process of recording from dictation would so slow the procedure as seriously to interfere with the flow of informant responses. Such mechanically recorded interviews could be linguistically processed during a separate work period, and their contents coded for analytic purposes. The analysis and coding should pace the interviews as closely as possible, so that sterile leads could be quickly abandoned and promising ones vigorously pursued. No materials should be destroyed, however, until the investigator is satisfied that they will yield no further information.

IX

The analytic processing of large quantities of linguistic materials is humanly possible only if machine aids to analysis are available. Machine aids store a large corpus of materials coded and fed into them, and produce on demand all items and sequences relevant to the solution of a particular problem. Such storage aids also may be equipped to handle all entries statistically. Frequency counts and transitional probability counts run on particular groupings often furnish valuable leads to problems worth investigating. Such counts run on completely analyzed materials from a variety of informants tell us significant things about the relative range and importance of particular patterns.

X

The procedure we have outlined, if applied, not merely to the forms of language and to other cultural forms in so far as they are reflected in language, but also to all other kinds of cultural activity, should make possible in the future controlled investigation of all the patterns of culture. Such investigation could then be based on actual individual cultural acts, elicitable and reproducible on demand, for any and all investigators. Statistical investigation of material so obtained and so analyzed would make it possible for the culture analyst to pace changes in culture as they happen, and, within limits, to predict them before they occur. The attributes of controllability, publicity, and predictability are those which will eventually appear in a science of culture.

REFERENCES CITED

BIRDWHISTELL, R.
1952 *Introduction to Kinesics.* Washington, D.C., Foreign Service Institute, Department of State.

BLOCH, BERNARD
1948 "A Set of Postulates for Phonemic Analysis," *Language* **24**:3–46.

HARRIS, ZELLIG S.
1951 *Methods in Structural Linguistics.* Chicago, University of Chicago Press.
1952*a* "Discourse Analysis," *Language* **28**:1–30.
1952*b* "Discourse Analysis (A Sample Text)," *Language* **28**:474–94.

HOCKETT, C. F.
1952 *Idiolect, Common Core, and Over-All Pattern.* Bloomington, Indiana University. Mimeog. tentative draft.

JOOS, MARTIN
1948 *Acoustic Phonetics.* Linguistic Society of America, Monograph No. 23.

PIKE, KENNETH L.
1943 *Phonetics.* Ann Arbor, University of Michigan Press.

SEBEOK, THOMAS A.
1950 "Cheremiss Dream Portents," *Southwestern Journal of Anthropology* **6**:273–85.

SMITH, H. L., JR.
1952 *An Outline of Metalinguistic Analysis.* Washington, D.C., Foreign Service Institute, Department of State. Mimeog. tentative draft.

SHAWNEE LAWS: PERCEPTUAL STATEMENTS FOR THE LANGUAGE AND FOR THE CONTENT

C. F. VOEGELIN, JOHN F. YEGERLEHNER,
AND FLORENCE M. ROBINETT

WE ARE OFTEN told by our informants that a certain part of their culture has a folkloristic origin, has existed in their own society from before contact with Whites until today; and here we can confirm our informants to the extent of knowing that the part of culture being discussed is indeed aboriginal—aboriginal in the sense of being non-European. Such persisting parts of culture we designate as stable, to distinguish them from acculturational changes, from culture which has appeared since White contact.

Shawnee Laws (šaawanwa kwteletiiwena) represent such a stable part of culture in a society in which some people are still trying to live like Indians rather than like Whites. A point by point morphemic transformation of kwteletiiwena = *advise-animate-reciprocal-inanimate thing-plural* = *laws;* hence, šaawanwa kwteletiiwena = *Shawnee Laws.*

The "language of the law" among us is specialized and in part archaic. To compare the language of Shawnee law with that of English law, we need first to produce a legal glossary in Shawnee. Legal glossaries in English are plentiful. From *Black's Law Dictionary* (third edition, St. Paul, 1933), we abstracted a few terms and categorized them as either externally perceived or internally experienced. The procedure for selecting the terms was to read the entries under the first ten letters of the alphabet and to note on separate slips a few English entries whose specialized meaning was recognized by us; we excluded all Latin terms and also all English terms which appeared to lack legal specialization. After collecting some fifty slips in this way, we read the definition of each, to confirm our guess as to the use of the term. We then classified the terms as either externally perceived or internally experienced, with an unexpected result—a neutralized category had to be added, as shown below.

Of a total of fifty technical terms selected, about half (24) fell into our externally perceived category, while less than a third (14) fell into our internally experienced category. For more than three fourths of the terms (38) there was coincidence in our independent judgments for these two categories. For the remaining one fourth of the terms (12) there was lack of agreement. Such terms, failing to gain confirmation for either of the two categories, have the effect of being neutralized in respect to the opposition set up by these categories.

Our externally perceived category includes: *abandonee, abator, back* (as in *indorse;* and again as in *back taxes*), *backwards and forwards* (as between ports at sea), *bail, cabotage, carrying away, case* (as in *case agreed upon;* and again as in *case for motion*); *damages, decision, earnest, ebb and flow, effluxion of time, ejectment, factor, grant, habitual, harbor, immovables, jetsam, John Doe,* and *joinder.*

Our internally experienced category includes: *bad* (as in *bad behavior*), *capable, capacity, civil death, easement, efficient cause, fabricate, faculties, false witness, fault, hang* (= remain undetermined), *illegal, immunity,* and *jeopardy.*

Our neutralized items are: *abandon, abet, bad* (as in *bad debt*), *debenture, debt, general exception, genuine* (as in *genuine bond*), *give notice, good* (as in *good cause*), *hearing, impeach,* and *judgment.* Our nonagreement suggests postulating a nonabsolute factor or, in other words, a relative factor, namely, the previous experiences of the perceivers. Whorf was on the side of regarding perception of Gestalt as absolute and hence universal. (All peoples see Ursa Major as one figure, he said; though we call this constellation of stars the "dipper," ways of speaking in other cultures may vary the figure to suit the culture. We question, however, whether all references in all cultures are to 4 + 3 stars. The Chukchee see 6 + 1 stars, with the last called a "double star"; moreover, they see two figures, the 6 = *men hunting* and the "double star" = *fox chewing on antlers.*)

Whether or not Gestalt gives us an absolute which can be used as a meter for universal measuring, some scholars have postulated one or another kind of absolute in semantic work, instead of resting content with translation meaning which merely switches codes from one language to another. Thus, in semantic studies of grading, totality, and end-point relation—more or less in collaboration with others who want ultimately to construct an international language—Edward Sapir tacitly assumed a kind of semantic absolute, which was in part configurational (Sapir 1930, 1944; Sapir and Swadesh 1932). The configurational absolute in Gestalt psychology can be discussed in terms of language structure, as well as in its traditional terms such as the equivalence of stroboscopic with mechanical movement.

If, like H. G. Barnett in *Innovation: The Basis of Cultural Change* (1953), we can convince ourselves that it is possible to have non-absolute Gestalten—configurations whose perception is determined by the prior experiences of the observer—then we can simply regard our neutralized terms as removed from the evidence which remains good in the agreed-upon categories. These suggest that the law in English is more inclined toward terms which are externally perceived; the terms in the Shawnee Laws, on the other hand, lean toward what we classify as internally experienced.

Whorf wrote a paper (1940) in which he exemplified his theory of the application of Gestalt techniques to the discovery of subtle features of the grammar of any language. Thus, in English, Gestalt considerations tell us why we use the simple present for certain verbs (*I hear you*) rather than the present progressive (*I am hearing you*); and why we use the present progressive for other verbs (*I am working*) rather than the simple present (*I work*). In Whorf's theory, Gestalt considerations and grammatical considerations from English structure are integrated into one statement. But for Shawnee it appears to be more difficult to state any integration between classes of distribution within the structure of the language—analogous to the simple and progressive present in English—and classes or subclasses of Gestalt distinctions. The results obtained by Whorf do not, in fact, integrate with Shawnee structure; they can, however, be stated in their own right, as, indeed, Whorf stated them.

We try again to obtain some integration or correlation between (1) grammatical categories and (2) perceptual categories; also between the latter and (3) the content of Shawnee Laws, which might be called the culture of the document, in contrast to the language of the document. If, now, we were to give our translation of the text called Shawnee Laws, we should obtain, *inter alia,* what is generally called "the content" of the document. But here we are not seeking ethnographic information as a whole, or specific legal-folkloristic points embedded in the document; instead we are seeking a procedure which will enable us to categorize morphological features of Shawnee in terms of perception, and a procedure which will allow us to categorize "the content" of our document in terms of perception, too—"the content" of the document in contrast to the morphology of the language in which it is written.

The categorizing of legal terms into two opposing groups is of dubious value, even for English, because the categories set up are invulnerable (not subject to being proved wrong). At best, we can get slight comfort from the fact that, though independent in our judgments, we generally agree. We do not attempt a vote to test agreement on Shawnee legal terms because, however we voted, we would fail to find a rationale for giving significance to the result; any such rationale would have to assume that the judges reacted in part from their intimate knowledge of the language being judged. In the case of Shawnee, the language whose terms were to be judged would be nonnative to the voters.

What we want for Shawnee is a procedure for arriving at categories relevant to some perceptual psychology like Gestalt, but we want our categories to be vulnerable. Perceptual categories are, in general, vague in definition, however clear they may look when projected visually. In order to have these more or less vaguely defined categories susceptible to being proved wrong, we correlate them with morphological features which are relatively precise and specific in definition. The latter then become the defining property of the former.

To this end, we set up two perceptual categories, defined by Shawnee morphemes which mark gender of nouns and actor of intransitive verbs, and which mark voice of transitive verbs; particles are selected for one of the categories irrespective of their referents, but their referents are always subsidiary to verbs and nouns.

1. All animate nouns are categorized as defining what is externally perceived, and as implying activity. In most instances Shawnee nouns are animate when their referents are animals, including humans, which are capable of mobility; in the common ancestor of Shawnee and the other Algonquian languages, according to Bloomfield, animate nouns included "all persons, animals, spirits, and large trees, and some other objects, such as tobacco, maize, apple, raspberry (but not strawberry), calf of leg (but not thigh), stomach, spittle, feather, bird's tail, horn, kettle, pipe for smoking, snowshoe" 1946: 94). In addition to animate nouns, intransitive verbs are categorized as defining the externally perceived when the actor is animate, irrespective of their meaning otherwise—whether of activity or of inert descriptiveness. So, also, all transitive verbs are categorized as defining the externally perceived, provided only that the transitive is nonpassive and noninverse, but irrespective of whether the verb marks animate or inanimate goal.

2. Every transitive verb that includes a preinflectional passive or inverse marking suffix is categorized as defining what is internally experienced; the same verb stem would accordingly fall into our

category 1, above, when lacking passive or inverse suffix, but into category 2, when so suffixed. So also all intransitive verbs with inanimate actor are categorized as defining the internally experienced. Besides these two types of verbs, both inanimate nouns and free particles are put into the category of the internally experienced or background phenomena rather than into the category of what is perceived as figure in the foreground.

When particles leading to one perceptual category are compounded with verbs leading to another, the word in question is neutralized so far as falling into one or another of our contrastive categories is concerned; so, also, when the translator introduces or injects an additional term into the record.

Morphological criteria for our perceptual categories are tentatively selected and subject to both revision and addition (in anticipation of obtaining more fruitful correlations). Though we throw all animate nouns into the externally perceived category, for example, we might, in another selection, distinguish between those animate nouns which are marked as more conspicuous from those which are marked as less conspicuous. The latter, known in Algonquian languages as "the obviative," might be placed in our internally experienced category in contrast to the other animate nouns, which would remain in the externally perceived category.

The first two paragraphs of Shawnee Laws are given below by way of illustration. Sentences are numbered consecutively, without breaks between paragraphs. The latter are marked by initial scope notes indicating the general range of content rather than a précis or itemization of content. The sentences themselves are printed in three varieties of type: roman for Shawnee words whose defining morphology throws them in category 1 (externally perceived); *italics* for words whose Shawnee morphology indicates that they belong to category 2 (internally experienced); SMALL CAPS for what has been described above as neutral or neutralized terms. As will presently be noted, fewer words appear in roman than in italics and small caps; this is true not only for the seventeen-sentence sample given here, but also for the entire text, which is now being prepared for publication in the *International Journal of American Linguistics*. The reader of this paper will understand, of course, that the following translation (like all translations) suggests only in part morphological criteria which serve to classify the translated words into two opposing categories besides a neutral one.

Scope Note 1–6 (Creator gives laws for men who are assured guidance from manitos): "(1) *Thus are* men *presented with a way provided by the Creator* that they may follow—SO THAT HENCEFORTH THEY WILL LIVE IN A SATISFACTORY MANNER, if they adhere to *the law* which she devised. (2) *Certainly, the law was made up for all of those* who are traveling in the direction *intended for* man. (3) *Thus* does one earn the right to the earth when he follows *these laws in the way arranged for him.* (4) *That is the reason* the Creator gave out THE LAWS and the reason men know them. (5) *That is the reason* she gave them out—so that those manitos *turned loose* IN THE WORLD may take pity on men. (6) *That is the reason* she provided men with a way to live."

Scope Note 7–17 (Sexual initiation with wife helped by husband's mother): "(7) Henceforth men teach one another *everything, in order that* they may respect their sisters. (8) WHEN a man IS TWENTY-FIVE YEARS OLD, *at the time he is customarily married off,* he *doesn't* know *a thing about the* way to have intercourse with his wife. (9) At the time they must marry, therefore, YOUNG MEN *are given personal instruction* in the way EACH ONE should try to act when having intercourse with his wife. (10) *It seems that once* a woman helped her son LEARN the way he should try to act. (11) 'You must pull over *your clothes like this,*' she said to her daughter-in-law, 'and you must lie *still,*' she told her. (12) She helped her son get an erection. (13) When he had an erection, he got on top. (14) 'Crawl off,' she told him. (15) *Properly* she directed HIS PENIS to the woman's vaginal orifice. (16) '*Now,* if you get it to go in, say "*all right*" to me, *and* I'll turn the two of you loose.' (17) *But* PEOPLE *become frenzied* when they do not follow exactly *the way as it was arranged for them, the way* they ought to follow, *the way it was intended for them.*"

Until publication of the actual Shawnee forms from which the above translation is derived, it is impossible for the reader to confirm our count—namely, that what is morphologically defined as falling into italics (internally experienced) and into small caps (neutralized) well exceeds what falls into roman (externally perceived). A traditional translation of the type here given is still suggestive; yet to extend this from the first seventeen sentences of the text to the entire text (1,214 sentences) would transform the present paper into a monograph.

The above procedure concerns perceptual categories correlated with morphology; the procedure following concerns perceptual categories correlated with content.

Though space limitations preclude continuation of the sample above—the sentence-by-sentence translation—it is possible to give all the scope notes for the entire Shawnee Laws text, and to classify them according to whether they are mostly Contemplative or mostly Eventful; or whether the two classifications are each conspicuous within one scope note, as in half-and-half proportion (C + E or E + C); or whether they are mixed (alternating between C and E). It is of course the translated sentences which are classified; then all sentences comprehended under one scope note (covering the content of one paragraph) are characterized as all Contemplative, or all Eventful, or mostly the latter with one or two paragraph initial sentences which strike a Contemplative tone as an introduction to sentences which are Eventful. By reading all the scope notes for Shawnee Laws, we can gain an overview of "the content" of the document—the culture of the document—and then compare this with the perceptual categories into which the language of the document falls.

FIRST LAW

All Contemplative (1–6): as above, Creator gives laws for men who are assured guidance from manitos. [Our definition of Contemplative includes what is normative rather than a statement of actualized event; also what is clearly fantasy rather than what is actualizable; also, whatever draws attention to moralistic desiderata rather than to actually overt, or as though overt, cultural happenings.]

Mostly Eventful (7–17): as above, Sexual initiation with wife helped by husband's mother. [The first sentence within this paragraph (7) is Contemplative, as is the last sentence (17); the others (8–16), flanked by the initial and final sentences, are Eventful. With subscript numbers to give the total of sentences within the scope which are Contemplative (C) and which are Eventful (E), we can write $C_1 + E_9 + C_1$. As a category opposing Contemplative, the Eventful comprehends what is said to be possible as a cultural happening, without regard to frequency or to typicality and without regard to overtness or to covertness—except for that part of the covert culture which is said to be entirely confined to what is talked about, and hence is not included in the Eventful.]

Half and half (18–25): Wife separates from husband for eight days each month. [One of the rarest things in the Shawnee Laws is an even division within a scope, as here ($C_4 + E_4$); the first four sentences are Contemplative (e.g., "That's the way people live"); the second four sentences are Eventful (e.g., "Eight days is the length of time a man does not sleep with his wife"). This raises an interesting question as to whether we have paragraphed advantageously; it might be cogently argued that this $C_4 + E_4$ scope proves nothing more than that the two paragraphs are called for; the first, all Contemplative; the second, all Eventful. *Per contra,* the sentiments of our C_4 are related to the action of our E_4; hence we have decided to combine the two into one paragraph.]

Mostly Eventful (26–28): Husband forbidden intercourse with pregnant wife; penalty for violation given. [This is the only scope begun and concluded by Eventful sentences, with intervening Contemplative ($E_1 + C_1 + E_1$).]

All Eventful (29–32): Test for boy arriving at manhood. [This is the only paragraph in which all sentences are Eventful.]

All Contemplative (33–36): Girl arriving at womanhood marries.

Mostly Contemplative (37–43): Infrequent intercourse conducive to health of husband, wife, and children. [This is an example of $E_1 + C_6$, the first sentence being Eventful, the rest Contemplative.]

All Contemplative (44–47): Men following the law will talk about the nature of things.

Half and half (48–60): Old men doctor overly virile young men. [This is an example of $E_6 + C_7$.]

All Contemplative (61–69): Socially beneficial laws oriented in direction of fire person.

Mixed (70–82): Injunction to talk about and to listen to laws of Creator; penalties mentioned. [This is an example of $C_{10} + E_2 + C_1$.]

The next two paragraphs are all Contemplative. First (83–94): Laws oriented in direction of earth person; then (95–109): Dualism, with hell for nonfollowers of law.

The next two paragraphs are mixed. First (110–123): Law prohibiting intercourse for six months after birth of child; then (124–138): Law against adultery for husband; penalties for violation specified.

The next two paragraphs are all Contemplative. First (139–143): Law is for the good of humans; then (144–153): Creator gives laws specifically for women.

Mixed (154–183): Law for women when menstruating; penalties specified [$C_1 + E_4 + C_{25}$].

The next three paragraphs are all Contemplative. First (184–202): The mystery of the law in relation to the mystery of motherhood; then (203–215): Law which recommends twelve children; then (216–219): Explication of four manitos or grandfathers.

Mixed (220–233): Grandfather in the winter. [This is an example of the most frequent mixed type, that with one or two Eventful sentences between two longer stretches of Contemplative sentences; thus, $C_6 + E_2 + C_6$.]

A solid block of twenty-two paragraphs now follows, which is all Contemplative. (234–241): Grandfather who sits in the west; (242–245): Grandfather who sits in the south; (246–252): Grandfather southerner of Spring; (253–257): Heaven is the end-point of law; (258–264): Creator and her manitos helpful when asked for help; (265–270): Heaven is objective, earth is a memory; (271–274): All kinds of languages spoken but Shawnee involved in repeating the laws; (275–280): Benefit from prayer in terms of paths or alternative directions; (281–286): Prayers which reach up to our grandmother in heaven are related to survival; (287–295): All are equal to the Creator who may not be all-powerful; (296–299): Devil tempts away; (300–324): Penalties (including insanity, half-witted visitors, sadism) for following what the Devil devises (e.g., liquor, different languages, different laws); (325–331): Plan of creation, including levels of heaven, not for benefit of men who are thoughtless of plan; (332–339): Benefit for those who follow laws, with provision for misunderstanding; (340–354): Instruction on how to receive knowledge of laws with notification (prophecy) year ahead of time to be interpreted as laws; (355–365): Fire person and water person, corn, bean, pumpkin created to help man; (366–373): Being humble, saying prayer, and "pity" gladden Creator and strengthen man; (374–390): Good results flowing from Creator's plan, as rain from water person, and as alternation of night and day; (391–409): Laws are good because Creator loves all, sees all (but is not herself seen until afterlife), and because they, as all created things, will never stop; (410–413): Do not doubt, because doubting makes duty and language appear disagreeable; (414–434): Hunting laws conveyed to animals as well as to humans; (435–447): Travel laws for humans and animals encountered in traveling to be learned before starting out on travels.

Mixed (448–459): Laws regulating women, with penalties (failure in health and hunting). [The actual mixture of sentences for this paragraph is $C_3 + E_1 + C_8$.]

The next eight paragraphs (the rest of the First Law) are all Contemplative. Their scopes are (460–470): Laws are unforgettable, but weakness and insanity result from neglect, in contrast to fulfilment for obedience; (471–493): Interpretation of laws in council and by grandfathers, as Eagle; (494–512): Omniscience of grandfathers, especially of the Thunderers, and their protective role toward man;

(513–517): Frequent prayer beneficial for Creator and grandfathers who listen, as at dances; (518–536): Grandfather Sun and Grandfather Moon carry man through day and urge preparation for following day, so all will be well; (537–562): Creator promises unidentifiable sound as signal to good persons among chiefs and councilors who are created with special insight, are faultless in speech, and able in translation of Creator's thought; (563–574): Leader to take his people for sojourn to father in heaven and after twelve days of rain to return to earth populated with animals, as at first creation; (575–594): Laws direct followers to little road on which all goes well until the earth burns, destroying all life, which will be re-created as at the first creation, with people descending from two men and two women.

SECOND LAW

Mixed (595–638): Continuity from generation to generation; from infancy to maturity, with sympathy from Creator, with constant values—all toward the increase of life [$C_{13} + E_2 + C_{29}$].

The next five paragraphs (the rest of the Second Law) are all Contemplative. The scopes are (639–649): Foods have savor because men possess laws for caring for everything and will transmit the laws to their children; (650–660): Manitos remember their grandchildren (humans) and are in sympathy with the laws, and humans remember manitos who talk to them; (661–677): Sun sees all, helps all in living now and into the future—as long as men follow rules handed down by the Creator who sits watching in heaven; (678–700): Law for snake and insect to serve as medicine to help those who have encountered the nonbeneficial—as long as Creator allows the earth to exist; (701–704): Man to live and multiply, never disappear entirely, and arrive in heaven.

THIRD LAW

Mixed (705–715): Law regulating deer to serve man by being eaten [$C_6 + E_1 + C_4$].

The next five paragraphs (the rest of the Third Law) are all Contemplative. (716–733): Deer's freedom from disease (gained by eating medicines) good for humans whose kind talk is good for deer; (734–751): Deer created as children of Earth Person; rules given so that no one will ever come to destroy deer; (752–761): Longevity of laws not known to Creator, who is gladdened when laws are currently followed; (762–778): What is sacred and what is to be pitied—both deer and man, for both will eventually go to heaven, in the morning, crying;

(779–791): Speech made on arriving at place where our grandchild lives gives prophecy of end of world, followed by the dead rising, and even the trees being renewed.

FOURTH LAW

Mostly Contemplative (792–801): Law regulating bear to serve man by being killed by him [$C_9 + E_1$].

Mixed (802–816): Disposal of bear entrails and their use by humans; fate of bear after being killed four times, and his speech to bear overseer [$E_2 + C_6 + E_4 + C_3$].

The remaining three paragraphs in the Fourth Law are all Contemplative. First (817–832): Bear to relay information from Creator to man, who passes information along to others with Creator notified by bear of man's action; then (833–837): Bear to live in wilderness; then (838–848): Bear to aid in bringing mankind to heaven at date unknown even to Creator.

FIFTH LAW

All Contemplative (849–854): Dog to help men when they hunt.

The next two paragraphs are mixed. First (855–866): Man is not to abuse dog but dog to be fed occasionally by man, who in turn is to profit by dog's premonitions [$C_7 + E_1 + C_4$]; then (867–873): Man enjoined never to kill dog; penalties mentioned [$C_1 + E_1 + C_5$].

The next five paragraphs (the rest of the Fifth Law) are all Contemplative. (874–877): Dog to be man's friend; (878–891); How the behavior of a certain dog will indicate the approach of the world's end; (892–902): Dog to be dressed and shod exactly like his grandchild; (903–914): Reason given why man hunts animals and how dog is to help man when man hunts; (915–927): Not all of the laws apply equally to all beings who populate the earth, but all beings are brought to heaven.

SIXTH LAW

The first two paragraphs are all Contemplative. First (928–939): Birds to warn men of things not beneficial to them; then (940–948): Birds are to pity men, especially when they pray.

Mixed (949–961): Birds and man to aid one another; birds to pray for man [$C_1 + E_1 + C_{11}$].

The remaining two paragraphs of this law are all Contemplative. First (962–968): Birds eventually to go to heaven, but while on earth they are not to wonder about things; then (969–976): Birds and men to dress in similar fashion; Creator gladdened and birds brought to heaven by following this rule.

SEVENTH LAW

The paragraphs of the Seventh Law total two; both are all Contemplative. (977–988): Wolf to live in wilderness and to act as intermediary between the guides and man; (989–1004): Man is notified of how the law applies to wolf so that both man and wolf know how they are to aid one another on mutual road to heaven.

EIGHTH LAW

The single paragraph of the Eighth Law is mixed. (1005–1041): Buffalo to be grandfather to man, who will not say anything bad about him, will feed him, and will kill, cook and eat him on earth, and share with him in heaven [$C_7 + E_1 + C_{13} + E_2 + C_{14}$].

NINTH LAW

The paragraphs of the Ninth Law total three, which are all Contemplative. (1042–1050): Creator interrogates raccoon as to what he will look like and how he will live; (1051–1071): Raccoon will never counsel his grandchild, but will help him find water; (1072–1078): Raccoon notified of where he is to live and when he will roam about.

TENTH LAW

All Contemplative (1079–1082): Turtle to live in water.

The two remaining paragraphs in the Tenth Law are mixed. First (1083–1091): Man kills turtle to make medicine and is strengthened by turtle's strength [$C_2 + E_3 + C_4$]; then (1092–1101): Turtle to be a rain maker for man [$C_3 + E_1 + C_6$].

ELEVENTH LAW

All Contemplative (1102–1107): Turkey to live in wilderness and sleep on tree.

Mixed (1108–1118): Turkey to be in same clan as man, to be leader of man's prayers, and to be eaten by him [$C_2 + E_1 + C_8$].

Mostly Contemplative (1119–1127): Man forbidden to use grease of turkey or to fry squirrel; penalty for violation given [$C_8 + E_1$].

Contemplative (1128–1134): Injunction to pity man.

TWELFTH LAW

Mixed (1135–1146): Crow to receive information in dreams which he will tell to man, who will eat him [$C_9 + E_1 + C_2$].

The remaining paragraphs in Shawnee Laws are all Contemplative. (1147–1155): Crow will dispose of the carcasses of dead animals at the beginning of winter and feed snakes and birds; (1156–1162): Crow will aid man in hunting and be fed by him; (1163–1165): Crow to have dreams after man defeats enemy in battle; (1166–1172): Crow to pity man and become a manito; man to respect crow and not come near him; (1173–1182): Creator will tell crow to warn man of things he will not be benefited by; crow will give man this warning and advice on children; (1183–1197): Laws given and manitos created so that Creator will keep man in mind and won't wonder about him, and so that man won't wonder about things; (1198–1214): Manitos promise to help man by listening to him through smoke from their place under the sun, and to give him Creator's instructions. [Though our phrasing of the scope notes for the first two paragraphs above—(1147–1155) and (1156–1162)—read as though the content were full of action, the Shawnee phrasing of the sentences in these paragraphs gives an opposite impression—mystical, allusive, otherworldly.]

In the perceptual categorization proposed above, two sets of single categories are opposed—in consideration of the linguistic structure alone (externally perceived versus internally experienced), and in consideration of the ethnographic content alone (Eventful versus Contemplative). We now suggest the possibility of an integration between the two sets which might lead to a contrast of greater depth than when single categories are opposed. Something less than an equation, perhaps a relationship of implication, might be expected between the members of the opposition set up for the language and the content, respectively. If a contrast of greater depth were obtainable, it would come out of combining, as pair (1), the externally perceived (1.1) with the Eventful category (1.2); and opposing this to pair (2), a combination of the internally experienced (2.1) with the Contemplative category (2.2).

In general, everything attributed to (1), both under (1.1) and (1.2), is concerned with the outline of Gestalten, with what is figural, either directly visual or inferred in space as figures projected from another sense. Everyday experiences—like the Doppler effect in hearing a higher pitch when a train is coming than when it is going away, or childhood experiences as discovering the shape of some object in playing blind man's touch—lead to an association of touch and shape, of sight and space, of sound and space, and of time and space. These associations must surely enter into our comprehension of motion, since motion goes on in space, and space is a characteristic component in such associations.

In general, everything attributed to (2), both under (2.1) and (2.2), is concerned with the field of Gestalten, with the filling-in of outline, the less conspicuous, the background. The associations for (2) can be stated as the converse of those for (1). The nonfigural, the field or background, is associated with the nonactive, with the passive, with what remains unmoving—this for the negative side; on the positive side, categories of type (2) are concerned with what is internal to the perceiver, and Whorf and others have extended this to include ego considerations—the egoic.

It is still not certain whether the proposal for combining categories in pairs would lead to useful correlations, or whether the categories are independent variables in respect to each other. We have not given the evidence on the distribution of (1.1) and (2.1), the morphologically defined categories; but we can anticipate that they might well be more evenly distributed throughout the document than (1.2) and (2.2), the content-defined categories.

As the record shows, nothing is more striking in the style of Shawnee Laws than the way the second kind of categories are scattered, beginning with some apparent alternation, and then proceeding to clusters or blocks of one category, with the Contemplative characterizing the larger blocks of paragraphs and also occurring more frequently than others. The first paragraph in the document is all Contemplative; this is followed by paragraphs which are mostly Eventful, then half and half, then mostly Eventful again, then all Eventful. Thereafter, and for the remainder of the document, blocks of Contemplative paragraphs are, in effect, merely flanked by paragraphs which are otherwise characterized as Eventful (E), mixed generally (M), or mixed half and half (HH). The inventory for the remainder of the document is given in tabular form to show the stylistic dominance of the contemplative over the other categories.

3 Contemplative paragraphs + HH + C + M paragraphs
2 Contemplative + 2M paragraphs
2 Contemplative + M paragraphs
3 Contemplative + M paragraphs
22 Contemplative + M paragraphs
8 Contemplative + M paragraphs
5 Contemplative + M paragraphs
6 Contemplative + M paragraphs
4 Contemplative + 2M paragraphs
7 Contemplative + M paragraphs
4 Contemplative + 2M + C + M paragraphs
2 Contemplative + M paragraphs
7 Contemplative paragraphs

REFERENCES CITED

Barnett, H. G.

1953 *Innovation: The Basis of Cultural Change*. New York, McGraw-Hill.

Bloomfield, Leonard

1946 "Algonquian." In: *Linguistic Structures of Native America*, pp. 85–129. Viking Fund Publications in Anthropology, No. 6.

Sapir, Edward

1930 *Totality*. Linguistic Society of America, Monograph No. 6.

1944 "Grading, A Study in Semantics," *Philosophy of Science*, **11**:93–116.

Sapir, Edward and Morris Swadesh

1932 *The Expression of the Ending-Point Relation in English, French, and German*. Linguistic Society of America, Monograph No. 10.

Whorf, Benjamin L.

1940 "Gestalt Techniques of Stem Composition in Shawnee," Prehistory Research Series, Indiana Historical Society, **1**, No. 9:393–406.

AN EXAMINATION OF THE CONCEPTIONS OF BENJAMIN WHORF IN THE LIGHT OF THEORIES OF PERCEPTION AND COGNITION

FRANKLIN FEARING

I. ASPECTS OF THE THEORY AS RELATED TO HUMAN COGNITION

BENJAMIN WHORF in a series of papers (1952*a*, 1952*b*) has presented a number of generalizations regarding the relation of thought and behavior to language, which have important implications not only for the linguistic sciences and anthropology but also for social psychology. These generalizations assert that the commonly held notion that the cognitive processes of all human beings possess a common logical structure (called by Whorf "natural logic") which operates prior to and independently of communication through language, is erroneous. It is Whorf's view that the linguistic patterns themselves determine what the individual perceives in his world and how he thinks about it. Since these patterns vary widely, the modes of thinking and perceiving in groups utilizing different linguistic systems will result in basically different world views. Briefly stated, according to Whorf, language shapes our ideas rather than merely expressing them.

These conceptualizations are derived primarily from analyses of certain exotic linguistic systems, notably those of the Hopi, Shawnee, and Nootka Indian cultures, which are compared with the family of languages called by Whorf SAE (Standard Average European). It is the purpose of the present paper to examine Whorf's assumptions regarding the unique relationship between language and thought, in the light of relevant findings and theory in those areas of psychology which are concerned with the interrelations between symbolic processes, thinking and perception.

Before undertaking these analyses it seems desirable briefly to recapitulate those aspects of Whorf's theory which are concerned with cognitive processes. For our purposes they may be summarized under four headings.

1. *The linguistic relativity principle.*—No individual is free to describe nature with absolute impartiality, but is "constrained to certain modes of interpretation even while he thinks himself most free.

. . . We are thus introduced to a new principle of relativity, which holds that all observers are not led by the same physical evidence to the same picture of the universe, unless their linguistic backgrounds are similar, or can in some way be calibrated" (1952*a:* 5). The linguistic relativity principle means "that users of markedly different grammars are pointed by their grammars toward different types of observations and different evaluations of externally similar acts of observation, and hence are not equivalent as observers but must arrive at somewhat different views of the world" (p. 11).

Experience of nature is segmented in a particular manner by particular linguistic patterns.

We cut up and organize the spread and flow of events as we do largely because, through our mother tongue, we are parties to an agreement to do so, not because nature itself is segmented in exactly that way for all to see. Languages differ not only in how they build their sentences but in how they break down nature to secure the elements to put in those sentences. . . . English terms like "sky," "hill," "swamp," persuade us to regard some elusive aspect of nature's endless variety as a distinct *thing*, almost like a table or chair. Thus English and similar tongues lead us to think of the universe as a collection of rather distinct objects and events corresponding to words. Indeed this is the implicit picture of classical physics and astronomy—that the universe is essentially a collection of detached objects of different sizes [p. 21].

The implications of this principle are far-reaching. For example, Whorf states (p. 44) that the concepts of time and matter basic to Western European science

are not given in substantially the same form by experience to all men but depend upon the nature of the language or languages through the use of which they have been developed. They do not depend so much upon *any one system* (e.g., tense, or nouns) within the grammar as upon the ways of analyzing and reporting experience which have become fixed in the language as integrated "fashions of speaking" and which cut across the typical grammatical classifications, so that such a "fashion" may include lexical, morphological, syntactic, and otherwise systematically diverse means coordinated in a certain frame of consistency. Our own "time" differs markedly from Hopi "duration." It is conceived as a space of strictly limited dimensions, or sometimes as a motion upon such a space, and employed as an intellectual tool accordingly. Hopi "duration" seems to be inconceivable in terms of space or motion, being the mode in which life differs from form, and consciousness *in toto* from the spatial elements of consciousness. Certain ideas born of our own time-concept, such as that of absolute simultaneity, would be either very difficult to express or impossible and devoid of meaning under the Hopi conception, and would be replaced by operational concepts. Our "matter" is the physical sub-type of "substance" or "stuff," which is conceived as the formless extensional item that must be joined with form before there can be real existence. In Hopi there seems to be nothing corresponding to it; there are no formless extensional items; existence may or may not have form, but what it also has, with or without form, is intensity and duration, these being nonextensional and at bottom the same.

SAE objectifies time as if it were a ribbon or scroll marked off in equal spaces. This is incompatible with the Hopi linguistic pattern, which is essentially ahistorical. The past for them is always implicit in the present. Whorf notes that a cultural resultant of the Western European view of time is our linguistically conditioned interest in record-keeping, diaries, histories, and the concern with the "past" generally, as well as our emphasis on devices such as clocks, calendars, and time graphs, for the exact quantification of time.

Perhaps the most important example of the relativity principle is found in the "use of language on data" (p. 11) that has made possible the scientific world view of Western European cultures. Whorf, however, is careful to state that Western European science is not *caused* by language, but is "simply colored by it" (p. 11). Historic, economic, and other forces happened to converge in a quarter of the world where certain linguistic patterns (SAE) were dominant, and the result was the kind of thinking and, as Whorf would say, talking which we know as science. But the kind of science which resulted in Western Europe could only have occurred in a culture possessing linguistic patterns of a particular character.

Comment.—The linguistic relativism of Whorf seems to be a special type of cultural-relativistic theory, with which social scientists are already familiar. Cultural-relativistic thinking emphasizes culture as a determiner of the individual's values, motives, needs, and, in general, his world view. Such theory stresses the diversity and role of cultures and minimizes the biologic universals as controlling factors in human behavior. The special character of Whorf's conception consists in the central role of linguistic patterns.

2. *Background and obligatory character of linguistic systems.*—The complex systems of linguistic patterns which are assumed to determine thinking are conceived to be outside the critical consciousness and control of the individual. The notion that when we talk we are completely free to express any ideas we wish to express is an illusion.

This illusory appearance results from the fact that the obligatory phenomena within the apparently free flow of talk are so completely autocratic that speaker and listener are bound unconsciously as though in the grip of a law of nature. The phenomena of language are background phenomena, of which the talkers are unaware, or, at most very dimly aware . . ." [Whorf 1952*a:* 11].

The phenomena of language are to its own speakers largely of a background character and so are outside the critical consciousness and control of the speaker who is expounding natural logic. Hence, when anyone, as a natural logician, is talking about reason, logic, and the laws of correct thinking, he is apt to be simply marching in step with purely grammatical facts that have somewhat of a background character in his own language or family of languages but are by no means universal in all languages and in no sense common substratum of reason [p. 4].

These background systems or grammars are not merely reproducing instruments for ideas, but shapers of ideas. They furnish the program and guide of the individual's mental activity and determine his syntheses and analyses. They are both unconscious and obligatory.

Thinking itself is, according to Whorf, "mysterious," but "by far the greatest light upon it that we have is thrown by the study of language" (1952*b:* 173). The linguistic pattern of each language or family of languages determines the course of thought. Thinking

follows a network of tracks laid down in a given language, an organization which may concentrate systematically upon certain phases of reality, certain aspects of intelligence, and systematically discard others featured by other languages. The individual is utterly unaware of their organization and is constrained completely within its unbreakable bonds [p. 177].

While thinking occurs "in a language" Whorf notes that it is not necessarily in *words.* "Much thinking never brings in words at all, but manipulates whole paradigms, word classes, and such grammatical orders 'behind' or 'above' the focus of personal consciousness" (p. 173 n.).

Comment.—It is difficult to disentangle the unconscious, obligatory patterning imposed by language from the data of experience on which it operates. Both are nonconscious. The formulations of Gestalt psychology, with which Whorf was much impressed, make a figure-ground experience a characteristic of primary awareness. However, this is itself a form of organization, and it is proper to ask at what point the linguistic patterns begin to operate.

3. *Processes which are prior to linguistic patterning.*—Whorf recognizes a form of experience which occurs irrespective of language. This primordial experience may be common to all men.

The tremendous importance of language cannot, in my opinion, be taken to mean necessarily that nothing is back of it, of the nature of what has traditionally been called "mind." My own studies suggest to me that language, for all its kingly role, is in some sense a superficial embroidery upon deeper processes of consciousness which are necessary before any communication, signalling, or symbolism whatsoever can occur and which also can at a pinch effect communication (though not true *agreement*) without language's and without symbolism's aid. I mean "superficial" in the sense that all processes of chemistry, for example, can be said to be superficial upon the deeper layer of physical existence, which we know variously as intra-atomic, electronic, or subelectronic [1952*a:* 21].

The different languages—for Whorf there is no such universal as Language—may have a "sublinguistic or superlinguistic" base. These, says Whorf (p. 21), may be "not altogether unlike, even if much unlike, what we now call 'mental.'" In another place Whorf states that "experience more basic than language tells us that if energy is expended effects are produced" (p. 38).

There is, according to Whorf, a prelinguistic apprehension of space. "The *apprehension* of space," he says, "is given in substantially the same form by *experience irrespective of language*" (p. 44, italics added). He refers to the experiments of the Gestalt psychologists to support this and makes the distinction between the *apprehension* of space which occurs independently of language and the *conceptualization* of space which is linguistically conditioned.

Although the Hopi see space-forms as we do, they do not use spatial concepts as surrogates for nonspatial relationships such as time, intensity, and tendency. This metaphorical reference to the nonspatial by the spatial was fixed, according to Whorf, by Latin. He says, "If we compare, say Hebrew, we find that while Hebrew has some allusion to not-space as space, Latin has more. . . . This is not true of all languages—it is quite untrue of Hopi" (p. 43). That the linguistic development in Latin, which markedly affected later tongues, was from the spatial to the nonspatial is responsible for the belief, which still persists, that "this is the natural direction of semantic change in all languages, and for the persistent notion in Western learned circles (in strong contrast to Eastern ones) that objective experience is prior to subjective" (p. 43).

Kinesthesia, the awareness of muscular movement, and synesthesia, the identification of the properties of one sense modality in terms of another, are both regarded as arising prior to language. However, both are made "more conscious" by particular linguistic patterns. Synesthetic experience is made

> more conscious by a linguistic metaphorical system that refers to non-spatial experiences by terms for spatial ones, though undoubtedly it arises from a deeper source. Probably in the first instance metaphor arises from synesthesia and not the reverse, yet metaphor need not become firmly rooted in linguistic pattern as Hopi shows [p. 42].

The effect of language on this nonlinguistic experience which occurs prior to language is to sharpen and channel it in a particular direction.

> What is significant for our thesis is that language, through lexation, has made the speaker more acutely conscious of certain dim psychic sensations; it has actually

produced awareness on lower planes than its own, a power of the nature of magic. There is a yogic mastery in the power of language to remain independent of lower-psyche facts, to override them, now point them up, now toss them out of the picture, to mould the nuances of words, to its own rule, whether the psychic ring of the sounds fits or not. If the sounds fit, the psychic quality of the sounds is increased, and this can be noticed by the layman. If the sounds do not fit, the psychic quality changes to accord with the linguistic meaning, no matter how incongruous with the sounds, and this is not noticed by the layman [1952*b:* 186].

Comment.—The question of the degree of organization or lack of it at the nonlinguistic levels of experience of the individual is left unclear by Whorf. It seems to be his conception that there is some sort of metaphoric-synesthetic experience common to all men which transcends cultural and linguistic patterning. To this experience he applies the term *apprehension,* which he distinguishes from the linguistically determined *conceptualization.* We are bound to inquire how it is, from Whorf's point of view, that the individual can apprehend independently of language and what form this nonlinguistic apprehension takes. The data on which the linguistic patterns operate are presumably the observer's experiences. But the "data" must somehow be selectively identified, and for Whorf this identification should reflect the observer's linguistic systems. This seems implied in the statement, quoted above, that the "users of markedly different grammars *are pointed by their grammars toward different types of observation* and different evaluations of externally similar acts of observation . . ." (italics added). But, in another place, Whorf refers to "experience more basic than language" (1952*a:* 38). This seems to suggest that there are mental processes which transcend and occur prior to language. This problem is critical with respect to the hypothesized relationship between language and perception.

4. *Historical relations between linguistic patterns and culture.*—Whorf assumes an interaction between cultural norms and linguistic patterns. There are "connections but not correlations or diagnostic correspondences between cultural norms and linguistic patterns" (1952*a:* 45). As to which was first historically, he says, "In the main they have grown up together, constantly influencing each other. But in this partnership the nature of the language is the factor that limits plasticity and rigidifies channels of development in the more autocratic way" (p. 43). Language "represents the mass mind," and while it is affected by innovations it is affected "little and slowly." It is this rigidity of linguistic patterns that obstructs the development of new world views, especially new scientific theory. Such obstructions can be overcome only, according to Whorf, by developing a new

language. "Science," he says, "is beginning to find that there is something in the cosmos that is not in accord with the concepts we have formed. . . . It is trying to frame a *new language* by which to adjust to a wider universe" (p. 41).

Comment.—While Whorf is properly noncommittal about the question of historical origins, he is emphatic regarding the dominant role which linguistic patterns play once they have been established. They "rigidify" the channels of development, and to individual "inventors and innovators [they] legislate with the decree immediate." This does not tell us much about the developmental sequence in the individual. In view of the compelling role which Whorf ascribes to language, we may inquire at what point it begins to operate.

In the following pages these conceptualizations are discussed with special reference to (*a*) their implications for a theory of knowledge and (*b*) their relation to relevant psychological theories of cognition and perception. The intent of this discussion is not to present any solution of the problems raised by Whorf but to indicate a context —certainly not the only context—within which his theory may be considered.

II. THE RELATIVISTIC HYPOTHESIS

A. THE IMPASSE CREATED BY THE RELATIVISTIC HYPOTHESIS

Since Whorf's formulations are concerned with psychological processes and concepts ("thinking," "communicating," "behavior," "meaning," etc.), and are based on inferences from anthropological (linguistic) data, the whole question of the psychological use of anthropological data and the anthropological use of psychological data is raised. The issues go far beyond questions of the methodological strategies of two scientific disciplines. The wealth of ethnological and psychological data which have established the reality and discrete character of cultures and their enormous potency in determining human behavior has not only made cross-cultural comparisons difficult but even implies that the attempt itself is invalid. In its extreme form the hypothesis of cultural relativism asserts that the mold of culture is absolute, final, and specific in determining all the characteristics of the individual. If he has been exposed to, and presumably internalized, the norms, values, "world view" of his culture, he may be said to be enculturated or, to use Mead's term (1946), "fully acculturated."

In Whorf's view, linguistic patterns, operating unconsciously, play the dominant role in the enculturating process. These patterns determine how the individual in Western European culture analyzes reality. Other cultures arrive at equally convincing but quite different analyses. This is the "new principle of relativity," which holds that all observers cannot arrive at the same picture of the universe unless their linguistic backgrounds can "in some way be calibrated."

This is not only a theory of cognition; it is a theory of cognition which asserts that the cognitive processes themselves are determined in such a manner as to create almost insurmountable barriers to cross-cultural comparisons. The prospects for "calibration" do not appear to be too bright. According to Whorf, we may not accept "the few recent dialects of the Indo-European family, and the rationalizing techniques elaborated from their patterns, as the apex of the evolution of the human mind . . ." (1952*a:* 7).

It is impossible to explore all the ramifications of these problems except to point out that the more extreme forms of the cultural relativistic hypothesis, of which Whorf's is an example, appear to have resulted in an impasse in which constructs designed to transcend culture are themselves culturally determined and hence, in a sense, suspect. The special field of inquiry concerned with these problems, sometimes called the sociology of knowledge, has recently been reviewed by Merton (1949). As he sees it, studies in this field are concerned with the examination of the "entire gamut of cultural products (ideas, ideologies, juristic and ethical beliefs, philosophy, science, technology)" from the point of view of their relations to other "existential factors in the society or culture" (p. 217).

He points out that the result of these inquiries has been to create a "context of distrust" (p. 217) in which the concern is not with the validity of the differing perspectives or world views which are revealed, but with *how it happened that such views came about.* These systems of ideas or world views are conceived as end products, the face value of which may be discounted since it is assumed that they were *unwittingly* determined. They are then examined in the new context which is concerned with their "real meaning." In many of its aspects Whorf's approach is an example of Merton's formulations. The individual's picture of the universe is *unwittingly* determined by linguistic patterns, and our attention is directed to these as the reality behind the picture.

In one of the few examinations by a psychologist of these problems, Köhler (1937: 273) raises the question regarding the fitness of persons trained in Western science to understand less intellectual cultures.

What are the objective facts of nature? What is the best access to objective knowledge in this sense? What influences on the other hand are apt to hamper our progress in this field? Since the 17th century such questions have gradually introduced a definite set of values which is now so dominant that far beyond the circle of scientists proper the outlook of civilized people is thoroughly governed by these particular ideals. A sober attitude towards a real world is instilled in children of our civilization by the words and actions of their parents. Long ago the most basic convictions of scientific culture lost the character of theoretically formulated sentences. Gradually they have become aspects of the world as we *perceive* it; the world *looks* today what our forefathers learned to say about it; we act and speak accordingly.

The point which Köhler stresses is that the world as perceived by man in our scientific culture is the product of complicated historical processes in which the orientations of Western physics and sensory physiology have played a dominant part. Whatever has not fitted into these orientations has gradually been "neglected and despised because of its 'subjective' nature. . . . Judged from a merely psychological standpoint and without any reference to physical reality this [the scientific] aspect of the world is therefore no more genuine than any previous appearance of man's perceived environment." Indeed, Köhler suggests that the more "natural" traits of perception may be found "where science has not exerted its modifying influence," i.e., in the world of the primitive. The study of this world presents difficulties. "The psychologist no less than other people has learned to see the world through the eye-glasses of natural science. . . . If primitives have such another view, their mystical thinking will be made responsible for it" (p. 275).

Köhler's analysis is particularly relevant to the present discussion because it states the problem in *perceptual* terms. Except that it does not refer to linguistic factors as such, it supports Whorf's thesis. Whorf's "fashions of speaking" become "fashions of perceiving."

A different but equally critical approach to the problem is that of Mead (1946). While pointing out the inutility of such concepts as "the primitive" who thinks prelogically and represents the childhood of the human race, she thinks that the more sophisticated concept of primitive man as a fully acculturated individual may be equally sterotypic. She suggests that the negative aspects of ethnological research—negative, that is, from the point of view of a comprehensive science of man that transcends cultural boundaries—may be offset by the fact that it takes advantage of two important characteristics of primitive societies: (1) they are social forms which we can neither produce experimentally nor derive by extrapolation, and (2) their relatively smaller size makes it possible to examine the individual within the whole society in a way that is impossible with larger groups in a highly stratified society. While not meeting in full the issues raised by the relativistic hypothesis, this formulation implies that significant generalizations may result from the comparison of data obtained from the study of nonliterate and civilized societies.

The relativistic hypothesis, especially Whorf's particular formulation, raises the question of the extent to which there exists a human nature which has a shape of its own, a shape which exists prior to, or underlies, and must in some manner interact with, the configuration of forces called culture, including language. Asch, for example, has recently trenchantly criticized the relativistic hypothesis especially as applied to the development of ethical values, on the ground that it assumes a "dynamically empty organism, lacking directed forces toward nature and society" (1952: 373). The relativistic hypothesis fails, he believes, "to describe the concrete cognitive and emotional operations one encounters in the social setting" (p. 374). For Asch, the psychological basis of cultural relativism can only be a simplified mechanistic stimulus-response psychology, the major constructs of which are "drive," "reward," and "response," and even though these may be adequate for infrahuman organisms, he regards it as "highly questionable whether they apply without modification to social action" (p. 374).

The current interest in the relations between personality structure and culture has resulted in an extensive literature, some of which bears on this question. There is general agreement that the individual's culture plays an almost all-powerful role in patterning his behavior, in determining what he believes in, what he strives for and how he strives for it, in a word, his personality structure. There is also a consensus—although somewhat less than unanimous—that there is some sort of underlying organization, possibly biological or "constitutional," common to all men with which culture may interact but which it may not eliminate. Such an assumption, according to Mead (1949: 111), enables us to understand "those widespread similarities in cultural behavior which occur in different parts of the world, at different levels of cultural development." Dennis' (1942) use of the terms "autogenous" and "sociogenous" to distinguish between personality manifestations which develop as a consequence of biological maturation, and those which are the result of cultural factors, recognizes this relationship.

The possibility of cross-cultural universals has recently been discussed by Redfield (1952, 1953). He is concerned with the world views of primitive and precivilized peoples in different societies, and particularly with the question of the extent to which they possess factors in common. "After denying for quite a time that psychic unity exists," he says, "anthropologists now take an interest in something not too different, universal human nature" (1953: 90). Redfield notes that concepts in this area are hardly developed and comparative studies barely begun. Nevertheless, he believes that certain assertions may be made which will hold for the world view of primitive man. He makes three such assertions: (1) For primitive man "the distinction between persons and things is not sharply made: all objects, not only man, are regarded somewhat as if they were persons" (1952: 34). (2) In the primitive world view the attitude of man toward not-man is one of "participant maintenance." Such an attitude implies mutuality rather than exploitation in the relation of man to "nature." (3) For primitive man the universe is morally significant. There is an universal moral order in which man, nature, and God participate.

In a somewhat similar vein, Murdock (1945) points out that certain recurrent stimulus patterns, such as meteorological phenomena, anatomical characteristics, or physiological cycles, are universally experienced and may be associated with cultural responses. There are in nearly all cultures, he says, beliefs about, and responses to, items such as "the sun and the moon, darkness, rain, thunder, the ocean, mountains, streams, blood, hair, the heart, the genitals, sneezing, breathing, menstruation," and many similar phenomena (p. 137). Feuer (1953), in a critical review of Whorf's linguistic relativity principle, also points out that all men in the struggle for survival have common problems. These, he believes, result in a "common, universal, scientific mode of thinking which manages to express itself in all languages" (p. 96). On this basis he rejects the Whorfian relativism.

The pros and cons of the argument regarding the relativistic hypothesis need not be expanded here. The examples given afford documentation for the considerable degree of ambivalence regarding it that Herskovits (1951) has noted. On the one hand, he points out (p. 162), the study of many cultures validates it, and, on the other, the absolutist tradition challenges it. It is necessary, he believes, to sift out the *universals* found in all human groups from the *absolutes* which members of a particular group may insist upon applying to groups with differing orientations. It is necessary to take into account the primary character of the enculturative experience which gives men their particular world view.

B. THE DEVELOPMENTAL HYPOTHESIS

An approach which certainly does not resolve all the difficulties of the relativistic hypothesis, and which has obvious difficulties of its own, is to consider the similarities and differences in the behavior of literates and nonliterates in the light of hypothetical developmental sequences analogous to the sequences of biological development. Such an approach might provide a set of co-ordinates within which the uniqueness and discreteness of cultural phenomena are recognized and at the same time ordered to constructs which may make cross-cultural comparisons possible. If, for example, as Whorf asserts, the substrata which determine the unique character of the cognitive activities in various cultures are linguistic, we might inquire regarding (*a*) the stage in the development of the individual at which these influences begin to operate, (*b*) the character of the organization of the individual's cognitive processes prior to the appearance of the linguistic influences, and (*c*) the extent to which nonlinguistic processes persist in all stages of development.

A systematic attempt to order the mental life of children, "primitives," and nonprimitives to hypothetical developmental sequences is that of Werner (1948). Using the comparative method, he finds that certain types of mental organization or structures are characteristic of particular levels of development. There are, he believes, certain parallels in the form and structure of the thinking, conceptualizing, and perceiving of primitives, children, and certain psychotics. These he conceives to be the bases for functional levels of development. Werner is careful to point out that the similarities in mental organization which he believes may be ordered to levels of mental development are not evidence for theories of cultural recapitulation, or historic-evolutionary development. He is not concerned with "an actual or speculative history of mankind. . . . We ask, for example, not whether a pattern of functions is relatively early or late in the historical scale, but whether it represents a low or high level of mentality" (p. 17). Further, the differences between primitive and the more advanced levels of development are conceived not as differences on a graduated quantitative scale, but as qualitatively distinct functional levels. Modes of thinking and perceiving of nonliterates and children are understood not as exotic or archaic departures from some "scientific" norm, but as modes which are adequate for their situations and levels of development.

The general direction of both organic and mental development is toward increasing differentiation and centralization or hierarchic integration. Werner conceptualizes this increasing differentiation of structure and function of mental phenomena by such terms as "syncretic-discrete," "diffuse-articulated," and "indefinite-definite." Although each of these pairs characterizes a specific dimension of this development, basically the distinction is between a mode of cognition in which the world is apprehended as dynamically related to, even dependent on, the individual, and one in which the world is apprehended as relatively static and independent of the observer. Werner's concept of syncretic organization, especially its particular manifestation in the field of perception known as *physiognomic* perception, is of special importance for present purposes and will be discussed in detail in a later section.

Although differing from Werner in several important respects, Mead (1946) also accepts some sort of developmental sequence, which distinguishes the differences between the child and the adult, and primitive and civilized peoples, in cognition, thinking and perceiving. Both Werner and Mead recognize differences between literate and nonliterate cultures and agree in rejecting the notion of the "primitive" who thinks "prelogically" and of the civilized man who thinks logically and abstractly. They also agree in rejecting biogenetic conceptions which assert that the child recapitulates the past history of the race or that existing primitive cultures represent earlier developmental stages of civilized cultures.

Regarding the question of the extent and significance of the parallels in the behavior of children in civilized societies and adults in primitive societies, there is some divergence in viewpoint. Mead is impressed by the fact that the

> only cases in which the savage adult can be compared with the child within our society are those in which primitive societies have failed to pattern some aspect of behavior which we have patterned extensively. In those cases the thinking of the primitive adult, not trained, for example, in scientific logic, may resemble to a certain extent the thinking of civilized children *not yet* trained in the methods of scientific thinking [1946: 667].

She recognizes, however, that a sequence of development holds for children of all cultures, but that different cultures "may select an earlier ontogenetic tendency than others for elaboration. When this occurs, we can find elaborations in given primitive cultures of types of behavior manifested for a brief period and within a restricting and limiting frame in our own culture." She finds, for example (p. 668), that there are cultures

> which develop the potentiality for animistic thought, as we can also find primitive societies which give their children a training which discourages animistic thought

even more rigorously than does our own, cultures which fail either to give encouragement and elaborate channeled forms, or to discourage, but leave man's capacity to begin thinking animistically, in childhood, so unpatterned that it will survive merely as an idiosyncracy in some adults confronted with a new situation.

Werner is more impressed with the parallels between the behavior of primitive man and children. He says (p. 28):

It is highly expedient to employ the principle of parallelism. If the peculiarly concrete thinking of the child is compared with certain forms of thinking typical of primitive people, if the drawings and the musical expression of early childhood are compared with the drawings of the Australian aborigines and with the songs of the Andaman Islanders and of the Vedda, certain striking parallels will be found. These parallels must be taken as such, as merely indicating a similar mental structure in a general and purely formal sense. In a particular and material sense, there will be irreconcilable differences in the behavior of the child and of the primitive man.

Werner (p. 28) is at some pains to indicate the specific character of these differences (as well as the parallels) between primitive man and children.

Formally considered, a child may exhibit concrete thinking quite as much as the primitive man. Since the child's thought, however, is in constant conflict with the abstract thinking of the adult world, this concrete mentality will not express itself explicitly in any characteristic language, as in the case of the primitive man, but will tend to translate the adult abstractions into words of concrete meaning. . . . Furthermore, because the child is but slightly conditioned and integrated socially, no more than fragmentary sociological parallels are possible. It is indeed true that we can find the beginnings of magic in the child's mentality, but only in very rudimentary forms. Magic achieves systematic expression only when it is a social, and not an individual phenomenon.

III. WHORF AND THE COGNITIVE PROCESSES

Whorf's statement that no individual is free to describe nature impartially but is "constrained to certain modes of interpretation even while he thinks himself most free" is essentially a statement of a theory of perception or, to use a more inclusive word, of cognition. Broadly speaking, Whorf's conception of the relationships among thought, behavior, and language may be considered as a series of assertions regarding a particular set of determinants and the individual's modes of cognizing his world. So considered, these assertions are concerned primarily with the perceptual rather than with strictly linguistic processes, and may be examined in the light of cognitive (perceptual) theory and analysis.

The phenomena with which we are here concerned have been variously designated by the terms "cognition," "perception," "abstraction," and "conceptualization." All these terms designate forms of interaction between the organism and its environment, in which the responses are *not governed exclusively by the energy properties of the stimulus or stimulus pattern.* These terms all refer to behavior in which the organism brings to bear resources of its own (both inborn and experiential) in reacting to the stimulus configuration. It is convenient, although somewhat arbitrary, to distinguish between two groups of factors: (1) those which are directly related to the properties of the stimulus configuration and (2) those which are related to properties "in" the organism itself. Included in the first group are the factors commonly referred to as "objective" or "physical." Included in the second group are the needs, motives, values, and previous experiences of the organism, in so far as they operate in a particular situation. These factors taken together underlie the interchange between the individual and the environment which constitutes in the broadest sense the basis of his contact with "reality."

In many discussions of these phenomena two levels of "contact" are distinguished, the perceptual and the conceptual or cognitive. This distinction usually refers to the degree to which properties of the stimulus field determine the response. In perception the contact is immediate, with a relatively greater opportunity for a feed-back from the stimulus field ("reality"), which serves as a check on the "accuracy" or appropriateness of the perception. In cognition (or conceptualization) there is a relatively greater opportunity for the operation of interpretive or inferential factors. Frenkel-Brunswik, in discussing the distinction, notes (1951: 356) that in perception "one is confronted with external stimuli actually present, whereas cognition deals with inferences from such data." Although a continuum may be assumed with "relatively clear-cut perception on the one end and relatively pure theoretical constructs on the other, we must not overlook the fact that there is some element of inference in every perception, and that conceptual constructs always relate to perceptual data." Heidbreder makes a similar distinction when she says (1945: 11–12):

> In attaining a concept [an organism] performs, at a level beyond the perceptual, a cognitive function very similar to that it performs when perceiving a concrete object. Nothing indeed is more trite than the statement that conceiving carries the function of cognition a step—or many steps—beyond perceiving; freeing the organism from what is immediately given, here and now, enormously increasing both the refinement and the range of its operations, enabling it to work symbolically with the absent and the distant, with the past and the future, and to go beyond the actual and construct the merely possible.

Similarly Bartlett (1932: 31) notes that, while perceiving is one of the simplest of all human cognitive reactions, "inextricably mingled with it are imaging, valuing, and those beginnings of judging which are involved in response to plan, order of arrangement and construction of presented material."

Psychologically, then, conceptualizing is not a qualitatively different kind of mental activity, as the terms "intellectual," "reasoning," and "thinking" seem to imply. Whatever point on the continuum we choose for analysis, whether it is a relatively direct and immediate perception of the external world or a highly generalized construct, we may assume an organism striving to achieve order and stability. *Cognition at whatever level is a structuring activity in which the organism seeks to establish a relatively stable environment in which to act.* The structuralizations are patterns which, within certain—sometimes exceedingly wide—limits, the organism *imposes* on the environment. They reflect an organization of forces within the organism itself and its need to maintain a frame of reference within which it may come to terms with the external world.

A. THE DEVELOPMENT OF PERCEPTION

With certain exceptions, to be discussed later, the world for Whorf is presented primordially "in a kaleidoscopic flux of impressions," which are unconsciously organized by linguistic processes. This appears to bypass any mode of prelinguistic perception and, in fact, to ignore entirely the possibility of developmental sequences.

The problem of the development of perception, or, rather, the problem of the emergence of the different levels of cognitive functioning, has been discussed in several recent papers.

Murphy and Hochberg (1951) have recently proposed a series of hypotheses regarding the development of perception. Perception is "a form of continuous adjustment to environmental requirements, involving not simply a 'sensorium' or seat of cognitive functions, but the whole organism" which "in coping with its environment, progressively alters its modes of perception and develops more and more complex ones that serve it better" (p. 332). The hypotheses which relate most directly to the present discussion follow:

1. "A primordial aspect of the structure of the percept is differentiation between figure and ground." Figure consists in "shaped regions" against a relatively unshaped ground. The differentiation between figure and ground exhibits varying degrees of sharpness. As Koffka says (1935), we see things and not the holes between them.

In looking at the landscape, we see the shape of *things* and not the sky—unless we have that particular orientation.

2. "Structure depends genetically upon two processes: (*a*) differentiation within a more-or-less homogeneous matrix, and (*b*) integrations of the differentiated phases." Here reference is made to the work of Werner and others who have noted that the child's earliest percepts show a diffuseness and "syncretic" lack of differentiation. "Progression from (*a*) homogeneous through (*b*) differentiated to (*c*) integrated characterizes, in principle, not only the stages through which the perceptual development of the maturing child passes, but also the course of every perceptual process regardless of age" (p. 334).

3. All the sense modalities "enter on an equal footing, but not always with equal weight, into the dynamics of perception." These modalities include the receptors which are stimulated by energies external to the organism (exteroceptors), those which respond to stimuli within the organism, especially in the visceral organs (interoceptors), and the receptors in the muscles and tendons (proprioceptors). Traditionally perceiving has been limited to the exteroceptive fields, especially vision and audition—as the sole mediators of external reality. Murphy and Hochberg regard the proprioceptive (kinesthetic) components as especially important. "Visual information must be pooled with proprioceptive information as to the position and motion of the receptor surfaces if effective contact with the outside world is to be maintained . . ." (p. 335). Interoceptive factors —those which yield "information" as to the internal bodily states and needs—is the third important component. "It is assumed that in the most primitive forms of perception all three sources of sensory information are present in an undifferentiated or partially undifferentiated state and that subsequent differentiation gradually achieves more and more separation of these factors" (p. 336). This is the basis for the type of perception, largely ignored by Whorf, which is called by Werner and others "physiognomic." "We should expect," say Murphy and Hochberg, "that *in primitive stages, perception of environmental objects would prove inextricably fused with the motion, position, and feeling state of the observer*" (italics added). Evidence of this type of perception is found in children and in brain-damaged individuals in which a dedifferentiation has occurred, and in schizophrenics in whom ego-object polarity is lost. These persons find it difficult to perceive objects-in-isolation or shapes-as-such. It is difficult to get evidence for the interaction of these components after differentiated perception is developed, because "the very structure of

our language is designed to make almost impossible the report on process or context rather than static and abstract identity, and in the laboratory an added effort has been made to rule out the 'subjective' variable presumably to be removed from science" (p. 337).

4. "It is meaningless to separate the cognitive, affective, and conative aspects of perception." In other words cognition, affection and conation are regarded as independent only in the context of scientific analysis and abstraction.

5. "Perception develops through experience as well as through neural maturation." In perception there is both a "systematic perceptual 'growth' dependent upon a general developmental principle of differentiation and integration" and the results of experience. It is noted that members of different cultures perceive as they have learned to perceive. Environments differ in the extent to which they force us to perceive in certain ways.

Heidbreder also recognizes (1945: 1) that the cognitive activities of the organism may be ordered to a developmental sequence.

Since they have presumably evolved along with other biological activities, it may be expected that this functional order is not unrelated to the phylogenetic sequence; that the dominant and typical mode of response [perception] is older and more deeply embedded in the organism, the distinctive mode [attainment of concepts] a later arrival and less solidly established.

The attainment of concepts she regards as a distinctive human activity involving the *interpersonal use of signs and symbols*. In literate cultures perception is typically the perception of concrete objects. It is an activity that presupposes an advanced position on the phylogenetic scale, and is closely linked with the development of a motor apparatus in the organism. By the perception of concrete objects she means that

under ordinary conditions, a person is more likely to see an apple than redness and roundness; more likely to see tables and chairs, on a floor, in a room, than a patterned arrangement of colored figures and ground; more likely to see a stable road on which his car and other cars are moving, more likely to see stable trees and filling stations in a stable landscape through which he is passing, than swirling masses of color and form. In other words, human beings are likely to respond at once with *more* than sensory reaction, with more even than perception of sensory patterns [p. 6].

With respect to the figure-ground differentiation, which is one of the distinctive contributions of Gestalt theory to the problems of perception, Heidbreder states that the perceptual field may be ordered with respect to "degrees of dominance." "Immediately figure-and-ground suggests itself as an illustration; with objects, the most prominent of figures, corresponding to the dominant perceptual response, and with ground, not at all thing-like, corresponding to the least dominant of perceptual reactions" (p. 7). An organization in which figures are prominent is one that leads itself to motor behavior in "animals living by locomotion and manipulation." The observed phenomenon in which ground becomes figure and figure becomes ground (illustrated by various types of "ambiguous" figures) indicates that "whatever the organism cognizes directly is likely to arouse a response as much like that of perceiving objects as the conditions of stimulation permit" (p. 7).

Since thing or object perception is regarded as characteristic of individuals in our own society, she raises the question whether persons in all cultures perceive objects.

> They seem to do so, though the fact ordinarily emphasized by students of culture is that the same or similar objects seem to be differently perceived in different cultures. . . . By comparing the perceptual reactions of members of different cultures, much might be learned about the psychological reactions involved in perceiving objects—not only about reactions characteristic of different cultures, and which escape notice and report, possibly because they are so basic that they are taken for granted [p. 3, n.; see also Hallowell 1951, esp. 178 ff.].

Piaget has dealt more extensively with the problems of the development of the cognitive processes in children than any other investigator. In a series of studies (1926, 1929, 1930, 1932) he has been concerned with the way in which the Western European child perceives and thinks about his world. Although Piaget's work has been the subject of considerable criticism, largely on methodological grounds (Deutsch 1937; Mead 1932), other investigators, notably Dennis and Russell (Dennis 1942, 1943; Hazlitt 1930; Russell 1940; Russell and Dennis 1939), have in the main confirmed his findings. (Vinacke [1951] presents a general review of the critical literature on Piaget. See also Dennis [1940] and McCarthy [1946].) Only the broader aspect of Piaget's extensive studies need concern us here. He finds that the child conceives itself and perceives its world in ways that are basically and qualitatively different from those of the adult. The thinking of children is characterized by *realism*, *animism*, and *artificialism*. By realism Piaget refers to the failure to clearly distinguish the self from the external world, the confusion of thought with the object of thought. By animism he means that tendency to regard objects as living and endowed with will. Artificialism is the tendency to regard things as the product of human creation, rather than to attribute creative activity to things themselves. Dennis (1940) found realism, animism, and artificialism typical of the concepts of Zuni and Navaho children.

Before reaching adulthood the child passes through intermediate stages which differ qualitatively from each other. It is in the intermediate and final stages of Piaget's hypothesized developmental sequence that the particular culture in which the child is reared exerts its influence. These stages, according to Dennis (1942: 307), "are, in all likelihood, compromise formations due to the conflict between the child's own views and those expressed by adults. If I understand Piaget correctly, the children of a society whose adults hold conceptions different from our own might go through intermediate stages different from those which he outlines for French and Swiss children." Dennis believes the primary stage is modified but slightly, if at all, by the culture in which the child is born. "The primary conception—whether of names, or of dreams, or of any other phenomenon treated by Piaget—is developed by the child himself. It is influenced by the environment only in the sense that it comes from the child's perception of and reflection upon the scene in which he lives" (p. 308).

B. NONLINGUISTIC PRIMITIVE FORMS OF COGNITION: PHYSIOGNOMIC PERCEPTION

The distinction regarding which the foregoing analyses seem to be in general agreement is admirably summarized by Allport in his Foreword to Werner's book (1948: xi):

> It is only in the most highly developed individuals that one finds a sharpening of the polarity between subject and world. Between the primitive or the child and his environment there exists a raw, syncretic relation illustrated by fusions between dreams or imagery and perceptions of outer reality. What to our minds is a mere poetic metaphor represents to the undeveloped mind a convincing causal relation. Notions of space and time, highly abstract to us, are egocentric and utilitarian in the primitive and in the child. Whereas our abstract concepts evolve through the repeated analysis of critical features embedded within complex situations, the less developed mind clings to salient signs or properties that are tangible, near and active. Preoccupation with global and salient structure prevents theoretical knowledge from accumulating. When theoretical knowledge is lacking, magical practice takes its place.

Reference has already been made to the characteristics which Redfield finds common to the world views of primitive peoples. Two of these seem to be clearly syncretic: the absence of a sharp distinction between that which is confronted and that which does the confronting, and the attitude of participative maintenance of man toward not-man. As Redfield suggests, the characteristic attitude of civilized man toward the cosmos is instrumental and pragmatic. This is the antithesis of the syncretic attitude.

There is no evidence that the "raw syncretic" or physiognomic relationship between the individual and his environment requires, or is dependent on, symbolic processes, although, if linguistic mechanisms are available, they may be used. There is a dearth of evidence on the earlier manifestations of nonlinguistic cognition, perhaps for the reason that it is difficult to establish the existence of cognitive structures in the individual except through linguistic mechanisms. For this reason a study by Spitz (1946) is notable. Using the smiling response, which appears very early in the infant, as an index of perceiving, he was able to establish that a selective (perceptual) response to a complex stimulus *configuration* occurs as early as the third month. The stimulus configuration was a "human" face consisting of two eyes, a nose, and movement. When these essentials were presented *together* in a full face (not in profile), whether in an actual face, a human face with a mask, or a "face" mounted on a dummy, the smiling response occurred and it did *not occur in response to any other stimulus pattern.* The "expression" of the face—smiling or scowling—did not matter. This is a very simple form of global perception which is not "learned," is certainly not present at birth, and does not differentiate between friend and stranger, or human beings and inanimate objects.

While physiognomic perception occurs more frequently in young children, it is experienced in some degree by all adults (as is reflected in our use of and response to metaphors), and is perhaps the dominant form of perception in certain adults. The frequency of physiognomic description in the autobiography of the artist Kandinsky seems to indicate that this was for him a primary mode of cognizing the world, not merely a facile use of poetic language. "On my palette sit high, round rain-drops, puckishly flirting with each other, swaying and trembling. Unexpectedly they unite and suddenly become thin, sly threads which disappear in amongst the colors, and roguishly skip about and creep up the sleeves of my coat . . ." (quoted in Werner 1948: 71).

It is frequently found in brain-damaged and schizophrenic individuals. Hanfmann and Kasanin (1942: 24) observed it in connection with the performance of schizophrenic subjects on tests involving the grouping of colored blocks according to certain categories.

> In physiognomic perception which has often been described as typical of a primitive mentality, there is no differentiation between the objective qualities of the ob-

jects and the emotions they arouse in the person. Objects appear not as large or small, having this or that color and shape, but as powerful, weak, harmonious, threatening, etc. In our experiments some subjects place blocks together describing them as "puny" or "well-behaved," or "strong in their healthy way." . . . Much more frequently, the physiognomic impression was not merely states as such, but led the subject to animate the blocks, ascribing to them traits and other human properties.

Heider and Simmel (1944) report an experiment in which the "movements" of several geometric figures (two triangles, a black disk, and a rectangle) as projected from a motion-picture film were perceived as actions of animated beings. The film on which the figures were drawn ran two and a half minutes, and the various objects "moved" in various directions and at various speeds. Groups of normal subjects were shown the films and instructed simply to write down what happened in the picture. In one group of thirty-four adults, only one described the animated sequences in "objective" geometric terms. The remainder ascribed various human characteristics to the movements of the figures. In other words, the figures were seen as having dynamic relations with each other. Asch has suggested (1952: 153) that cause-and-effect relations have the same immediacy in perception as shape, or figure-ground. This is the "dynamization of things" to which Werner has referred. It is especially important in the perception of movement whether apparent (as in films) or actual or of animate or inanimate things. It is probably involved in all perceptions in which one individual perceives another as possessing specific motivations, personality characteristics, etc.

Stimulus configurations which are perceived as possessing these dynamic-affective qualities are said by some investigators to be "expressive." Arnheim in two recent articles (1947, 1949) discusses the reaction to, and creation of, art forms in the context of a theory of the physiognomic perceptions of expressive qualities. In the first paper Arnheim is concerned especially with the ambiguity in the usage of the term "abstraction" in connection with cognitive processes. Abstraction, he believes, is not the result of highly intellectual processes, but rather a characteristic of primitive perceiving. The simple global forms in children's drawings or in "primitive art" are not the result of intellectual processes; rather they reflect the world as directly perceived, and are abstract only in the sense that they are perceptual simplifications. The order of development is from the simple, global forms which are directly perceived to forms which show greater and greater "realistic" detail. The child first perceives the simple functional characteristics which a group of objects may have in common—the "roundness" of heads, the "verticality" of trees—without, of course, any concept of roundness or verticality. To represent this perceptual experience which is abstract in the sense that "realistic" details are ignored in the interest of simple global forms, the child creates within a particular medium an equivalent of the perceptual experience. The representation—requiring a medium and a modicum of skill—is *not* a copy of the percept or of reality, but rather an interpretation of the individual's perceptual experience, which expresses a certain attitude toward the world. Children's drawings and so-called primitive art, according to Arnheim, directly reflect but do not copy the percepts, the primary content of which is concerned with the "friendly, hostile, or otherwise relevant environmental forces to which the organism must react."

The phenomena of synesthesia possess physiognomic aspects. Recent investigations of Karwoski, Odbert and others (Karwoski and Odbert 1938, 1942) have been concerned with the relations between synesthesia, and thinking and language. These studies indicate that synesthesia is much more frequent than earlier studies had suggested. Karwoski and Odbert, for example, found that thirteen per cent of Dartmouth College students regularly experienced color-music synesthesia. Osgood, in reviewing this work (1952), notes that "exciting music might be pictured by the synesthete as sharply etched, bright forms." Others would characterize it by terms such as "red-hot," "bright," and "fiery." Osgood raises the question whether this synesthetic experience indicates a rare capacity, or whether it is merely an overt expression of linguistic relationships implicit in our culture. In this connection he studied anthropological field material from a number of primitive cultures. Although the results were only suggestive, "nevertheless the generality of certain relationships was quite striking. For example, *good* things, places, social positions, etc., were regularly *up* and *light* (*white*) in relation to *bad* things, which were *down* and *dark* (*black*)" (pp. 225–26).

On the basis of these and other findings, Osgood has developed a method for measuring what he terms the "semantic" relations involved in synesthesia and metaphor. The latter he regards as occurring on the same continuum with synesthesia. His procedure consists in presenting the subject with a series of pairs of polar opposites, e.g., angular-rounded, weak-strong, small-large, good-bad, fresh-stale. The subject is given a word and instructed to indicate where it "belongs" on the seven-step scale which separates each of the polar opposites. If the word were "eager," for example, the subject would indicate where it "belonged" on the angular-rounded, weak-strong, good-bad, fresh-stale scales. From this a profile may be constructed for a particular word which would reveal its various "semantic" dimensions. Osgood believes this method may be useful in studying the development of meaning in children as well as for cross-cultural comparisons. Osgood's work is relevant to the present discussion because it implies the existence of synesthetic-physiognomic cognitions which in some manner are reflected at relatively sophisticated levels of linguistic development.

A linguistic phenomenon described by Sapir (1929) seems also to indicate a physiognomic relationship between certain verbalizations and "meaning," although at a much simpler level than that found by Osgood. Sapir hypothesized that, in addition to the arbitrary associations between combinations of vowels and consonants and "meanings" (the phonetic entity "boy" and the idea "boy"), there is a psychologically more primary "meaning" in which certain vocalic and consonantal contrasts express meanings in terms of their sound alone. For example, ". . . English-speaking society does, for some reason or other, feel that of these two vowels, *a*, by and large, is possessed of a greater potential magnitude symbolism than the contrasted vowel *i*" (p. 65). These relationships between meaning and sound Sapir calls "phonetic symbolism," or "referential symbolism." He tested various age groups in both English-speaking and Chinese subjects and found evidence for this type of symbolism in all groups beginning at the age of eleven. He believes these symbolisms "constellate in accordance with an unconscious or intuitive logic which is not necessarily based on experience with the stimuli in their normal, functional aspect." In another place he calls them "unsocialized symbolisms" and states that the "ordinary specific, functional language factors need not be invoked" to explain them.

C. PHYSIOGNOMIC PERCEPTION AND METAPHOR

In his discussion of the relations between synesthesia and metaphor Whorf comes closest to identifying a nonlinguistic form of cognition. Metaphor, he thinks, arises out of synesthesia, which is a nonlinguistic, presumably primitive, mode of experience. Metaphor itself, however, as a linguistic pattern, is characteristic of certain languages and not of others and serves to heighten the consciousness of synesthesia. He suggests the possibility that its use in European art may have a "far reaching value . . . *leading toward a more direct apprehension of underlying unity behind the phenomena so variously re-*

ported by our sense channels" (1952*a:* 42, italics added). This seems to indicate that metaphor is not merely a peculiarity of SAE linguistic patterns, but refers to a fundamental nonlinguistic mode of perception. The frequency of metaphor in primitive languages, its relation to the physiognomic form of cognition, and its dependency on linguistic expression need further exploration. The problem of the relations between metaphor and physiognomic perception and a program of relevant research have recently been outlined by Werner (1953).

It seems reasonable to postulate a relationship between physiognomic experience and metaphorical reference. Richards (1936, 1947), Burke (1935, 1941, 1945, 1950), Empson (1952), and others have pointed out the metaphorical overtones which pervade all language experience. Richards (1936: 116–17) seems to be specifically describing physiognomic experience when he says,

> I . . . include as metaphoric, those processes in which we perceive or think of or feel about one thing in terms of another—as when looking at a building it seems to have a face and to confront us with a peculiar expression. I want to insist that this sort of thing is normal in full perception and that study of the growth of our perceptions (the animistic world of the child and so on) shows that it must be so.

Burke (1941: 152) states that "every perspective requires a metaphor, implicit or explicit, for its organizational base." Earlier (1935: 119), in a discussion of "perspective by incongruity," he noted the revealing character of the "hitherto unsuspected connectives which we may note in the progressions of a dream." These are significant because they reveal relationships between objects which our "customary rational vocabulary" ignores.

Burke elaborates this in his distinction (1941: 138–68) between "poetic" and "semantic" meaning. Poetic meanings are metaphorical and orient the individual toward objects in the external world establishing a motivational, attitudinal, and emotional context. The individual is invited to participate maximally in the situation, and hence is oriented for action. Semantic meaning, on the other hand, is merely the neutral naming of the object. It is perception without affective overtones. This is the "geometrical-technical" perception to which Werner refers (1948: 69), in which, to a maximum degree, the subject and the object are separated from each other.

It is strictly in accord with the Whorfian thesis that the linguistic basis of Western European science should codify experience so as to separate subject and object. This insistence on a neutral vocabulary has led to a culturally rooted tradition in which nonneutral, i.e., metaphoric descriptions (or perspectives in Burke's sense) are regarded with suspicion. In spite of this it appears, according to Whorf, that metaphoric experience may lead to a more direct apprehension of the unity underlying sense experience.

Whorf's studies, it should be noted, are exclusively concerned with the fully enculturated adult, as are, I suppose, most linguistic investigations. If the reality and frequency of occurrence of physiognomic or syncretic types of cognition are accepted, their relation to more "advanced" types of cognition—the attainment of concepts, for example—in which, presumably, symbolic processes play a necessary role, is of primary importance. In other words, we may not assume, as does Whorf, that primordial experience is characterized by kaleidoscopic confusion, but, on the contrary, that it is a structured unity and expresses a dynamic relation between the individual and the environment. Nor is all the experience of the enculturated adult wholly ordered by linguistic patterns peculiar to a specific culture, although, as Whorf so clearly indicated, these factors are tremendously potent. Perhaps the most important issue demanding clarification is the extent and character of nonlinguistic cognition, and the dynamics of the interplay between it and more developed forms of cognition.

D. SUMMARY

Although more data and further systematic analysis are needed, the evidence seems to be conclusive that there is a type of cognition in which the individual is in immediate contact with the external world, that in its simplest form it is probably the same for all men irrespective of culture, and that symbolic processes, including language, are not necessary for it to occur, although when linguistic patterns are available they may be utilized to express it, probably in the form of metaphor. Important characteristics of this experience are the blurring or abolition of the subject-object polarity and the high degree to which the object is endowed with dynamic-affective qualities. In some form or other it may occur at all age levels, although it is more frequent in children and "primitives." With respect to the latter more evidence is needed.

Although Whorf makes certain rather oblique references to types of apprehension which "transcend language," especially the apprehension of space, and to synesthesia and kinesthesia as processes which arise prior to language, in general, he ignores or gives but slight attention to nonlinguistic cognition. Whorf does not, of course, completely rule it out, especially as regards the apprehension of space or "space forms" (1952*a:* 44). He appears also to recognize the existence of nonlinguistic primordial experience in which language "for all its kingly role" is a superficial embroidery. Kinesthesis is specifically referred to as arising prior to language. But until linguistic patterns supervene, these processes apparently play a negligible role in so far as the individual's cognition of himself in relation to the external world is concerned. They are considered to be background phenomena with respect to consciousness.

IV. THE ATTAINMENT OF CONCEPTS AND COMMUNICATION

The distinction between physiognomic perception and the more developed forms of cognition is, as has been indicated, more or less arbitrary. However, it seems clear that as the individual is separated in time or space from the stimulus field, there is opportunity for experiential, attitudinal, or other "existential substrata" (to quote Merton) to operate. These are the conceptual resources of the individual of which he may or may not be conscious. They are specific for the individual perceiver and the culture in which he lives. In utilizing his repertory of available concepts, he codifies and thus transcends that which is immediately given in experience. The examination of these processes is especially important in the critical consideration of Whorf's theory, since *the linguistic patterns which, under the theory, constrain the individual to certain modes of interpretation, "even when he thinks himself most free," appear to have the properties of concepts.*

Vinacke's comprehensive review of the extensive literature on the attainment of concepts (1951) summarizes the problems in this field. A first problem is concerned with conceptualizing ability.

> We do not really know for certain that there is an ability to conceptualize which might be distinguished from other perceptual and intellectual functions. Undoubtedly, children's concepts change with age, but whether or not this reflects development in a general function to form and use concepts has not been convincingly demonstrated [p. 27].

A second problem is concerned with the acquisition of a repertory of concepts. Regarding this, Vinacke believes much more is known.

> Here it has been found that concepts tend to change with increasing age, becoming more numerous, more complex, and more "logical." It has been tentatively ascertained that children acquire concepts in a definite order [pp. 27–28].

The third problem is concerned with the formation of a particular concept.

> Among the characteristics noted are the tendency for subjects to evolve concepts gradually, the occasional attainment of concepts without awareness of the concept

itself, the development of inconsistent as well as consistent concepts, the tendency for concepts to be learned in a definite order, and the occurrence of varying degrees of concrete and abstract approaches to, and use of, concepts [p. 28].

A. THE ROLE OF SYMBOLIC PROCESSES

The transition from perceiving to conceptualizing may be crudely illustrated by the following example. If the mass of clouds on the horizon is perceived as "threatening," we have a simple, direct, physiognomic type of perception. If some quality of the cloud formation is isolated and reacted to as a *sign of an approaching storm*, it is still a perception but interpretive components are present. If language or other signs (flags as storm warnings, for example) are produced by a human agent and reacted to as substitutes for and identical with the cloud-as-a-sign-of-storm, we are still further removed from the "pure" perception and have moved into the region of the conceptual. We can now *talk* about storms. A necessary condition for this last stage is the existence of persons in a communicative relationship. This last step involves a symbolic process and conforms to Morris' definition (1946: 25) of a symbol as a sign "produced by its interpreter which acts as a substitute for some other sign with which it is synonymous."

An investigation which bears directly on this point is that of Neff (1937). He exposed various kinds of visual stimulus material, which ranged from pictures of specific objects to highly abstract drawings, to adult observers, and found evidence for five modes of perceptual activity. He says (p. 417):

> These five modes of performance may be taken to constitute stages in a functional continuum from perceiving to understanding. The *figurational* and *depictive* forms closely adhere to the region of the object. The last three, however, depart from that sphere and strike out in increasing measure for new psychological regions. The *abstractive* variety takes the object as a representative of some other object; the *generalized* mode carries through a topical kind of reference, the object standing for a class, and the *symbolical* mode regards the object merely as a surrogate, as a "sign" of some topic, subject, or other object quite different from that implied by its directly perceived characteristics.

The same point is made by Heidbreder when she notes that perception is the experience of palpable and manipulable objects perceived as together in space and time, whereas in the attainment of concepts the organism elaborates, selects, and organizes. The result is a construct "suitable to another mode of reaction, the symbolic."

Conceptual activity always involves some form of comparing and relating. Maslow (1948) calls this "rubricizing" and suggests that language plays a crucial role. He believes that when we use language, instead of attending to the fresh, idiosyncratic characteristics of a stimulus situation, we give only a stereotyped, rubricized recognition in which the event or situation is merely catalogued within a set of existing categories. "True perception," he says, "which would encompass the object, play over all of it, soak it in, and understand it, would obviously take more time than the fraction of a second which is all that is necessary for labelling and cataloguing" (p. 27). He believes that "to the extent that language forces experiences into rubrics, it is a screen between reality and the human being." Without necessarily accepting such a negative interpretation of language, we may recognize that the distinctive character of the more differentiated forms of cognition is the relation of the particular as related to the generic, and that language is involved.

Werner distinguishes two separate phases in the thought-processes of comparison. The first is the formation of a perceptual relationship —the relation between two parts is grasped in a certain configuration. The second is the derivative abstract form of the relationship as expressed in a verbally constituted judgment. When perceptual relationships are *represented by mediation*, e.g., words or pictures, we have the emergence of symbolic function. Werner states (1948: 248–49):

> Even though this "symbolic function" reaches its fullest expression on an advanced level, we must recognize that representation is already effective in the primitive sphere. The fundamental difference is that in the latter case we are dealing no longer with a representation that is relatively pure and abstract, but with one bound syncretically to a concrete series of events.

The syncretic form of representation, Werner believes, may even be found in the higher vertebrates. A similar distinction is made by Hallowell (1951: 172 ff.).

Arnheim, as we have seen, also makes the distinction between *perceiving* and the *representation* of percepts. The latter activity does not result in a simple copy of the percept; the individual has to *invent* a pattern in a particular medium which interprets the percept.

> Undoubtedly the young child who draws the circle sees more than sheer roundness when he looks at a human head. Before he can draw at all he is capable of telling different people from each other. The perceptual pattern is refined beyond anything indicated by the child's drawings. Nor can the difference between what is perceived and what is produced on paper simply be explained as a lack of technical craftsmanship. By and large the young child, and certainly the primitive artist possess enough motor skill and visual control to produce the image they intend to [1947: 71].

The point at which representational, that is, symbolic, activities occur is particularly important from the point of view of Whorf's general theory for it is here that the individual utilizes whatever symbolic, particularly linguistic, equipment he possesses. These, as we have said, have the properties of concepts. It seems inconceivable that these symbolic facilities could have been acquired except through specific social processes, that is, through communication. If this is true it becomes necessary to consider Whorf's general theory in the context of a social-psychological theory of communication.

B. COMMUNICATION

Communication may be conceived as a pattern of interpersonal relationships occurring in a social field possessing certain specific properties. The important characteristic of these relationships is that both the communicator and the interpreter must be able to perceive the other (in the sense of George Mead 1934) as capable of reacting in certain ways to a particular kind of stimulus material (symbols) *produced* by one of them. Further, the individuals participating in this transaction must perceive each other in specific ways. The communicator, for example, must *perceive* the potential interpreter as an entity who-can-be-moved-by-the-produced-content, and the interpreter must perceive the content as produced by a human agent. In other words, it is here postulated that for communication to occur both the producer of the communication and the interpreter must be in each other's field, if not physically at least psychologically. (Fearing 1953 sets forth this theory in detail.)

Malinowski gives an admirable statement of the same idea when he says:

> Each verbal statement by a human being has the aim and function of expressing some thought or feeling actual at that moment and in that situation, and *necessary for some reason or other to be made known to another person or persons—in order either to serve purpose of common action, or to establish ties of purely social communion, or else to deliver the speaker of violent feelings or passions* [1949: 307, italics added].

In this sense the "meaning" of communications content can be understood only in terms of these relationships and the situation in which they occur. As Malinowski makes clear, the categories of primitive philosophy and the language on which it may be based are not evidences of crude attempts at theory-making or metaphysical speculation, but are reflections of specific experience (read: cognitions) in particular communicative situations. Language and communication for the civilized intellectual, on the other hand, is "a condensed piece of reflection, a record of fact or thought. In its primitive uses, language functions as a link in concerted human activity, as a piece of human behavior. It is a mode of action and not an instrument of reflection" (p. 312). Both the primitive and the civilized use of language (concepts) requires a communicative relationship. For the primitive the conceptualization is much closer to the immediate demands of the communicative situation—perhaps it more frequently requires that "the other" be physically present. In Werner's sense, it is more syncretic. For the intellectually more advanced person "the other" need not be present—but certainly "records of fact and thought" are not made unless they are to be reacted to by somebody, sometime.

If communication is conceived as an activity involving particular kinds of interpersonal relationships, the question is raised whether it can occur *until the individual has developed the forms of cognition in which concepts are attained and representations (symbols) made.* It seems doubtful, for example, whether representation, in Arnheim's sense, is ever undertaken except in the context of communication—a context in which the individual perceives "the other" and uses symbolic material to affect him in some manner. Unless there is an act of "pure expression," the question is raised whether a child or primitive artist would represent anything (in Arnheim's sense) without the actual or implied presence of others who could be affected. In other words, the attainment of concepts (as distinct from primitive perceptions), the production and use of symbols, and the interpersonal relationship demanded by the communicative situation are co-existing activities. Each requires the other—in the development of the individual they must appear together.

Métraux's definition of the image (1953: 350) is suggestive in this connection. An image "stands for any unit in the perceptual system through which individuals are related to one another in a culture." In this sense an image would occur most frequently in the communicative situation, although presumably it might be purely expressive. Métraux notes that similes and metaphors are verbal expressions of clusters of images.

At the syncretic level of organization the individual does not clearly differentiate between himself and the external world, including "others." It is possible that at this stage some form of vocalization might exist and be used for expressive purposes—this is a point which needs further examination. Sapir's statement that the "purely communicative aspects of language have been exaggerated" implies that language may be used for expressive as well as representational (instrumental) purposes, although it does not seem possible that it could have developed except in the context of communication.

Piaget's distinction (1926), which has been confirmed by McCarthy (1946) and others, between the *egocentric* and *social* functions in the language development of children, supports this view. In egocentric speech the child is not concerned with a listener or whether he is being listened to. He takes no account of the other (hearer). In socialized speech, on the other hand, the child addresses his hearer and tries to influence him. Piaget finds a higher percentage of egocentric speech at the earlier ages (three to five). Werner also stresses the physiognomic character of primitive language as distinct from the more advanced stage when it is used as a medium of communication.

Whorf's neglect of the relationships between linguistic processes and communication does not, of course, vitiate his theory. The analyses of Whorf are concerned almost exclusively with the conceptualizing process. At this level of cognition symbolic processes are essential, and it may be assumed that a communicative situation is necessary for their appearance. The evidence indicates that there are ways of cognizing the world which exist not only prior to but concurrent with those involving concepts and symbols. Whorf does not take these other forms of cognition into account, nor does he explore the relationships between linguistic processes and the dynamic properties of the communication situation.

REFERENCES CITED

ARNHEIM, RUDOLPH

1947 "Perceptual Abstraction in Art," *Psychological Review* **54**:66–82.

1949 "The Gestalt Theory of Expression," *Psychological Review* **56**:156–71.

ASCH, SOLOMON E.

1952 *Social Psychology*. New York, Prentice-Hall.

BARTLETT, F. C.

1932 *Remembering: A Study in Experimental and Social Psychology*. London, Cambridge University Press.

BURKE, KENNETH

1935 *Permanence and Change*. New York, New Republic.

1941 *Philosophy of Literary Form*. Baton Rouge, La., Louisiana State University Press.

1945 *Grammar of Motives*. New York, Prentice-Hall.

1950 *A Rhetoric of Motives*. New York, Prentice-Hall.

DENNIS, WAYNE

1940 "Piaget's Questions Applied to Zuni and Navaho Children," *Psychological Bulletin* **37**:520.

1942 "Piaget's Questions Applied to a Child of Known Environment," *Journal of Genetic Psychology* **60**:307–20.

1943 "Animism and Related Tendencies in Hopi Children," *Journal of Abnormal and Social Psychology* **38**:21–36.

DEUTSCH, J. M.
1937 *The Development of Children's Concepts of Causal Relations.* University of Minnesota Institute of Child Welfare Monograph Series. Minneapolis, University of Minnesota Press.

EMPSON, W.
1952 *The Structure of Complex Words.* New York, New Directions.

FEARING, FRANKLIN
1953 "Toward a Psychological Theory of Human Communication," *Journal of Personality* **22**:71–88.

FEUER, L. S.
1953 "Sociological Aspects of the Relation between Language and Philosophy," *Philosophy of Science* **20**:85–100.

FRENKEL-BRUNSWIK, ELSE
1951 "Personality Theory and Perception." In: *Perception: An Approach to Personality* (by ROBERT R. BLAKE and GLEN V. RAMSEY), pp. 356–419. New York, Ronald.

HALLOWELL, A. IRVING
1951 "Cultural Factors in the Structurization of Perception." In: *Social Psychology at the Crossroads* (eds. J. R. ROHRER and M. SHERIF), pp. 164–95. New York, Harper.

HANFMANN, E. and J. S. KASANIN
1942 *Conceptual Thinking in Schizophrenia.* Nervous and Mental Disease Monograph Series, No. 67.

HAZLITT, V.
1930 "Children's Thinking," *British Journal of Psychology* **20**:354–61.

HEIDBREDER, EDNA
1945 "Toward a Dynamic Psychology of Cognition," *Psychological Review* **52**:1–22.

HEIDER, F. and M. SIMMEL
1944 "An Experimental Study of Apparent Behavior," *American Journal of Psychology* **57**:243–59.

HERSKOVITS, MELVILLE J.
1951 "Cultural and Psychological Reality." In: *Social Psychology at the Crossroads* (ed. J. R. ROHRER and M. SHERIF), pp. 145–63. New York, Harper.

KARWOSKI, T. F. and H. S. ODBERT
1938 *Color Music.* Psychological Monographs 50, No. 2.
1942 "Studies in Synesthetic Thinking: II. The Roles of Form in Visual Response to Music," *Journal of General Psychology* **26**:199–222.

KÖHLER, W.
1937 "Psychological Remarks on some Questions of Anthropology," *American Journal of Psychology* **50**:271–88.

KOFFKA, KURT
1935 *Principles of Gestalt Psychology.* New York, Harcourt, Brace.

MCCARTHY, D.
1946 "Language Development in Children." In: *Manual of Child Psychology* (ed. L. CARMICHAEL), pp. 476–581. New York, Wiley.

MALINOWSKI, BRONISLAW

1949 "The Problem of Meaning in Primitive Languages." In: *Meaning of Meaning* (by C. OGDEN and I. A. RICHARDS), pp. 297–336. 10th ed. London, Routledge and Kegan Paul.

MASLOW, A. H.

1948 "Cognition of the Particular and the Genetic," *Psychological Review* **55**:22–40.

MEAD, GEORGE

1934 *Mind, Self, and Society*. Chicago, University of Chicago Press.

MEAD, MARGARET

1932 "An Investigation of the Thought of Primitive Children with Special Reference to Animism," *Journal of the Royal Anthropological Institute* **62**:173–90.

1946 "Research on Primitive Children." In: *Manual of Child Psychology* (ed. L. CARMICHAEL), pp. 666–706. New York, Wiley.

1949 "Anthropological Data on the Problem of Instinct." In: *Personality in Nature, Society and Culture* (ed. CLYDE KLUCKHOHN and C. MURRAY), pp. 109–13. New York, Knopf.

MERTON, ROBERT

1949 *Social Theory and Social Structure*. Glencoe, Illinois, Free Press.

MÉTRAUX, RHODA

1953 "Resonance in Imagery." In: *The Study of Culture at a Distance* (ed. MARGARET MEAD and RHODA MÉTRAUX), pp. 342–63. Chicago, University of Chicago Press.

MORRIS, CHARLES

1946 *Signs, Language and Behavior*. New York, Prentice-Hall.

MURDOCK, GEORGE PETER

1945 "The Common Denominator in Cultures." In: *The Science of Man in the World Crisis* (ed. RALPH LINTON), pp. 123–42. New York, Columbia University Press.

MURPHY, GARDNER and J. HOCHBERG

1951 "Perceptual Development: Some Tentative Hypotheses," *Psychological Review* **58**:332–49.

NEFF, W. S.

1937 "Perceiving and Symbolizing: an Experimental Study," *American Journal of Psychology* **49**:376–418.

OGDEN, C. and I. A. RICHARDS

1949 *The Meaning of Meaning*. London, Routledge and Kegan Paul.

OSGOOD, C. E.

1952 "The Nature and Measurement of Meaning," *Psychological Bulletin* **49**:197–237.

PIAGET, JEAN

1926 *The Language and Thought of the Child*. New York, Harcourt, Brace.

1929 *The Child's Conception of the World*. New York, Harcourt, Brace.

1930 *The Child's Conception of Physical Causality*. New York, Harcourt, Brace.

1932 *The Moral Judgement of the Child*. New York, Harcourt, Brace.

REDFIELD, ROBERT
1952 "The Primitive World," *Proceedings of the American Philosophical Society* **96**:32–36.
1953 *The Primitive World and Its Transformations*. Ithaca, Cornell University Press.
RICHARDS, I. A.
1936 *The Philosophy of Rhetoric*. New York, Oxford University Press.
1947 *Principles of Literary Criticism*. New York, Harcourt, Brace.
RUSSELL, R. W.
1940 "Studies in Animism: II. The Development of Animism," *Journal of Genetic Psychology* **56**:353–66.
RUSSELL, R. W., and WAYNE DENNIS
1939 "Studies in Animism: I. A Standardized Procedure for Investigation of Animism," *Journal of Genetic Psychology* **55**:389–400.
SAPIR, EDWARD
1929 "A Study in Phonetic Symbolism." In: *Selected Writings in Language, Culture and Personality* (ed. DAVID MANDELBAUM), pp. 61–72. Berkeley and Los Angeles: University of California Press, 1949.
SPITZ, R. A.
1946 "The Smiling Response: A Contribution to the Ontogenesis of Social Relations," *Genetic Psychology Monographs* **34**:57–125.
VINACKE, W. E.
1951 "The Investigation of Concept Formation," *Psychological Bulletin* **48**: 1–31.
WERNER, HEINZ
1948 *Comparative Psychology of Mental Development*. Chicago, Follett.
1953 *A Program for the Psychological Investigation of Expressive Language*. Worcester, Mass., Psychology Department, Clark University. Mimeog.
WHORF, B. L.
1952*a* *Collected Papers on Metalinguistics*. Washington, D.C., Department of State, Foreign Service Institute.
1952*b* "Language, Mind and Reality," *Etc.: A Review of General Semantics* **9**, No. 3:167–88.

SEMANTIC PROBLEMS IN GRAMMATICAL SYSTEMS AND LEXEMES: A SEARCH FOR METHOD

STANLEY NEWMAN

I

AFTER COMPLETING a linguistic description of Yokuts, I attempted to find structural clues for characterizing Yokuts style as expressed in its folk tales (Gayton and Newman 1940: 4–8). This Yokuts study was aimed at only one aspect of the broader field encompassed in the Whorf hypothesis. Whereas Whorf attempted to demonstrate that a linguistic system shaped the thought world of its speakers, I limited my approach to a demonstration of how the Yokuts language shaped the stylistic values of its speakers. Both of these approaches, however, attempt to characterize the semantic patterns of an entire linguistic system, and, therefore, encounter many of the same problems.

Investigations of this type have as their goal the identification of the dominant conceptual categories of a language. For this task the investigator must try to assess the relative weights of the many categories presented by the language—those expressed in structural features such as inflections, derivations, morpheme and word classes, and syntactic units, as well as the conceptual patterns expressed in lexemes. So far as I am aware, linguists (including myself) have tackled this problem by making an intuitive leap, selecting from the numerous categories in a language only those whose meaning content appears to have some striking significance for interpreting the manner of thought of a people.

Before one can arrive at any formulation of the conceptual system of a language, it is necessary to have a descriptive account of the conceptual categories themselves. Some linguists have taken pains to include in their grammars a careful treatment of the meaning content of structural forms and classes. It is not surprising that Whorf gave meticulous attention to the description of conceptual categories even in his technical linguistic papers, such as his grammatical sketches of Hopi and Aztec (Hoijer and others 1946: 158–83, 367–97). But, on the whole, linguists have tended to slight this aspect of their descriptive task. A semantic inventory, however, is the first step toward interrelating the categories of meaning into a system, and there are certain criteria that can be utilized to determine the relative prominence of the various categories within the system.

One criterion involves the distinction between obligatory and optional categories. It can be stated as a proposition that the concepts expressed by obligatory forms and classes carry greater weight than those contained in optional categories. Yokuts nouns must be defined in one of the six cases; number, on the other hand, may be left ambiguous. The obligatory case system, consequently, can be regarded as having a more dominating influence than number concepts in the semantic scheme of Yokuts speakers. Their language suggests that they need be less concerned than speakers of English in defining the single versus the plural occurrence of a noun-entity or noun-event, but that they place more emphasis on specifying the function of the noun as agent, as possessor, as direct or indirect recipient of the event, or as the locus toward which or away from which the event is directed.

Another criterion applies to the variable range of conceptual categories. Some have an extensive range in a language, while others are limited in scope. In terms of their ubiquity in the structural system, the case functions are again emphasized in Yokuts. In all of the noun classes the same paradigm of six cases reappears, sometimes with different suffix forms. The expression of case is obligatory for all Yokuts nouns, which are subdivided into classes on the basis of distinctive stem and suffix forms and not on any functional basis. Further than this, case relations are also expressed in verbs. On one level, certain suffixes of voice attached to Yokuts verbs indicate whether, for example, the grammatical subject functions as the agent of an active-verb event, the direct recipient of a passive-verb event, or the recipient of an agentless, mediopassive-verb event. On another level, verb roots are themselves defined in the category of voice: selectively they express either the active or the mediopassive. The case functions and their associated concepts of voice represent the most extensive category of Yokuts.

Compared to the case-voice category, which spans both the nouns and the verbs, the expression of mode is somewhat more limited. Although the distinction between indicative and other modes is obligatory in Yokuts, it functions only in the verbs and does not extend among the nouns. Even more restricted are concepts such as the inchoative or the habitual, which are given expression in a subtype of one of the five verb classes of Yokuts.

This subclass of the Yokuts verb manifests a number of other anomalous features. It is formed by a proclitic stem added to the root wiyi, *do*. Proclisis, or any other type of compounding, occurs nowhere else in the language. Furthermore, many of these wiyi verbs are onomatopoetic, and such mimetic play with sounds is also absent outside this verbal subclass in Yokuts. In applying the criterion of extensiveness, the characteristics limited to a small segment of the class system provide negative clues, indicating the features that occur but are given little prominence in the language.

Problems arise in attempting to assess the relative weights that should be assigned to the various classes themselves. In my field work with Yokuts, I made special efforts to obtain as many wiyi verbs as I could. Although I badgered my informants to give me additional examples, since these verbs were very rare in the texts, I was able to collect less than a hundred stems. In contrast, hundreds of verb-stems of other subclasses kept appearing, with no direct effort on my part to elicit them. On this basis I would consider the wiyi verb as a relatively small subclass and would give its conceptual categories less prominence than those expressed in other subclasses. Much less ambiguous as a factor for rating the size of a class is the distinction between open and closed classes. The personal pronouns of Yokuts represent a closed class; there are three pronominal stems and no more. The expression of singular, dual, and plural number is obligatory in these pronouns, in contrast to the optional category of singular-plural number expressed in Yokuts nouns. But, because the obligatory expression of number is limited to a closed class, it would be assigned little importance in the conceptual scheme of Yokuts. The same factor would apply in estimating the weight of the English case system, which is also restricted to the closed class of pronouns.

A third criterion, and one which I emphasized in my treatment of Yokuts style, involves the selection of optional features. This is essentially a frequency criterion. It attempts to correct the skewed semantic picture offered in a grammatical description, which merely states the functional potentialities of a linguistic structure without committing itself to any statement of the degree to which these potentialities are actualized. A structural description of Yokuts, for example, would classify suffixes into the following three types: thematizing, auxiliary, and final. There are no other affixes. Grammatically speaking, the word may contain any number of thematizing suffixes, one auxiliary suffix, and one final suffix. Since the thematizing suffixes are the only ones that can occur in theoretically unlimited combinations within the word, it might be assumed that the concepts they express should be given special prominence. But, regardless of the potential importance of the thematizing suffixes and their conceptual content, they are actually not frequent in occurrence.

In order to obtain a rough statistical indication of the frequency of the various suffix types, I analyzed five hundred verbs occurring in my texts—a sampling of five randomly selected series, each of one hundred consecutive verb forms. Because one final suffix is obligatory in Yokuts inflected words, this type of suffix could be counted on to appear in every verb. The great majority of the verbs which were analyzed, about 80 per cent, contained no other suffixes beyond the single final suffix; about 15 per cent were made up of one thematizing and one final suffix; almost 5 per cent were composed of one thematizing, one auxiliary, and one final suffix; and less than one-half of 1 per cent contained two thematizing suffixes in addition to the final suffix.

Formally elaborate words containing three or four thematizing suffixes can be constructed. As part of my field procedure I invented many such complex words, which my informant dutifully translated, though with obvious amusement. These heavily suffixed words were grammatically unobjectionable. But they were the creations of a structurally oriented linguist, not those of native speakers who collectively impose selective limits upon the structural potentialities of their language.

In terms of its selective habits, Yokuts sets a low limit on exploiting the potentialities of its thematizing suffixes, which give expression to conceptual categories such as voice and aspect and which perform the class-changing functions of verbalizing nouns and nominalizing verbs.

The same tendency to avoid formal elaboration is to be found in Yokuts syntax. Just as the language possesses the formal machinery for modifying a root morpheme by the addition of many suffixes, it also has a syntactic device for modifying a noun. There is no class of adjectives. But a noun may function as a modifying term by being linked in a parallel series to another noun, and potentially any number of such modifying terms can be juxtaposed with a noun. But, with the exception of demonstrative and quantifying nouns, even a single modifying term linked to a noun-head rarely appears in my textual material. Yokuts speakers prefer to make separate predications: their selective habits would lead them to break down a sentence such as "He saw the tall man" into "He saw the man, and that one was a tall one." Similarly, the language has the morphological and syntactic tools for constructing complex sentences. In fact, several different types of subordinate clauses can be formed by suffixes which are part of an obligatory category: each verb must be formally marked as either a main or a subordinate verb. And, in line with the morphological regularity of Yokuts, the linguist can form an infinite number of subordinate verbs by attaching any one of the subordinating suffixes to the appropriate stem of every verb. But, here again, the Yokuts themselves make little use of these potentialities. Verbs containing subordinating suffixes are extremely rare in the texts I collected. The great majority of verbs are simply main verbs. Throughout its grammatical system, Yokuts plays down its structural potentialities for modifying stems, nouns, or main clauses.

The three criteria I have enumerated do not, I am sure, exhaust the methodological controls that can be employed in trying to determine the relative prominence of the concepts and conceptual categories expressed in a language. But these criteria have the advantage of using the system of structural form as a point of departure, and this is the system in which linguists feel most at home. The utilization of structural clues is not the only way of tackling semantic problems, for the study of lexemes offers another approach. But we have come to know a great deal about the nature of structural systems. By using this knowledge as a relatively firm base from which to operate, we may come to know something about the nature of semantic systems associated with linguistic structures and to understand in what senses we can talk about systems of meaning. This, it seems to me, is one of the steps we must take before we can proceed to make valid statements about the relation between the semantic system of a language and the nonlinguistic thought world of its speakers.

II

During the academic year of 1951/2 I worked with a Zuni informant on the standard type of linguistic research. Having obtained a fairly clear idea of Zuni structure, I devoted the next year to a study of semantic problems in Zuni lexemes. Linguists, of course, gather semantic data in the normal course of their field work. They obtain translation definitions of the lexemes occurring in their textual material, and, particularly when they come upon near synonyms, they usually try to elicit definitions that are as distinctive as their informant can give them. But such data are gathered haphazardly, as a side line to the structurally significant material. My present work with Zuni is directed primarily toward the semantic study of lexemes, in an attempt to develop definable procedures and to arrive at some systematic results.

An assumption basic to this study is that Zuni lexemes can be utilized as clues to the way in which experience is conceived by Zuni speakers as either segmented or interrelated. Unavoidably I have had to depend upon English translations for defining the semantic content of Zuni lexemes, but I see no other satisfactory method of making an initial approach to semantic problems in a language of which I am not a native speaker. It is taken for granted, as a matter of procedure, that no English lexeme is a perfect semantic equivalent of a Zuni lexeme. Consequently, a Zuni word must be translated through several English equivalents. Being modified by multiple equivalents, the range of meaning of a Zuni term is extended in certain directions and delimited in others. Another step in the translation procedure involves defining a Zuni lexeme in phrase and sentence contexts. With translations of both the lexeme and the total contexts, the semantic content of the lexeme can then be identified as the increments of meaning expressed by that lexeme in its various contexts.

From his fundamental assumption of linguistics, Bloomfield derives the implication that "each linguistic form has a constant and specific meaning. If the forms are phonemically different, we suppose that their meanings also are different" (1933: 145). It is assumed, then, that discriminations of meaning in Zuni are indicated by distinctive lexemes; conversely, associations of meaning are indicated by the semantic range of a single lexeme. As an example of discriminated meanings, Zuni has two lexemes expressing the literal notion of the color "yellow." Lexeme A would be used in contexts such as "yellow shirt, yellow paint." Lexeme B is employed in combinations such as "yellow skin, yellow leaves." The difference is not one of hue. Rather, lexeme A covers many shades of yellow characterizing an object, while lexeme B refers only to an object that has become yellow (or a related hue, which might be translated by English "pale" or "rusty") as a result of ripening or aging. In itself, such a distinction has no wide significance, except perhaps to suggest that an investigation of color terms must recognize that such terms may express discriminations other than those involved in the color spectrum.

The semantic range of lexeme B, in various morphological combinations, indicates the manner in which certain concepts are linked in terms of Zuni cultural associations. In its singular form lexeme B refers to any ripened or aged yellow object. In the plural it is specialized to refer to pollen or corn meal, a culturally important linkage for other related meanings of this lexeme. When it is preposed to an element meaning "stretching across," it forms the prayer term for "road" and, by extension, "the road of life." Reference here is to the ceremonial sprinkling of corn meal to form a path, symbolizing the sacred road.

In this semantic study I have been exploring the distinctions and associations expressed within certain arbitrarily selected categories. For example, I have collected Zuni expressions comparing persons to animals. The overwhelming majority of these comparisons assigns some physical characteristic of an animal to a human being: an individual's hands are rough like the feet of a turkey; he is bald or downy-headed like an eaglet; he has protruding eyes like a rat; he has bony legs like a bird. In contrast, expressions based upon similarities in behavior or "personality" are extremely rare, and in nearly all such cases the comparison involves a post-Conquest animal with a Zuni name borrowed from English or Spanish: a stubborn and disobedient child is like a donkey; an overactive child is like a monkey (from English "monkey"); a flighty person is like a young goat (from Spanish "chivato"). The basic Zuni conception of man's affinity to animals, then, is limited to overt physical likenesses. The notion that there are psychological similarities between human beings and animals appears to be a borrowed idea incorporated into Zuni expression.

Another category which I am attempting to cover is that dealing with expressions of affective and related physiological states. The concept of experiencing an emotional shock, for example, is expressed by an inchoative morpheme added to the stem meaning "thyroid." Other expressions containing a reference to the thyroid, such as "his thyroid came out," provide the native context: the thyroid gland is conceived as an organ that moves up into the throat at an emotional shock and causes a sharp intake of breath or a choking sensation. The heart is the seat of emotional disturbance: to be "heartsick" is to be sad or angry in an overtly manifested manner. The opposite emotion, an overtly manifested happiness, is expressed by a distinct lexeme. In contrast to these visible emotions are the subjectively perceived psychosomatic states, which are referred to by phrases containing a term that my informant translates as "thinking": when one's thinking "is good," one feels internally happy and has a sense of physical well-being; when one "is full" of thinking, one is sick and feels sad or anxious, as in brooding over a dead relative or in worrying over being accused of witchcraft.

This presentation of human and animal comparisons and of expressions regarding affective states is merely a sketch of the type of semantic description which, I hope, can be developed on a broader scale and more systematically as the study progresses. Other semantic categories that I am emphasizing are the references to non-Zuni groups (whites, Mexicans, Indian groups in contact with the Zuni), terms denoting polar contrasts (black : white, bad : good, hard : soft), expressions used by adults in correcting children, and expressions used only by men or only by women. These categories, of course, are no more than convenient foci of attack.

The most difficult problem in this lexemic study is that of establishing valid methods for identifying the Zuni configurations of concepts. The basic assumption is that lexemes provide a formal framework that corresponds to an organization of meanings. It is true that lexemes do not manifest formal features that are as regularly patterned as those of morphological structures, but they can be utilized as formal markers for piecing together the systematic characteristics of meaning expressed in the language. Thus, the single lexeme is accepted as a form unit expressing a bundle of associated concepts, its range of meaning being determined by the linguistic contexts in which it may be used. Distinct lexemes are regarded as expressing concepts distinct to the Zuni, regardless of the supposed affinity of concepts on the basis of English lexemes or on philosophical grounds. Formally complex lexemes are analyzed into their constituent morphemes, which indicate the constituent concepts that are combined or fused in such lexemes. Certain lexemes are identified as borrowed forms, which may be suspected of expressing meanings borrowed from another culture.

In addition to these formal characteristics, certain semantic regularities have proved helpful in this study. My informant finds no difficulty in giving me the "opposites" of many lexemes: states of happiness can be contrasted with states of sadness. Such opposites are purely semantic, having no overt reflection of their contrastive relationship. They represent the tendency to refer to certain continua by means of lexemes expressing the polar extremes of such continua. Lexemes which discriminate between the poles of a continuum are to be regarded as semantically related in terms of culturally given experience: happiness of an overtly manifested type is culturally conceived, but not formally expressed, as the Zuni opposite of a sadness that is also overtly manifested. This is a different type of discrimination from that expressed in the lexemes referring, on the one hand, to overtly manifested sadness and, on the other, to the internally felt state of sadness combined with physical illness. These latter two lexemes have reference to the poles of two different continua, whose reality can be demonstrated by the occurrence of two pairs of lexemes, each pair covering the opposite poles of a single continuum, and one pair having reference to a semantic continuum distinct from the other. The two kinds of sadness, then, are to be regarded as unrelated poles of two distinctive continua in Zuni. Another type of semantic regularity is exemplified in the expressions used by parents in correcting or criticizing their children: one group of expressions refers to hearing, such as "You are becoming deaf," "You have no ears," "Listen!" Here, again, the various expressions cannot be linked by correspondingly related formal features, nor can they be associated along a single continuum. Their association is based, rather, on an empirical relationship between the references (becoming deaf, having no ears, listening) within one situational context (parental correction of children).

In short, this study utilizes criteria of lexical form wherever possible, but it recognizes that there are semantic regularities not manifested in form. In either case, the aim is to bring together recurrent types of associated or discriminated concepts in an attempt to find the dominant and more systematic characteristics of the Zuni arrangement of meanings.

III

In the preceding sections I have avoided any direct discussion of the thought-world concept. This omission has not been due to any feeling on my part that the problem is unimportant, nor that it is outside the proper confines of linguistics. The growing interest among ethnologists and other social scientists in formulating the system of motivations among a people—a conception variously designated as world-view, ethos, culture configurations, basic patterns, absolute logics, orientations, themes, values—this trend attests to the importance of the problem. And I am convinced that the linguist can contribute, and contribute significantly, to the clarification of this problem.

The measure of the linguist's contribution, however, will depend upon his ability to devise linguistically oriented methods for dealing with semantic data. Just as the thought-world problem is not an exclusively linguistic concern, so semantic investigations are not the prerogative of the linguist alone. A variety of approaches to the study of verbal meanings has been devised by philosophers, psychologists, and social scientists. Each of these specialists utilizes language materials in his own way and in terms of the methods and aims which have developed in his own discipline. In the same way, the unique contribution of the linguist will lie, not in any priority he may claim in dealing with semantic data, but rather in the distinctive methods that he can bring to bear upon the common problem. Despite the fact that the linguist's tools, when applied to the neglected field of semantics, will necessarily lack the rigor and precision attained in structural linguistics, this direction holds out a better promise than purely structural investigations for his participation in the broader problem which has attracted the efforts of many ethnologists.

Although a large part of the ethnological literature on the thought-world problem is either theoretical or intuitive, there are some empirical studies in which methods have been formulated and applied to the culture of a specific people. One investigation of this type has been carried on by Opler with the Lipan Apache (1946), and a more ambitious project is being conducted by the Values Study with the Navaho, Zuni, and three non-Indian groups in the "Rimrock" area of New Mexico. (For an outline of the Values Study and a list of its publications, both printed and in preparation, see Vogt 1951: vii–xi.) The results of such empirical studies made by specialists in other disciplines, it seems to me, offer a particularly valuable frame for comparison with the conclusions which can be reached independently by linguistic methods.

REFERENCES CITED

Bloomfield, Leonard
1933 *Language*. New York, Henry Holt and Company.

Gayton, A. H. and S. S. Newman
1940 *Yokuts and Western Mono Myths*. University of California Anthropological Records **5,** No. 1.

Hoijer, Harry and others
1946 *Linguistic Structures of Native America*. Viking Fund Publications in Anthropology, No. 6.

Opler, Morris
1946 "An Application of the Theory of Themes in Culture," *Journal, Washington Academy of Sciences* **36**: 137–66.

Vogt, Evon Z.
1951 *Navaho Veterans: A Study of Changing Values*. Papers of the Peabody Museum of American Archaeology and Ethnology, Harvard University **41,** No. 1.

THE SAPIR-WHORF HYPOTHESIS

HARRY HOIJER

THE SAPIR-WHORF HYPOTHESIS appears to have had its initial formulation in the following two paragraphs, taken from an article of Sapir's, first published in 1929.

> Language is a guide to "social reality." Though language is not ordinarily thought of as of essential interest to the students of social science, it powerfully conditions all our thinking about social problems and processes. Human beings do not live in the objective world alone, nor alone in the world of social activity as ordinarily understood, but are very much at the mercy of the particular language which has become the medium of expression for their society. It is quite an illusion to imagine that one adjusts to reality essentially without the use of language and that language is merely an incidental means of solving specific problems of communication or reflection. The fact of the matter is that the "real world" is to a large extent unconsciously built up on the language habits of the group. No two languages are ever sufficiently similar to be considered as representing the same social reality. The worlds in which different societies live are distinct worlds, not merely the same world with different labels attached.
>
> The understanding of a simple poem, for instance, involves not merely an understanding of the single words in their average significance, but a full comprehension of the whole life of the community as it is mirrored in the words, or as it is suggested by their overtones. Even comparatively simple acts of perception are very much more at the mercy of the social patterns called words than we might suppose. If one draws some dozen lines, for instance, of different shapes, one perceives them as divisible into such categories as "straight," "crooked," "curved," "zigzag" because of the classificatory suggestiveness of the linguistic terms themselves. We see and hear and otherwise experience very largely as we do because the language habits of our community predispose certain choices of interpretation." [In Mandelbaum 1949: 162.]

The notion of language as a "guide to social reality" is not entirely original with Sapir. Somewhat similar ideas, though far less adequately stated, may be found in Boas' writings, at least as early as 1911. Thus we find in Boas' introduction to the *Handbook of American Indian Languages* a number of provocative passages on this theme, to wit:

> It seems, however, that a theoretical study of Indian languages is not less important than a practical knowledge of them; that the purely linguistic inquiry is part and parcel of a thorough investigation of the psychology of the peoples of the world [p. 63].

. . . language seems to be one of the most instructive fields of inquiry in an investigation of the formation of the fundamental ethnic ideas. The great advantage that linguistics offer in this respect is the fact that, on the whole, the categories which are formed always remain unconscious, and that for this reason the processes which lead to their formation can be followed without the misleading and disturbing factors of secondary explanation, which are so common in ethnology, so much so that they generally obscure the real history of the development of ideas entirely [pp. 70–71].

As Greenberg points out in a paper contained in this volume, approaches somewhat similar to the Sapir-Whorf hypothesis may be found among European writers, and are "particularly strong in the German-speaking world," where they can be "traced back at least as far as Herder in the latter part of the eighteenth century" (p. xx). Alexander von Humboldt is mentioned as having a profound influence in this development, together with more modern scholars like Ernst Cassirer, Johann Leo Weisgerber, and Jost Trier. To these we should probably add Charles Bally, Marcel Granet, Claude Lévi-Strauss, Jean Piaget, Alf Sommerfelt, and L. Wittgenstein.

The Sapir-Whorf hypothesis, however, gains especial significance by virtue of the fact that both these scholars had a major interest in American Indian languages, idioms far removed from any in the Indo-European family and so ideally suited to contrastive studies. It is in the attempt properly to interpret the grammatical categories of an American Indian language, Hopi, that Whorf best illustrates his principle of linguistic relativity, the notion that "users of markedly different grammars are pointed by their grammars toward different types of observations and different evaluations of externally similar acts of observation, and hence are not equivalent as observers but must arrive at somewhat different views of the world" (1952: 11).

The purpose of this paper is threefold: (1) to review and clarify the Sapir-Whorf hypothesis, (2) to illustrate and perhaps add to it by reference to my own work on the Navaho language, and (3) to propose a series of studies intended to test and further develop the hypothesis.

The central idea of the Sapir-Whorf hypothesis is that language functions, not simply as a device for reporting experience, but also, and more significantly, as a way of defining experience for its speakers. Sapir says (1931: 578), for example:

Language is not merely a more or less systematic inventory of the various items of experience which seem relevant to the individual, as is so often naïvely assumed, but is also a self-contained, creative symbolic organization, which not only refers to experience largely acquired without its help but actually defines experience for us by reason of its formal completeness and because of our unconscious projection of its implicit expectations into the field of experience. In this respect language is very much like a mathematical system which, also, records experience in the truest sense of the word, only in its crudest beginnings, but, as time goes on, becomes elaborated into a self-contained conceptual system which previsages all possible experience in accordance with certain accepted formal limitations. . . . [Meanings are] not so much discovered in experience as imposed upon it, because of the tyrannical hold that linguistic form has upon our orientation in the world.

Whorf develops the same thesis when he says (1952: 5):

. . . that the linguistic system (in other words, the grammar) of each language is not merely a reproducing instrument for voicing ideas but rather is itself the shaper of ideas, the program and guide for the individual's mental activity, for his analysis of impressions, for his synthesis of his mental stock in trade. . . . We dissect nature along lines laid down by our native languages. The categories and types that we isolate from the world of phenomena we do not find there because they stare every observer in the face; on the contrary, the world is presented in a kaleidoscopic flux of impressions which has to be organized by our minds—and this means largely by the linguistic systems in our minds.

It is evident from these statements, if they are valid, that language plays a large and significant role in the totality of culture. Far from being simply a technique of communication, it is itself a way of directing the perceptions of its speakers and it provides for them habitual modes of analyzing experience into significant categories. And to the extent that languages differ markedly from each other, so should we expect to find significant and formidable barriers to cross-cultural communication and understanding. These barriers take on even greater importance when it is realized that "the phenomena of a language are to its own speakers largely of a background character and so are outside the critical consciousness and control of the speaker" (Whorf 1952: 4).

It is, however, easy to exaggerate linguistic differences of this nature and the consequent barriers to intercultural understanding. No culture is wholly isolated, self-contained, and unique. There are important resemblances between all known cultures—resemblances that stem in part from diffusion (itself an evidence of successful intercultural communication) and in part from the fact that all cultures are built around biological, psychological, and social characteristics common to all mankind. The languages of human beings do not so much determine the perceptual and other faculties of their speakers vis-à-vis experience as they influence and direct these faculties into prescribed channels. Intercultural communication, however wide the difference between cultures may be, is not impossible. It is simply more or less difficult, depending on the degree of difference between the cultures concerned.

Some measure of these difficulties is encountered in the process of translating from one language into another that is divergent and unrelated. Each language has its own peculiar and favorite devices, lexical and grammatical, which are employed in the reporting, analysis, and categorizing of experience. To translate from English into Navaho, or vice versa, frequently involves much circumlocution, since what is easy to express in one language, by virtue of its lexical and grammatical techniques, is often difficult to phrase in the other. A simple illustration is found when we try to translate the English phrases *his horse* and *his horses* into Navaho, which not only lacks a plural category for nouns (Navaho łį·ʔ translates equally English *horse* and *horses*) but lacks as well the English distinction between *his, her, its,* and *their* (Navaho bìłį·ʔ may be translated, according to context, *his horse* or *horses, her horse* or *horses, its horse* or *horses,* and *their horse* or *horses*). These Navaho forms łį·ʔ, bìłį·ʔ make difficulties in English also because Navaho makes a distinction between a third person (the bì- in bìłį·ʔ) psychologically close to the speaker (e.g., *his* [that is, a Navaho's] *horse*) as opposed to a third person (the hà- of hàłį·ʔ) psychologically remote (e.g., *his* [that is, a non-Navaho's] *horse*).

Differences of this order, which reflect a people's habitual and favorite modes of reporting, analyzing, and categorizing experience, form the essential data of the Sapir-Whorf hypothesis. According to Whorf (1952: 27), it is in these "constant ways of arranging data and its most ordinary every-day analysis of phenomena that we need to recognize the influence . . . [language] has on other activities, cultural and personal."

The Sapir-Whorf hypothesis, it is evident, includes in language both its structural and its semantic aspects. These are held to be inseparable, though it is obvious that we can and do study each more or less independently of the other. The structural aspect of language, which is that most easily analyzed and described, includes its phonology, morphology, and syntax, the numerous but limited frames into which utterances are cast. The semantic aspect consists of a self-contained system of meanings, inextricably bound to the structure but much more difficult to analyze and describe. Meanings, to reiterate, are not in actual fact separable from structure, nor are they, as some have maintained (notably Voegelin 1949: 36), to be equated to the nonlinguistic culture. Our interest lies, not in questions such as "What does this form, or form class, mean?" but, instead, in the question, "In what manner does a language organize, through its structural semantic system, the world of experience in which its speakers live?" The advantage of this approach to the problem of meaning is clear. As Bloomfield long ago pointed out, it appears quite impossible, short of omniscience, to determine precisely the meaning of any single form or form class in a language. But it should be possible to determine the limits of any self-contained structural-semantic system and the ways in which it previsages the experiences of its users.

To illustrate this procedure in brief, let us turn again to Navaho and one of the ways in which it differs from English. The Navaho color vocabulary includes, among others, five terms: łìgài, dìłxìł, łìžìn, łìčį·ˀ, and dò·ƛ̀ìž, to be taken as one way of categorizing certain color impressions. łìgài is roughly equivalent to English *white*, dìłxìł and łìžìn to English *black*, łìčį·ˀ to English *red*, and dò·ƛ̀ìž to English *blue* or *green*. Clearly, then, the Navaho five-point system is not the same as English white-black-red-blue-green, which also has five categories. English *black* is divided into two categories in Navaho (dìłxìł and łìžìn), while Navaho has but one category (dò·ƛ̀ìž) for the English *blue* and *green*. We do not, it should be noted, claim either that English speakers cannot perceive the difference between the two "blacks" of Navaho, or that Navaho speakers are unable to differentiate "blue" and "green." The difference between the two systems lies simply in the color categories recognized in ordinary speech, that is, in the ordinary everyday ways in which speakers of English and Navaho analyze color phenomena.

Every language is made up of a large number of such structural-semantic patterns, some of which pertain to lexical sets, as in the case of the Navaho and English color terms, and others of which pertain to sets of grammatical categories, such as the distinction between the singular and plural noun in English. A monolingual speaker, if his reports are to be understood by others in his speech community, is bound to use this apparatus, with all its implications for the analysis and categorization of experience, though he may of course quite often select from a number of alternative expressions in making his report. To quote Sapir again (Mandelbaum 1949: 10–11):

> . . . as our scientific experience grows we must learn to fight the implications of language. "The grass waves in the wind" is shown by its linguistic form to be a member of the same relational class of experiences as "The man works in the house." As an interim solution of the problem of expressing the experience referred to in this sentence it is clear that the language has proved useful, for it has made significant use of certain symbols of conceptual relation, such as agency and location. If we feel the sentence to be poetic or metaphorical, it is largely because other more complex

types of experience with their appropriate symbolisms of reference enable us to reinterpret the situation and to say, for instance, "The grass is waved by the wind" or "The wind causes the grass to wave." The point is that no matter how sophisticated our modes of interpretation become, we never really get beyond the projection and continuous transfer of relations suggested by the forms of our speech. . . . Language is at one and the same time helping and retarding us in our exploration of experience, and the details of these processes of help and hindrance are deposited in the subtler meanings of different cultures.

It does not necessarily follow that all the structural-semantic patterns of a language are equally important to its speakers in their observation, analysis, and categorizing of experience. In describing a language, we seek to uncover all its structural-semantic patterns, even though many of these exist more as potentialities of the system than in actual usage. For ethnolinguistic analysis we need to know, not only that a particular linguistic pattern exists, but also how frequently it occurs in everyday speech. We also need to know something of the degree of complexity of the pattern of expression. There are numerous patterns of speech, particularly among peoples who have well-developed arts of oratory and writing, that are little used by any except specialists in these pursuits. The patterns of speech significant to ethnolinguistic research fall clearly into the category of habitual, frequently used, and relatively simple structural-semantic devices; those, in short, which are common to the adult speech community as a whole, and are used by its members with the greatest ease.

Not all the structural patterns of the common speech have the same degree of semantic importance. In English, for example, it is not difficult to ascertain the semantic correlates of the structural distinction between singular and plural nouns; in most cases this is simply a division into the categories "one" versus "more than one." Similarly, the gender distinction of the English third-person singular pronouns, as between "he," "she," and "it," correlates fairly frequently with the recognition of personality and sex.

In contrast to these, there are structural patterns like that which, in many Indo-European languages, divides nouns into three great classes: masculine, feminine, and neuter. This structural pattern has no discernible semantic correlate; we do not confuse the grammatical terms "masculine," "feminine," and "neuter" with the biological distinctions among male, female, and neuter. Whatever the semantic implications of this structural pattern may have been in origin, and this remains undetermined, it is now quite apparent that the pattern survives only as a grammatical device, important in that function but lacking in semantic value. And it is perhaps significant that the pattern is an old one, going back to the earliest history of the Indo-European languages and, moreover, that it has disappeared almost completely in some of the modern languages of this family, notably, of course, in English.

In ethnolinguistic research, then, it is necessary to concentrate on those structural patterns of a language which have definable semantic correlates, and to omit those, like the Indo-European gender system, which survive only in a purely grammatical function. The assumption behind this procedure is as follows: every language includes a number of active structural-semantic categories, lexical and grammatical, which by virtue of their active status serve a function in the everyday (nonscientific) analysis and categorizing of experience. It is the study of these categories, distinctive when taken as a whole for each language, that yields, or may yield, significant information concerning the thought world of the speakers of the language.

One further point requires emphasis. Neither Sapir nor Whorf attempted to draw inferences as to the thought world of a people simply from the fact of the presence or absence of specific grammatical categories (e.g., tense, gender, number) in a given language. To quote Whorf (1952: 44) on this point: the concepts of time and matter which he reports for the Hopi

> do not depend so much upon any one system (e.g., tense, or nouns) within the grammar as upon the ways of analyzing and reporting experience which have become fixed in the language as integrated "fashions of speaking" and which cut across the typical grammatical classifications, so that such a "fashion" may include lexical, morphological, syntactic, and otherwise systematically diverse means coordinated in a certain frame of consistency.

To summarize, ethnolinguistic research requires the investigator to perform, it seems to me, the following steps:

1. To determine the structural patterns of a language (that is, its grammar) as completely as possible. Such determination should include not only a statement of the modes of utterance but as well a careful indication of the frequency of occurrence of these modes, lexical and grammatical, in the common speech.

2. To determine, as accurately as possible, the semantic patterns, if any, that attach to structural patterns. This is a task neglected by most structural linguists who, as is repeatedly mentioned in the discussions that follow, are frequently content simply to label rather than to define both lexical units and grammatical categories. In this

connection it is important to emphasize that the analyst must not be taken in by his own labels; he is to discover, where possible, just how the form, or form class, or grammatical category functions in the utterances available to him.

3. To distinguish between structural categories that are active in the language, and therefore have definable semantic correlates, and those which are not. It goes without saying that such distinction requires a profound knowledge of the language, and possibly even the ability to speak and understand it well. Mark Twain's amusing translation of a German folktale into English, where he regularly translates the gender of German nouns by the English forms "he," "she," and "it," illustrates, though in caricature, the pitfalls of labeling the grammatical categories of one language (in this case, German gender) by terms belonging to an active structural-semantic pattern in another.

4. To examine and compare the active structural-semantic patterns of the language and draw from them the fashions of speaking there evidenced. As in Whorf's analysis of Hopi (1952: 25–45), while clues to a fashion of speaking may be discovered in a particular grammatical category or set of lexical items, its validity and importance cannot be determined until its range and scope within the language as a whole is also known. Whorf's conclusions as to the nature of the concept of time among speakers of English rest not alone on the tense distinctions of the English verb (mixed as these are with many other and diverse distinctions of voice, mode, and aspect) but as well on techniques of numeration, the treatment of nouns denoting physical quantity and phases of cycles, and a host of other terms and locutions relating to time. He says (1952: 33):

> The three-tense system of SAE verbs colors all our thinking about time. This system is amalgamated with that larger scheme of objectification of the subjective experience of duration already noted in other patterns—in the binomial formula applicable to nouns in general, in temporal nouns, in plurality and numeration.

5. Taken together, the fashions of speaking found in a language comprise a partial description of the thought world of its speakers. But by the term "thought world" Whorf means

> more than simply language, i.e., than the linguistic patterns themselves. [He includes] . . . all the analogical and suggestive value of the patterns . . . and all the give-and-take between language and the culture as a whole, wherein is a vast amount that is not linguistic yet shows the shaping influence of language. In brief, this "thought world" is the microcosm that each man carries about within himself, by which he measures and understands what he can of the macrocosm [1952: 36].

It follows then that the thought world, as derived from ethnolinguistic studies, is found reflected as well, though perhaps not as fully, in other aspects of the culture. It is here that we may search for connections between language and the rest of culture. These connections are not direct; we see, instead, in certain patterns of nonlinguistic behavior the same meaningful fashions that are evidenced in the patterns of the language. Whorf summarizes this facet of his researches in a discussion of "Habitual Behavior Features of Hopi Culture and Some Impresses of Linguistic Habit in Western Civilization" (1952: 37–52).

It may be helpful to outline briefly some aspects of Navaho culture, including the language, as illustration of the Sapir-Whorf hypothesis. In particular, I shall describe first some of the basic postulates of Navaho religious behavior and attempt to show how these fit in a frame of consistency with certain fashions of speaking evidenced primarily in the morphological patterns of the Navaho verb.

A review of Navaho religious practices, as described by Washington Matthews, Father Berard Haile, and many others, reveals that the Navaho conceive of themselves as in a particular relationship with the environment—physical, social, and supernatural—in which they live. Navaho man lives in a universe of eternal and unchanging forces with which he attempts to maintain an equilibrium, a kind of balancing of powers. The mere fact of living is, however, likely to disturb this balance and throw it out of gear. Any such disturbance, which may result from failure to observe a set rule of behavior or ritual or from the accidental or deliberate committal of some other fault in ritual or the conduct of daily activities, will, the Navaho believe, be revealed in the illness or unexplained death of an individual, in some other personal misfortune or bad luck to an enterprise, or in some community disaster such as a food shortage or an epidemic. Whereupon, a diviner must be consulted, who determines by ritual means the cause of the disturbance and prescribes, in accordance with this knowledge, the appropriate counteracting religious ceremony or ritual.

The underlying purpose of the curing ceremony is to put the maladjusted individual or the community as a whole back into harmony with the universe. Significantly, this is done, not by the shaman or priest acting upon the individual and changing him, nor by any action, by shaman or priest, designed to alter the forces of the universe. It is done by re-enacting one of a complex series of religious dramas which represent, in highly abstract terms, the events, far back in

Navaho history, whereby the culture heroes first established harmony between man and nature and so made the world fit for human occupation. By re-enacting these events, or some portion of them, the present disturbance, by a kind of sympathetic magic, is compensated and harmony between man and universe restored. The ill person then gets well, or the community disaster is alleviated, since these misfortunes were but symptoms of a disturbed relation to nature.

From these numerous and very important patterns of Navaho religious behavior, it seems to me we can abstract a dominant motif belonging to the Navaho thought world. The motif has been well put by Kluckhohn and Leighton, who also illustrate it in many other aspects of Navaho culture. They call it, "Nature is more powerful than man," and amplify this in part by the Navaho premise "that nature will take care of them if they behave as they should and do as she directs" (1946:227–28). In short, to the Navaho, the way to the good life lies not in modifying nature to man's needs or in changing man's nature but rather in discovering the proper relation of nature to man and in maintaining that relationship intact.

Turning now to the Navaho language, let us look at some aspects of the verb structure, illustrated in the following two forms:

nìńtį *you have lain down.*
nìšíńłtį *you have put, laid me down.*

Both these verbs are in the second person of the perfective mode (Hoijer 1946); the ń- marks this inflection. Both also have a prefix nì-, not the same but subtly different in meaning. The nì- of the first means [*movement*] *terminating in a position of rest,* that of the second [*movement*] *ending at a given point.* The second form has the causative prefix ł- and incorporates the first person object, expressed in this form by ši-. The stem -tį́, common to both forms, is defined *one animate being moves.*

The theme of the first verb, composed of nì- . . . -tį́, means *one animate being moves to a position of rest,* that is, *one animate being lies down.* In the second verb the meaning of the theme, nì- . . . -ł-tį́, is *cause movement of one animate being to end at a given point* and so, by extension, *put an animate being down* or *lay an animate being down.*

Note now that the first theme includes in its meaning what in English we should call both the actor and the action; these are not, in Navaho, expressed by separate morphemes. The subject pronoun prefix ń- serves then simply to identify a particular being with the class of possible beings already delimited by the theme. It functions, in short, to individuate one belonging to the class *animate being in motion to a position of rest.* The theme of the second verb, by reason of the causative ł-, includes in its meaning what in English would be called action and goal. Again the pronoun ši-, as a consequence, simply identifies or individuates one of a class of possible beings defined already in the theme itself. It should be emphasized that the forms used here as illustration are in no sense unusual; this is the regular pattern of the Navaho verb, repeated over and over again in my data.

We are now ready to isolate, from this necessarily brief analysis, a possible fashion of speaking peculiar to Navaho. The Navaho speaks of "actors" and "goals" (the terms are inappropriate to Navaho), not as performers of actions or as ones upon whom actions are performed, as in English, but as entities linked to actions already defined in part as pertaining especially to classes of beings. The form which is glossed *you have lain down* is better understood *you [belong to, equal one of] a class of animate beings which has moved to rest.* Similarly the second form, glossed *you have put, laid me down* should read *you, as agent, have set a class of animate beings, to which I belong, in motion to a given point.*

This fashion of speaking, it seems to me, is wholly consistent with the dominant motif we saw in Navaho religious practices. Just as in his religious-curing activities the Navaho sees himself as adjusting to a universe that is given, so in his habits of speaking does he link individuals to actions and movements distinguished, not only as actions and movements, but as well in terms of the entities in action or movement. This division of nature into classes of entity in action or movement is the universe that is given; the behavior of human beings or of any being individuated from the mass is customarily reported by assignment to one or other of these given divisions.

Analyses such as this one, though admittedly incomplete, point up the potential value of the Sapir-Whorf hypothesis in cross-cultural understanding. Further work is obviously needed, on languages and cultures as diverse as can be found, to develop the hypothesis. To this end, I venture to suggest the following study, arising mainly from my own experience, and designed to examine the question: If the thought world implies, as we have said, the existence of significant connections between language and the rest of culture, how are we to account for the fact that peoples very similar in the rest of their culture speak languages that are wholly unrelated, and that closely related languages are frequently spoken by peoples very different in the rest of their culture?

The data for a project centering about this question are already in large part collected; they require only to be completed and analyzed in terms of the Sapir-Whorf hypothesis. The project involves researches on the following cultures, chosen for their similarities and differences in culture area and linguistic affiliations.

1. The Navaho, who share a number of nonlinguistic culture patterns with their Hopi neighbors, speak a language (of the Athapaskan stock) that is not in the least related to Hopi (of the Shoshonean stock). There is already a great deal of linguistic and other cultural data on both these groups, though much is as yet unpublished. A Navaho grammar is now in preparation, and studies of Navaho nonlinguistic culture, published and in preparation, are numerous and detailed. For Hopi there is perhaps less published linguistic material but a considerable amount of data on the rest of the culture. A beginning has also been made on the characterization of the Hopi thought world; Whorf's Hopi studies are the most complete of his works (see especially 1952: 25–45).

Preliminary comparisons indicate that the Hopi and Navaho thought worlds are very different, despite the similarities between the two groups in certain overt cultural patterns. It should be kept in mind, however, that the likeness of Navaho to Hopi culture has probably been exaggerated; most of the similarities that led Wissler and others to put them into the same culture area are indeed superficial.

2. The Hopi and the Hopi-Tewa (the pueblo of Hano) offer a far better contrast. Here we find two peoples who, already sharing a general Puebloan culture, have lived in close association on First Mesa since about 1700. Their languages, however, are very divergent; the language of Hano is of the Tewan family and has its closest affiliations to the Rio Grande pueblos farther east. Data on Hano nonlinguistic culture have recently been collected by E. P. Dozier, who is now preparing them for publication. Unfortunately, there is as yet little work on the Tewan languages, though a beginning has been made on the Santa Clara dialect. It is interesting that the differences between Santa Clara Tewa, spoken in the Rio Grande region, and the Tewa of Hano are minor.

A study of one or more of the Rio Grande Tewa-speaking pueblos should be included in this project. In this comparison between Hopi, Hano, and the Tewa speakers of the Rio Grande, there are unusual possibilities. Some of the questions that now appear important are: How wide are the differences between the Hopi culture of First Mesa, that of the Hano, and that of the Rio Grande Tewa? To what extent have the Hano been acculturated to the Hopi? Is there a greater similarity between the Hopi and the Hano thought worlds than between those of the Hano and the Rio Grande Tewa? Since the move of the Hano people to First Mesa can be dated with some precision, it is possible in this project to gain some indication of the extent to which a thought world may change relative to changes in the rest of the culture.

3. The Hupa should be studied and contrasted with the Navaho. Here is an instance where two languages are indubitably and closely related; both Hupa and Navaho are of the Athapaskan stock. The nonlinguistic cultures, however, are widely divergent. Hupa has a northern California culture, very different from that of the Southwestern Navaho. Field data on the Hupa language are complete; the material is now being prepared for publication. Much material on Hupa nonlinguistic culture is already published and, more is in preparation.

4. A final phase of this project might involve a contrast of the Hopi with the Southern Paiute. The languages are related (both belong to the Shoshonean stock), but the nonlinguistic cultures offer the same order of difference as exists between the Navaho and the Hupa. There is much useful data on the Southern Paiute language, published by Sapir some years ago, and some published material on their nonlinguistic culture. It is probable, however, that more data may be needed.

It may be useful, in conclusion, to speculate a bit on the possible results of the project outlined above. The following quotation (Hoijer 1953: 567) is relevant.

> If language and culture have been regarded by some as distinct variables . . . it is perhaps because (1) they define language too narrowly and (2) they limit culture (especially in establishing culture areas) to its more formal and explicit features, those which are most subject to borrowing and change.
>
> It is quite possible that the features of a language (largely phonemic) by means of which we link it to others in a stock or family are among the least important when we seek to connect it to the rest of culture. The fashions of speaking that Whorf finds so important to habitual behavior and thought are, after all, derived from the lexical, morphological, and syntactic patterns of a language, and these, in turn, are arrangements of phonemic materials. Two or more languages, then, may well have their phonemic materials from the same historical source and yet develop, under the stimulus of diverse microcosms, quite different fashions of speech. In short, the fact that languages belong to a common stock does not prove that they have the same fashions of speaking; such proof, if it is forthcoming at all, must be demonstrated empirically.

The cultures included in the same culture areas, on the other hand, tend to resemble each other only in discrete cultural features, those which are easily diffused, and not necessarily in the ways in which these features are combined into fashions of behaving or in the basic premises to which such fashions of behaving may point.

REFERENCES CITED

BOAS, FRANZ (ed.)
1911 "Introduction," *Handbook of American Indian Languages*, Part 1. Washington, D.C.

HOIJER, HARRY
1946 "The Apachean Verb, Part III: The Prefixes for Mode and Tense," *International Journal of American Linguistics* **12:**1–13.
1953 "The Relation of Language to Culture." In: *Anthropology Today* (by A. L. KROEBER and OTHERS), pp. 554–73. Chicago, University of Chicago Press.

KLUCKHOHN, CLYDE and DOROTHEA LEIGHTON
1946 *The Navaho*. Cambridge, Harvard University Press.

MANDELBAUM, DAVID G. (ed.)
1949 *Selected Writings of Edward Sapir*. Berkeley and Los Angeles, University of California Press.

SAPIR, EDWARD
1931 "Conceptual Categories in Primitive Languages," *Science* **74:**578.

VOEGELIN, C. F.
1949 "Linguistics without Meaning and Culture without Words," *Word* **5:**36–42.

WHORF, BENJAMIN L.
1952 *Collected Papers on Metalinguistics*. Washington, D.C., Department of State, Foreign Service Institute.

CHINESE VERSUS ENGLISH: AN EXPLORATION OF THE WHORFIAN THESES

CHARLES F. HOCKETT

THIS PAPER consists of two parts. In the first, the writer attempts to classify the various points of contact between language and culture, linguistics and ethnography. The interrelations of the two disciplines, and of their subject-matters, are far more numerous than a narrow preoccupation with Whorf's writings would suggest. If we are to attempt verification or extension of his theories, we must first see them in proper perspective.

In the second part, we shall examine a number of points of difference between Chinese and English—with no effort to avoid the trivial—to see whether that particular pair of languages, contrastively examined, can shed any light on Whorf's theses.

I. POINTS OF CONTACT OF LINGUISTICS AND ETHNOGRAPHY

By "linguistics" we mean the study of human language (in the narrow sense accepted by most linguists; that is, excluding writing or other derivative communicative systems); by "ethnography" we mean the study of all of human culture. There is no need for us to dwell here on the long-standing and still unsettled terminological disputes about the precise coverage of the term "culture." The writer prefers a definition broad enough to guarantee that language is part of culture—broad enough, in fact, so that the epithet "human" in the phrase "human culture" is not redundant. Such a definition seems logically and ontologically possible.

By virtue of these definitions, the relations between linguistics and ethnography are relations between a daughter discipline and a more inclusive parent discipline. The histories of the two fields, and the current organizational status of the two on university faculties and in learned societies, are of course other matters. The logical and the institutional interrelationships of the two fields should not be confused. An explorer from Mars might be justified in trying to deduce the nature of the fields from the kinds of activities carried on by linguists and ethnographers. We who are actually in the fold cannot properly take any such circuitous approach; we must concern ourselves not only with what we have done and said heretofore, but also with what we ought to say and do in the future if the goals of our activity are to be approached.

The following is a possible outline of the points of contact with which we are concerned:

I. Existential
   A. General—for the whole human race
   B. Specific—to one or another community
II. Methodological
   A. Use of results attained in one field for purposes sought in the other
   B. Development of methods for use in one field on the basis of methods already in use in the other

By "existential" we mean the various relationships between language and any other phase of human culture, whatever the relationships may be, and whether anyone has noticed and reported on them or not. Existential problems are problems to be worked on with whatever methods can be devised; methodological problems start at the other end, and investigate how much and what kind of yield can be obtained with a stated method.

We shall discuss each of the four subdivisions briefly.

I. A. Language is a human universal, but is also exclusively human. There are other exclusively human patterns and institutions, some of them universal, some of them merely widespread. In what ways does language interrelate, causally or otherwise, with these other phenomena? What does language do for humans which nothing does for our closest nonhuman cousins, the anthropoids? The behavior of humans is different from that of other so-called "social animals"; to what extent and in what ways is language responsible for the differences? Humans are domesticated animals, but human behavior differs in many ways from that of other domesticated animals, despite the similarities. To what extent and in what ways is language the responsible factor here? The search for answers to these questions requires the marshaling of evidence by various disciplines: the problems escape the bounds of ethnography, and stand as key puzzles in comparative zoology, in the determination of "Man's place in nature."

These questions have also a historical phase. In the unfolding of human history, what role has language played in the emergence of distinctively human modes of behavior (other than, circularly, language itself)? What role has language played in the rise of other communicative systems? Are some communicative systems older than language—gesture systems, for example? If so, what role did these older systems play in the emergence of language? Of course, there are problems here which may never be solved, for lack of surviving evidence. Few of us, however, would be so narrowly operationalist as to assert that the absence of evidence renders the problems meaningless.

In the search for the human common denominator and its history, anthropologists still often lead themselves astray by the easy resort to mentalistic and finalistic terms such as "mind" or "idea." Under the tutelage of Leonard Bloomfield, linguists have for the most part learned to avoid pseudo explanations cast in such phraseology. The lesson badly needs learning in anthropology as a whole. A pseudo explanation, involving a parameter which is actually eliminable but not recognized as such, is worse than no explanation at all, since it puts a stop to further inquiry.

I. B. When we examine different human communities (what many ethnographers call "different cultures"), either as they function at a given time or as they change their ways of life with the passage of time, we find both similarities and differences. Specific linguistic patterns vary from community to community along with almost everything else. Despite all the work of anthropologists for the past half century or so, we still have very few adequate yardsticks for the measurement of differences from community to community, and very few satisfactory rubrics for the typological classification either of whole "cultures" or of specific phases of culture. This is as true for languages as for religions, housing-habits, folklores, social organizations, or agricultural practices. We cannot blithely say, "Menomini is a language of type 1-A2-3X, whereas Mandarin is of type 2-A1-7Y," or anything remotely approaching this.

Therefore the search for correlations between patterns in speech and patterns in other aspects of behavior is largely impressionistic. Of course we all know of low-level correlations: the Eskimos have many terms for different kinds of snow (so do English-speaking ski addicts); Arabs do not talk about the weather (neither did Mark Twain in *The American Claimant*); some Australian aborigines cannot count higher than three or four (why should they bother?). The vocabulary of a people reflects their experiences and interests. It is here that we find the most reliable and the dullest correlations between the rest of culture and language. Whorf sought to dig deeper—to find correlations, not between the things and activities which environ a group and its lexicon, but rather between what we might now call the "themes" of a community's culture, on the one hand,

and, on the other, the general grammatical and semantic tenor of the associated language. More specifically, he sought evidence for instances in which the state of affairs in a language was either (*a*) symptomatic of underlying cultural themes, or perhaps even (*b*) causally responsible for the choice of one course of action rather than another in given circumstances.

One technique which it would be well to use more extensively in this connection is to observe what difficulties a people encounters in trying to speak of new experiences. Settle a group of Arab families in central Minnesota, and see what they manage to do about speaking of the weather. Try to teach arithmetic and algebra to Australian aborigines in their own language. We know from many well-attested instances that, given time enough, the linguistic pattern of a community adapts quite efficiently to new living requirements. But we do not know for sure how quick and easy the adaptation is; it may be that for a measurable period the inherited linguistic pattern is the dead hand of the past, delaying adaptation in specific ways which could be described. Whorf's example of the blower installed incorrectly in the fur-storage warehouse is an instance of this if his analysis is right: the installer thinks the task out at least partly in words, and the connotations of the word "blower" lead to the faulty performance.

II. A. The use of linguistic results for ethnographic purposes is too familiar to belabor: native language as a tool in field work, linguistic relationships as partial evidence for the reconstruction of aboriginal history, and so on. It is worth while to point out that excellent work of this kind was done long before terms such as "ethnolinguistics" or even "cultural anthropology" were invented: nineteenth-century classical philologists undertook to determine the whole pattern of ancient Roman and Greek life as attested by documentary evidence, and as an intermediate step the analysis and constant reanalysis of Latin and Greek was necessary. It is well recognized that linguistics has its historic roots in philology; it should be recognized that ethnography also has some of its roots therein.

Similarly, the use of ethnographic results for linguistic purposes needs little detailing here. Whenever a linguist deals with the meanings of forms—and regardless of his theoretical stand on the matter he is constantly forced to do so—he is dealing with ethnographic information. The practical task of learning or teaching a foreign language cannot be successfully performed in an ethnographic vacuum. Without ethnographic (and historical) information, the Algonquian comparativist would be free to conclude that the pre-Columbian speakers of Proto-Central-Algonquian had guns and whiskey.

Some problems require such a close intermingling of linguistic and other techniques that they can hardly be classed as examples of the use of linguistic evidence for ethnographic purposes or vice versa; indeed, for the most part—despite the instances mentioned in the two preceding paragraphs—we ought not to raise the issue of scholarly hegemony. It does not matter whether we call the puzzle of the homeland of the speakers of Proto-Indo-Hittite a narrowly linguistic or a broadly ethnographic problem; it will be solved, if at all, only by taking all of the linguistic, cultural, historical, and archeological evidence into account.

II. B. Of all the sister fields, named or nameless, which lie close compacted within ethnography, linguistics has without doubt attained, to date, the clearest methods and the most reliable results. Those who are aware of this fact are by and large hesitant to state it openly, for obvious reasons of professional politeness. But there is no reason for such hesitancy: if linguistics has progressed further, the chief reason is the relative simplicity of its subject-matter as compared with that of its sister disciplines or of ethnography as a whole. Language is complex enough, but its complexity is as nothing in comparison with that of the whole fabric of life of a community, of which language is but one part. Linguists deserve no special credit for having made more progress; rather, they would deserve censure if they had not.

However, this state of affairs suggests that linguistics may have methodological lessons for other phases of ethnography. In a few instances the analogical extension of methodology is fairly obvious: for example, in the study of writing-systems (which the present writer has recently ventured to call "graphonomy"). It might seem much less likely that some phase of so-called "material culture," say house-building practices, could be studied more effectively by methods extrapolated from those of linguistics—but it would be wrong for us to jump to this conclusion. Theoretically we can divide the techniques of linguistics into two sets: those which work, in the analysis of language, because language is culture; and those which work because of the special characteristics which distinguish language from all other phases of culture. If we knew just which techniques belonged to each of these sets, then we could proceed to generalize those in the first set for use on other phases of culture. Actually, of course, only diligent trial and error will reveal the proper assignment of each individual procedure or approach.

As has already been indicated, the work of Whorf falls into our category I. B. The extensive attention which has been devoted in recent years—primarily under Whorf's stimulus—to problems in this category, is, positively speaking, highly commendable. Negatively, however, this has resulted in neglect of problems in the other three categories. We must not allow this neglect to continue. If work in the border area between linguistics and ethnography is to achieve such importance that a name for it, such as "ethnolinguistics," "metalinguistics," or "exolinguistics," is to become well established, then we must make sure that the term subsumes all of the types of problems which have been outlined above.

II. CHINESE AND ENGLISH

In this part of our paper we take up a number of aspects of Chinese and English, beginning with those which are certainly most trivial. We are concerned largely with colloquial forms of the two languages, on the assumption that "thinking in words" is more apt to be colloquial than literary. Chinese is represented by the variety of northern Mandarin spoken by educated people in Peiping; citation is in Yale Romanization. For consistency and clarity, cited Chinese forms are italicized, while both English glosses and cited English forms are placed between quotation marks.

TRAINS. *Hwǒchē* '(railroad) train'; *hwǒ* 'fire'; *chē* 'car, cart, wheeled vehicle'. The tendency, in talking in English about the Chinese words just listed, is to say something like "Chinese *hwǒchē*, the word for 'train', means literally 'fire-cart' ". Now we can be sure of two things:

(1) When steam rail transportation was introduced into China, the term *hwǒchē* came into use because of the fire-spitting locomotive;

(2) The formal structure of *hwǒchē* is still validly to be described as a compound of *hwǒ* and *chē*, as listed and glossed above.

However, the remark given in double quotes above is misleading. Currently, *hwǒchē* means almost exactly what 'train' means—there is no necessary image of a fire-spitting locomotive inside the speaker's head when he uses or hears the word. Evidence for this is that 'electric train' (as on an electrified railroad) is *dyànlì-hwǒchē*, where *dyànlì* means 'electric power'; such a train does not have a fire-spitting locomotive.

This first example is given to illustrate the danger inherent in a study of this kind when the non-native language is not thoroughly controlled—a danger not altogether avoided in the present study, though all points made have been carefully checked with native speakers of Chinese whose control of English is considerably better than the writer's control of Chinese. What is apt to be called the "literal" meaning of a Chinese (or other) form in terms of English is very often the poorest possible basis for any judgment. No doubt the childish errors of nineteenth-century European students of comparative semantics stemmed from just such a basis: for example, the oft-repeated assertion that the Algonquians can say 'my father', 'thy father', or 'his father', but have no way of saying just 'a father', and hence "lack powers of abstraction."

CITIES AND WALLS. *Chyáng* 'wall (of a room, house, city)'; *chéng* 'city, city wall'; *chéngshr̀* 'city, municipality'; *chéngchyáng* 'city wall'; *dzài chénglǐ* 'be in the city'; *dzài chéngwài* 'be outside the city, be in the outskirts'; *cháng* 'long'; *wànlǐ* 'ten thousand Chinese miles'; *chángchéng* or *wànlǐ chángchéng* 'The Great Wall'. The form that is central to our interest is *chéng*. The range of meaning of this element cannot be understood in terms of Western culture, but is immediately obvious when we recall that Chinese cities (except Shanghai) are universally enclosed in a square wall. With the exception of Shanghai, a clustering of dwellings and other structures which is not so enclosed is not a *chéng*, but a *tswēndz*, which we can gloss as 'village' if we are willing to redefine the English word for the purpose.

Here is a correlation between a particular segment of Chinese culture other than language and certain semantic features of the language. The correlation is different from that found in the English-speaking community. We fully expect that any two languages, chosen at random, will display a welter of such low-level differences; indeed, an exact match is a rarity worthy of notice.

AGE. In stating a person's age in English we use a cardinal number, followed, if necessary for clarity, by 'years old' or 'years of age'. In Chinese, one uses a cardinal number followed by the measure *swèi*. The possible matchings of English and Chinese expressions under various conditions can be shown as follows—where in English we assume that age is given to nearest birthday:

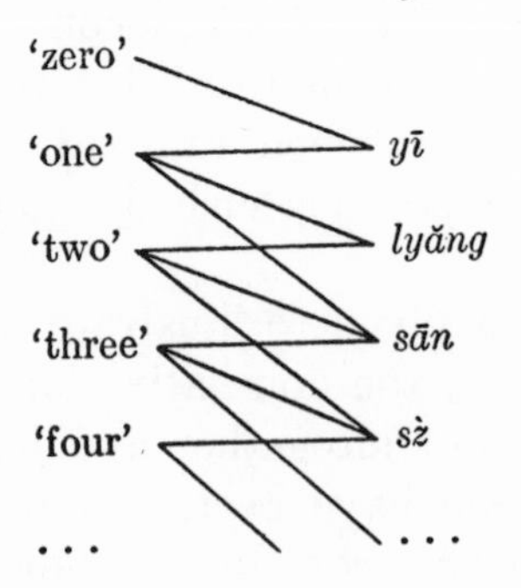

The absence of exact matching can be accounted for in terms of the meaning of the measure *swèi*. We can describe this as 'number of calendar years during all or part of which one has been alive'. In either language one can be far more precise in stating an age than these most customary expressions allow; in both languages the age of an infant is usually given in months, or months and days, rather than by any approximate formula. There are perhaps fewer occasions in Chinese culture in which such precision is called for than there are in English culture. To say 'so-many-years old' in Chinese, *swèi* in English, is possible but awkward. In ordinary usage one way of stating approximate age is as accurate, by and large, as the other.

Yet many Western scholars, approaching Chinese with too large a dose of glottocentrism, have passed snap judgment on the Chinese habit by saying something like, "In China [or: In Chinese] you are a year old when you are born."

FRUITS AND NUTS. If one has just eaten some strawberries, one can report the event in English by saying 'I just had some ———', filling the blank with 'strawberries', 'berries', 'fruit', or perhaps (this will not concern us) some even more generic term such as 'food'. A similar frame in Chinese, reporting the same event, could be filled with *yángméi* or *tsăuméi*, with *shwĕigwŏ*, or with *gwŏ*. In both languages the terms listed are idiomatic, not nonce-formations or especially coined descriptions. They line up as follows:

'strawberries'	*yángméi, tsăuméi*
'berries'	-----
'fruit'	*shwĕigwŏ*
-----	*gwŏ*

By this alignment we mean to indicate, for example, that 'berries' is a more inclusive term than *yángméi* or *tsăuméi*, but less inclusive than *shwĕigwŏ*.

Here there is close matching only at the most specific level. One can coin an expression in Chinese which will describe what 'berries' means in English; the expression is necessarily fairly long. Similarly, *gwŏ* can be paraphrased in English as 'fruits and/or nuts'. Neither the Chinese paraphrase for 'berries' nor the English paraphrase for *gwŏ* would ever naturally be used in the framework listed earlier. 'Strawberry' is a compound: it designates a kind of berry, and 'berry' is a single morpheme. *yángméi* and *tsăuméi* are both compounds, designating (the same kind of) *méi*, but *méi* does not mean 'berry'. This particular morpheme *méi*, in fact, does not occur as a whole word;

there is a homophonous morpheme *méi* which does occur alone and which means something like 'plum'.

Where English has a single morpheme 'fruit', Chinese uses a compound *shwěigwǒ* 'moist or watery *gwǒ*'. *Gwǒ* which is not *shwěigwǒ* is *gāngwǒ* 'dry *gwǒ*', but this does not match the English 'nuts', since *gāngwǒ* includes both nuts and dried fruits. Finally, there is no close match in Chinese for English 'nuts'.

The hierarchy of terms for specific items and various more inclusive classes of items, illustrated here in the field of fruits and nuts, is in any given language the product of a vast number of historical accidents; identical coverage of generic terms in two unrelated languages would be a second-order accident. There is a special idiom within the general framework of most Western languages in which the effect of these accidents is removed and categorization is based on actual structural similarities. This is the idiom of science—for fruits and nuts, the terminology of botanical taxonomy. Botanically speaking, the class of items which in everyday parlance are called 'berries' does not constitute a meaningful category. The idiom of science constantly replaces haphazard classifications by more objective ones. It is to be doubted whether any one language equips its speakers better than any other for the kind of semantic purification which the scientific approach necessitates. The Whorf approach suggests the value to an individual of learning a language of a type really alien to that of his own as a "second window" through which to view the universe. One may suspect that scientifically oriented study of the world about us is a more fruitful and enlightening experience of this sort than any study of a second language.

Random Holes in Patterns. In any language we can expect to find points on which the grammatical pattern is such as to make speech awkward. In English it is difficult to ask an ordinary colloquial negative question with subject pronoun 'I' and verb 'be' in the present tense. In the past tense it is easy enough: 'Wasn't I with you at the time?' With a different pronoun it is easy enough: 'Aren't we all going together?' At a more elevated style level it is easy enough: 'Am I not going with you?' At a substandard style level it is easy enough: 'Ain't I going with you?' But at the precise place—stylistically, and with the stated subject, verb, and tense—described above, there is a hole in the pattern. There is no ordinary colloquial contraction of verb-form 'am' and negative element 'not'. The only one ever used besides 'ain't' is 'aren't', and 'Aren't I going with you?' is either pseudo-elevated or vulgar, not ordinary colloquial speech. The only thing for a speaker to do when the need to ask such a question arises is to ask some slightly different question instead: 'I thought I was going with you; isn't that right?'

One does not expect matching from language to language in this connection. It would be surprising if Chinese had this particular hole, or even grammatical patterns so similar that a closely comparable hole would be possible. But Chinese has its own holes. For example, it is difficult to distinguish between 'We all read those books' and 'We read all those books.' The 'all' is expressed with an adverb *dōu*, which grammatical habits require to be placed directly before the verb or separated therefrom only by one or more other adverbs. This adverb collectivizes a plurality itemized earlier in the sentence or in some previous utterance. 'I read all those books' is *nèisyē shū wǒ dōu nyàn le*, where *nèisyē shū* 'those books' comes at the beginning of the sentence and is collectivized by the *dōu*. 'We all read that book' is *nèiběn shū wǒmen dōu nyàn le*, where *wǒmen* 'we' precedes and is collectivized by *dōu*. The sentence *nèisyē shū wǒmen dōu nyàn le*, where *dōu* is preceded by two substantive expressions which might be collectivized by it, means indifferently 'We all read those books', 'We read all those books', or even 'We all read all those books'.

Needless to say, fluent speakers of a language find their way around such holes without falling in. But even native speakers of a language can be inept, and a list of the pattern holes in a language is a good index of what specific ineptnesses will appear in the speech of a native speaker who has poor control of his language.

SUBJECT OF STUDY AND THE STUDY OF THE SUBJECT. Once the writer said to a chemist: "After all, all of chemistry can be regarded as a part of human history." His reply was "No; all of human history can be regarded as a part of chemistry." Both statements were potentially true, since the word 'chemistry' was being used in two different senses. In the first statement, the word meant 'the study of a particular range of phenomena'; in the second, it meant 'a particular range of phenomena', whether studied or not.

In a few cases, including chemistry, this same ambiguity is possible in Chinese. In others, e.g., physics or geography, it is not: *wùlǐ* 'physics (as an object of study)' : *wùlǐsywé* 'physics (as the study of an object)'; *dìlǐ* 'geography (as object)' : *dìlǐsywé* 'geography (as study)'. The cases in which the ambiguity is possible are mainly new importations from the West: *hwàsywé* 'chemistry' (either sense); *shùsywé* 'mathematics' (either sense, for the modern Westernized field). In these cases, the importation of perhaps desirable features of Western culture into China has been accompanied by the importation of a kind of terminological confusion from which Chinese had theretofore been largely free.

INSTANCE AND VARIETY. In the discussion of codes and messages (including language) it is necessary to distinguish between an occurrence of an element (e.g., a signal, a phoneme) and a kind of element which can occur. This is sometimes confusing in English and other Western languages. The problem of "one phoneme or two" is thus two problems: single phoneme-occurrence versus cluster; two allophones of one phoneme versus two allophones of two different phonemes.

In his "The Non-Uniqueness of Phonemic Solutions of Phonetic Systems" (*Academia Sinica, Bulletin of the Institute of History and Philology* IV [1933], 363–97), Yuenren Chao got around the difficulty by an importation from Chinese via "pidgin-Chinese": 'one-piece-sound' versus 'one-kind-sound'; in Chinese *yíge* 'one piece' versus *yìjǔng* 'one kind', with different measures. This particular stylistic difficulty is less apt to arise in Chinese than in English.

NUMBER. Most English substantives are subject to the obligatory distinction of singular versus plural; exceptions, such as 'sheep', 'deer', superficially resemble all Chinese nouns, for which there is no such obligatory category. Because of the prevalence of the contrast in English, such a sentence as 'If you take that road watch out for the deer' may leave us unsatisfied: does the speaker mean one deer or an unknown plurality? This dissatisfaction has even led some interpreters of English grammar to insist that 'deer' and 'sheep' have plurals just like other nouns, except that in these cases the plurals are made by "zero change"—an interpretation which renders the cited sentence grammatically ambiguous rather than just semantically so.

On this score English and Chinese do not differ as to what it is possible to specify, but as to what is relatively easy, or hard, to specify. To indicate a particular variety of substance or thing (for which a noun exists), without any implication whatsoever as to quantity, is easy in Chinese. In English it is accomplished in certain contexts with a generic singular ('Man wants but little here below'), in others by a generic plural ('Professors shouldn't do things like that'), but in still other contexts it is accomplished only quite awkwardly: 'That student or those students who arrives or arrive after the assigned time . . .' . Legal English shows many such awkwardnesses.

In English, on the other hand, it is easy to specify an indefinite plurality (that is, any number from two on up, but not just one). This is awkward in Chinese; expressions such as those equivalent vaguely to 'a few', 'many', and the like are of course otherwise matched in English, and cannot be counted as performing the specific semantic function of which we are speaking.

With its obligatory categories, certain nouns in English show fluctuation in the agreeing verb: 'My family is coming to see me'; 'Are your family all well?' The choice between agreement and nonagreement is semantically functional on the stylistic level; Chinese, lacking the number categories, is forced to make do with other devices, none of which exactly matches this one.

CHANNELS OF METONYMY FOR MOTION AND LOCUS. In English, and probably generally in Western languages, verbs of motion from one place to another are also freely used to express constant spatial locus of an object, or change of spatial relationship of parts of an object as in growth:

- 'fall': 'A man fell from the top of a building'; 'The land falls about ten feet behind the house'; 'The cake fell'.
- 'run': 'He ran around the lake'; 'The road runs around the lake'; 'They ran the road around the lake'.
- 'split': 'His lip (was) split in the fight'; 'The treetrunk splits into three large branches close to the ground'.

In Chinese, verbs which carry the central meaning of motion are not used in such extended senses. The few exceptions must be suspected of having developed under Western influence.

TAKING AND HOLDING. Here the situation seems to be reversed. In English, 'take', 'grab', 'snatch', 'pick (up)', 'lift', 'seize', and the like refer only to the event of passing from non-possession to possession of an object, while other verbs, such as 'carry', 'hold', 'guard'—a smaller number, less highly differentiated—refer to the state of possession. 'Take' is marginal, verging on 'carry'. The progressive construction with 'keep' underscores the difference: 'He kept taking candy from the bowl' is a repetitive in meaning, whereas 'He kept (on) holding the spoon' is continuous.

In Chinese, on the other hand, there are a large number of verbs which denote, in themselves, simply the grasping or holding of an object in a particular way, with one or another body part or associated artefact: *nyē:* between the fleshy part behind the nails of thumb and forefinger; *jwā:* in fingers partly closed, palm downwards; and many others. Any of these can be used inceptively (*tā bǎ jēn nyē-*

chilaile 'He picked up the pin') or continuatively (*tā nyēje jēn jǎu syàn* 'Holding the pin between her fingers she looks for the thread'); the difference depends on other elements in the sentences.

BREAKING. We have many words in English for various kinds of breaking: 'shatter', 'crumble', 'tumble', 'crack', 'split', 'tear'. Many of these are used, however, mainly when especially called for, rather than whenever the opportunity presents itself. If a window has shattered to splinters, we will normally report—if the report is unemotional—simply 'The window broke' or 'The window was broken'. To say 'The window (was) shattered' either is more emotional or is in response to a request for further detail.

In Chinese the normal unemotional report of any such event will usually use a more specific verb, of the kind first listed above. Individually these do not exactly match the English words, as these examples show:

dwàn: transverse breaking into segments of a long thin object, e.g., a pencil or tree branch;
lyè: to split without coming apart, as of a pane of glass with one or two long cracks, or a board or a drying surface;
swèi: to shatter into many small pieces, no longer in place relative to each other, as a pane of glass or a dish;
pwò: to break into a number of relatively larger pieces, most of which still hang together, as a pane of glass through which a bullet has passed, taking one small piece of glass away and leaving radial cracks, or a skull which has received a hard blow;
tā: to crumble down, collapse, as an old wall or house;
jà: to burst or explode outwards, as a bomb or balloon.

The word *hwài* is broader: 'to be or get out of order', as a watch or other mechanism, or an egg or piece of meat which is too old to eat, or a chair which still looks intact but which is apt to collapse (*tā*) if one sits on it. But *hwài* is not a generic for the specific terms listed above. When the window breaks, the normal Chinese report cannot be completely general; it will use *lyè, pwò, swèi,* or *jà* as the facts require.

In this and the two immediately preceding sections the examples seem to be more along the line of Whorf's interest than were those first given. We may perhaps call the example about cities and walls a "zero-order" difference: this is the kind we expect to find between any two languages. The fruits-and-nuts instance deserves then to be called a "first-order" difference: the point in this example is not that the semantic ranges of two relatively concrete nouns differ in the two languages (which would be a zero-order difference) but rather that there is divergence in the coverage of more inclusive generic terms. And if this is justified, then the motion-and-locus example deserves to be called a difference of even higher order. We have in it a situation in which not just one form from each language, but a whole semantically defined family of forms from each, have similar types of metaphorical or metonymic extension in English but not in Chinese. A higher-order difference, then, is establishable when a whole set of zero- or first-order differences seem to manifest parallelism. The writer does not wish, however, to push this sorting-out of orders of difference too far, nor for the reader to expect any great precision in it—the writer has no idea, for example, what the difference between a "second-order" difference and a "third-order" difference would be.

HANDLING TIME AND SPACE. Whorf made so much of the difference between Hopi and Standard Average European in this connection that it would be unfortunate not to examine other languages in the same connection. But the writer has only one comment to offer; the details need much more close analysis.

Whorf claims that we handle time like space, or like a thing, whereas the Hopi do not.

In a footnote in *Language* (**24** [1948], 160), Fang-Kuei Li writes, "These two villages are only a few miles distant from each other, but there are already slight dialectal differences."

What concerns us is the use of the word 'already'. Conceivably this sentence was "thought out" purely in English, so that the 'already' introduces a real reference to time: the relevant connection is not the short spatial distance between the two villages, but an implied relatively short interval of time since all the speakers of both villages were in intimate contact. It seems more likely that 'already' is Chinese *yǐjing* or *jyòu;* that is, that 'already' was inserted in the English sentence because in many contexts it is equivalent to *yǐjing* or *jyòu,* though in this specific context it is not. In Chinese—if our exegesis is correct—the reference is not to time at all, but genuinely to space, to the relatively short spatial distance between the villages; but it is a reference to space *handled like time.*

Or, put a bit differently, one could say that here, as in some other contexts, the Chinese make use of the linguistic machinery which they have on hand primarily for discussing temporal sequence and separation, in extended senses which are alien to English. A Chinese will say *Jèijāng jwōdz bǐ nèijāng cháng sāntswèn*. 'This table than that long three-inches'—'This table is three inches longer than that'. On occasion one will hear *Jèijāng jwōdz cháng sāntswèn le* 'This table long three-inches (particle for new state)'—'This table is three inches too long'. In the second one has, again, the use of a fundamental temporal element (the particle *le*) in an extended sense. The most tempting explanation is to say that the speaker has been looking for a table of a certain length, and has been examining a series of tables to find an appropriate one, so that upon examining the particular one on which the sentence comments, there has actually been a temporal sequence of events: the *le* means not that the table under discussion has changed its length, but that we, in looking at successive ones, have now arrived at one which is three inches too long. But this explanation is English, not Chinese; the writer fears that it is not really relevant. The safest statement we can make would probably be that in Chinese there is machinery used with reference to a variety of sequences and processes, some of which coincide with what we take as temporal. When the specific reference is temporal, the usage strikes us as normal; when it is not, it strikes us as alien.

Pigeonholes and Scales. Chinese verbs include a subclass which are "stative" and "intransitive," which for simplicity we can call adjectives. Individually, Chinese adjectives have meanings much like those of English adjectives: big, small, tall, short, and so forth. Many, but not all, are paired: *dà* and *syǎu* 'large, small'; *gāu* and *ǎi* 'tall, short'; *gāu* and *dī* 'high, low'; *cháng* and *dwǎn* 'long, short'. This pairing is not just semantic; it is also shown structurally. In each pair, one member is the "major" member; this is shown by the selection of that member, rather than the other, in asking a colorless question about the degree of the particular quality. For example, just as in English, the normal question is 'How tall (*gāu*) is that building?'—and such a question as 'How short (*ǎi*) is that building?' is most unusual.

Theoretically one can produce a grammatically complete sentence in Chinese by using a single substantive as subject and a bare adjective as predicate: *tā ǎi* 'He's short.' In practice such sentences occur only in response to questions of the form *tā ǎi buǎi?* 'Is he (relatively) short or not?' In making de novo statements, a predicate which includes a stative verb invariably also has modifiers—the negative modifier *bù* 'not', or some indication of degree like *hěn* 'quite', *dzwèi* 'very', *jēn* 'really'.

This last is the most frequent style of adjectival predicate. We may say that a pair of Chinese adjectives establishes a scale, and specifies one direction on that scale as "positive." The normal adjectival predicate then serves to locate the subject somewhere along that scale, but always more or less relatively to other items, never in an absolute way. That is, Chinese adjectives most normally handle qualities overtly as matters of degree of difference, rather than as matters of kind (pigeonhole).

A point of departure for the relative judgment of some given object can be supplied using the coverb *bĭ* 'as compared with': *Jèijāng jwōdz bĭ nèijāng cháng* 'This table is longer than that one.' The relative judgment can then be rendered quantitative by using, after the stative verb, a combination of numeral and measure: *Jèijāng jwōdz bĭ nèijāng cháng sāntswèn* 'This table is three inches longer than that one.' If the *bĭ* phrase is omitted, this becomes, as already stated in the preceding section, a judgment of amount of undesirable excess: 'This table is three inches too long'. A different pattern states the length (or other quality) of an object in terms of metric units, which are of course overtly relative: *Jèijāng jwōdz yŏu sānchř cháng* 'This table is three feet long'. These are the various possible modifications of the essentially relativistic use of stative verbs.

There is also a pigeonhole pattern; one adds *de* to the adjectival predicate, nominalizing it so that it names a class or pigeonhole, and the statement asserts the membership of the subject in that class: *Nèijāng jwōdz (shr̀) chángde* 'That table is one of the long ones' or '. . . is a long one'. Such a statement, with this particular adjective, is made only in a context where some preceding act or speech has set up the classifications in question.

A few Chinese adjectives are used, in the predicate, only in this pigeonholing manner: *nán* and *nyŭ* 'male, female', for humans; *gūng* and *mŭ* 'male, female' for animals. Thus 'male' and 'female' are never matters of degree or relativity in Chinese; they are absolute pigeonholes. A few other adjectives tend to be used in this pigeonholing way at least as often as they are used in the relativistic patterns, if not somewhat more often: the five adjectives for the five fundamental tastes 'sweet', 'bitter', 'salty', 'sour', and 'peppery-hot'; perhaps color adjectives. Except for 'male' and 'female', adjectives which are structurally paired are used normally in the relativistic patterns, in the pigeonholing pattern only when special contexts render such usage appropriate.

Now we may ask whether there is any attribute of Chinese culture with which this habitual relativism correlates. It will be recalled that the Chinese "philosophy of life," as often reported from observation and as codified in some of the Chinese philosophico-religious systems, particularly Taoism, emphasizes a "doctrine of the mean": never get too happy, or you may also become too sad; moderation in all things. The writer does not know certainly that the speech-habit outlined above is an old one; literary Chinese is so divergent that judgment would be precarious if built on it, and what is needed is extensive dialect comparison. If the speech-habit is indeed old, then there may very well be a correlation between the speech-habit and the "philosophy of life."

This suggestion is put forward with great hesitation. There are several crucial problems in addition to the one already mentioned. For one, if there is indeed a determinable correlation, then it would impress the writer that the direction of causality in the matter is in all probability from "philosophy of life" to language, rather than vice versa—though, of course, the linguistic habit might serve as one of the mechanisms by which the philosophical orientation maintains its existence down through the generations. Even more disturbing is the possibility that careful examination of the use of adjectives in English and other Western languages might reveal that we have much the same semantic pattern as has been described above for Chinese. If so, then what becomes of our pretty hypothesis? We would have a similar linguistic pattern in Chinese and in the West; in Chinese it would be hooked up with a philosophy of life, but in the West it obviously would not.

SUMMARY. From a tentative discussion one can draw only tentative conclusions. Yet the following three generalizations seem to be reasonably well supported in the specific case of Chinese versus English. The writer feels that they probably hold for languages in general, and they have been phrased accordingly:

1. The most precisely definable differences between languages are also the most trivial from the Whorfian point of view. The more important an ostensible difference is from this point of view, the harder it is to pin down.

2. Languages differ not so much as to what *can* be said in them, but rather as to what it is *relatively easy* to say. In this connection it is worthy of note that the history of Western logic and science, from Aristotle down, constitutes not so much the story of scholars hemmed in and misled by the nature of their specific languages as the story of a long and successful struggle against inherited linguistic limitations. From the time when science became observational and experi-

mental this is easy to see: speech-habits were revised to fit observed facts, and where everyday language would not serve, special subsystems (mathematics) were devised. But even Aristotle's development of the syllogism represented a sort of semantic purification of everyday Greek.

3. The impact of inherited linguistic pattern on activities is, in general, least important in the most practical contexts, and most important in such goings-on as story-telling, religion, and philosophizing—which consist largely or exclusively of talking anyway. Scientific discourse can be carried on in any language the speakers of which have become participants in the world of science, and other languages can become properly modified with little trouble; some types of literature, on the other hand, are largely impervious to translation.

PART II

THE DISCUSSIONS

FIRST SESSION

INFERENCES FROM LINGUISTIC TO NONLINGUISTIC DATA

THE SESSION opened with a statement by the chairman of the purposes of the Conference (see Preface). Greenberg then introduced his paper, which served as the starting point for the discussion.

HOCKETT: I would like to add one set of differences to the framework Greenberg has given us. I think it is important to distinguish between what people in a given culture speaking a given language can say, what they do say, and what they can say more easily than they can say something else.

The ordinary structural description that modern linguists turn out is almost always defective in that it is not qualified; it does not give the frequencies of occurrence of various forms and structures. Now, if we take a nonqualified description of a grammatical system and put together in various ways everything that it provides for, we will get a large number of possible utterances of different lengths, many of which might never be used. We might say that these represent what the people who speak this language can say. Inferences from the total possible utterances as to what the rest of the culture is like would be trivial or perhaps nonexistent. I do not think they would be relevant except in so far as some of the deductions from obligatory categories would be involved.

But we can go to the other extreme. We can try to infer things from what people do say, and this, of course, is done all the time when we base ethnographic analysis on texts or on what we elicit from an informant. This is also too trivial to be of primary concern.

The point of importance for our present purposes is what people can say more easily or less easily in a particular linguistic system. For example, it is easier for a speaker of Chinese to refer to a thing without any specification as to number than it is for a speaker of English. Although it is not impossible for a speaker of English to refer to something without specifying number, and it is certainly possible for a speaker of Chinese to refer to any specific number he wants to although he has a harder time specifying a number greater than one.

In opposition to some of Whorf's statements, I think we would find in the history of Western logic and science, from Aristotle right down through modern science, that people were indeed struggling because the language that they spoke made it easier to say certain things than certain others. But the positive accomplishment of logicians and scientists has been the beginning of the fight against these enforcing tendencies of language. The important thing about Aristotle's logic is not the extent to which it is conditioned by the structure of predication but the extent to which he broke through that structure and distinguished between different meanings and functions.

LOUNSBURY: I just want to comment briefly by way of giving examples on two points: Greenberg's comment with regard to compulsory categories and Hockett's with regard to what people can say or can say more easily.

First, though, I want to state that Whorf, in his writings dealing with so-called Hopi metaphysics and in his speculation as to what Hopi physics would be like, seems to assume a dependence of the kind of thinking the Hopi can do upon certain of the compulsory categories in their language. It seems to me that the ability to develop a physics involving time as one of the significant concepts does not in any manner depend upon the presence of grammatical tense in a language. Rather, it depends upon words for units of time and words for numbers so that these units can be counted.

If I may give an analogous example, are the Chinese, whose language lacks grammatical number, inhibited in developing an arithmetic or a mathematics? No! The fact is that mathematics depends not upon compulsory grammatical categories, but rather upon freely manipulable terms for certain concepts. If it depended upon grammatical categories of the compulsory variety, then people like the Kiwai Papuans should be mathematicians par excellence, because in the inflection of their verbs it is obligatory to specify, by means of grammatical affixes, the number of both the subject and the object of the verb. Furthermore, they distinguish not just singular and plural, as we do, nor singular, dual, and plural as in Iroquois and Greek, but singular, dual, trial, and plural, and they do this for both subject and object. It happens that these people are not mathematicians par excellence. Their numerical vocabulary goes only to five. This is to illustrate what I feel is a wrong emphasis—that a people's ability to develop a physics, let us say, does not depend upon what is in the concrete relational apparatus in their morphology.

Another example is found among the Bororo of South America, who have only two distinct number words. The first signifies "one," the second "two"; for "three" they use the phrase "this pair and this one which lacks a partner." This does not mean, however, that the Bororo lack concepts of higher numbers or the means to express them linguistically. One man gave me number terms to thirty-eight, another to seventeen. Up to five there was complete agreement, between five and ten a little variation, and beyond ten each man was on his own. Now, what must a Bororo's mathematics consist of? Not more than a single proposition, one and one makes two, because beyond that he would be saying two and one makes two and one, which is not an equation but an identity. Saying one and one makes two gives some new information about the language. Saying two and one makes two and one does not.

HOIJER: I would like to introduce an objection: I certainly do not think, from my study of Whorf, that he was so naïve as to draw from a consideration of a single compulsory category the kind of conclusions that Lounsbury has just suggested. Indeed, he makes explicit that the kind of conclusions he is drawing about the nature of the thinking of a people derives not from a consideration of a single category nor even from the structural aspect of language alone. They come instead from a totality of categories cutting across lexical, morphological, and syntactical materials plus the impresses of these upon other behavior which is nonlinguistic.

LOUNSBURY: I admit that I am doing Whorf an injustice by referring only to one particular item in one paper. Actually, what I said would be an incorrect representation of all of Whorf's thinking. I do not think it is an incorrect interpretation of his "Hopi physics," however.

HOIJER: I do not think Whorf would have said that the Hopi could not have developed a physics based upon time. The development of a physics is not a mere matter of language; it is a matter of experiencing on a large scale. He did, in fact, point out that Hopi experiencing was, as is demonstrated by all of Hopi culture including the language, oriented in ways quite different from ours, and in ways which might have led, had the Hopi developed a physics, to a physics quite different from our own.

HOCKETT: We perhaps agree that the impact of a linguistic system on what people do say, because it is more easy for them to say this than something else, is apt to be more active in those circumstances in which people are using the extreme forms of displaced speech than when they are using language in an immediately instrumental way in connection with other activities.

In this connection it occurs to me that the Kiwai Papuan language, with its many number distinctions, might serve as an inhibiting factor for the development of arithmetic and mathematics, rather than as a promoting factor. It has a machinery which takes care of the operational needs of the mathematical kind that this particular community has, and this machinery is of such a nature that it is not apt to thrust itself forward as a basis for casual speaking unrelated to operational needs. The mechanism would be something like that which apparently was involved—I am not sure of the history here—in the history of Chinese, when the invention of the abacus stopped the development of higher mathematics which might otherwise have taken place. The abacus was a device which took efficient care of their real computational needs, and so they were not inclined to speculate about higher mathematics.

HOIJER: There are plenty of instances where an elaborate formalism in vocabulary, a profuseness of terms, is accompanied by a kind of ceremonial treatment of the topics which are being expressed by this terminology, to the extent that the terminology is not useful for any purpose falling outside that ceremonial tradition. An excellent example is found in religious terminology and the distinction often made between sacred and secular terminology. Note the instance of the California tribes who have systems of numbering which apply only to woodpecker scalps—systems obviously useless for anything else, because they belong to particular rituals.

GREENBERG: I would like to return to the point raised by Lounsbury in regard to Whorf and Einstein, if I may put it that way, with a proviso that this is not all of Whorf. I am discussing at its face value what he says on this.

There seems to me a curious contradiction in Whorf's idea here (Whorf 1952: 6–7), and in the article on relation of habitual thought to behavior (1952: 25–46). He tells us that if conditions had been favorable, the development of some kind of Einsteinian theory of the universe would have been facilitated among the Hopi by their conception of time. However, Whorf talks as though Einstein's theory were a way of conceiving the universe, a philosophical theory about what time is like. But, as I understand it, Einstein used time as an operational variable, which was put in the equation because it was needed to account for certain observed phenomena. Time in this connection means a quantity that clocks measure, a quantified time.

That means one has to be able to speak of a certain number of units of time.

Now, according to Whorf, the Hopi cannot say things like "ten days" and "eleven days." He has to say, "I waited until the eleventh day"; he cannot say, "I waited ten days." That means that the Hopi language would prevent him from quantifying time and using it as an operational variable. This, if true, contradicts Whorf's hypothesis that Hopi is better adapted than English to an Einsteinian physics.

I would like to bring up just one other thing in this connection, i.e., the distinction between the influence of grammar, which is what one says about language, and the influence of language itself. A lot of the so-called influence of language on philosophy, thinking, etc., is not the influence of what English actually is, but the influence of grammatical doctrine about English. Whorf's discussion of English tense is illustrative, because as far as I can see, functionally, English does not have a past, present, and future. It was from Latin, on the basis of Latin facts, that we got these standard grammatical terms. Actually we see that the so-called future "I will go" is, from the point of view of English structure, on all fours with forms like "I can go," and so on. It is not an elementary meaning unit in the terminology of my paper, as a matter of fact; it is a complex unit.

If we take the simple inflected forms of the English verb, we have, first of all, a so-called present. But, as Whorf himself admits, it is not really a present; it is used only for a general truth; thus, "Iron melts at such and such a temperature." There is another form, which is called participle. It refers to action going on at any time at all. Then there is the part participle, which means that an action has been carried out. The only honest-to-goodness temporal form of the English verb is the past tense, which does refer to something in the past. But if you are one of the speakers who says, "If I was you," for "If I were you," and so confuse the conditional with the past tense, you then have lost every vestige of a category having to do with tense.

If we really think about time—past, present, and future—as units on a line, I do not see how Whorf could have got this conception from the actual structure of the English language. Rather, I think I know where he did get it—he got it from grammatical doctrine about English. That is another matter.

NEWMAN: The same point troubled me in trying to get what I thought of as categories out of grammatical forms. Usually in linguistic work we are concerned mainly with the form categories. Then, of course, we give these form categories names, which are very often functional, and we may get taken in by the functional name. If we have, let us say, two forms, a past and a nonpast, we will fall into the error of thinking that the past always refers to past time and the nonpast always refers to some kind of time that is not actually past. But as soon as we get into the problem of trying to define what the functions are, and that, I think, is the point that we are trying to get at when we think of meaning categories, we will find very often that even two opposed forms may overlap in function, and each form certainly will have a great many different functions. The job really comes down to one of trying, from a sampling of material, to cover the great variety of functions that our form categories indicate.

I do not think that we want to throw out work of this sort. My own feeling has been that it is much harder to deal with functions through grammatical forms than through lexicon. Now I would rather work with lexical material because it is easier—because one does not get taken in by—how shall I put it—the phony functional unity of a grammatical form.

But it is clear that there are a great many lexical items that will have reference to the same kind of function that we have in grammatical forms. If, for example, a past refers in part to a past, we will also have lexical items that will give us various elements of past time. Lexical and grammatical analysis can go hand in hand. Work with lexical items is probably safer but is not necessarily the only kind of work that we can carry on in this sphere.

KROEBER: In that case Whorf's semantic papers on Hopi verbs and the kind of meanings they express would be more productive in the present juncture than what he said about Hopi tense or lack of tense. We remember the kind of verbs he categorized. I would not want to summarize, but there are whole sets of meanings expressed in classes of Hopi verbs which have no English parallel.

NEWMAN: Yes, I would say that, mainly because, I suppose, I would suspect Whorf of doing the same thing that I do in working with grammatical form. We simply do not get a sampling of a given form in a large enough variety of situations. We nail down the meaning too fast. That, I think, has been a field procedure that has been common in the American linguistic field.

HOCKETT: I am not sure that I understand the distinction that is being made now. It may be because, having worked so long with Chinese, I am trying to make all languages work like Chinese does, but I do not see that one works with anything except forms and the positions in which they occur. I do not understand the distinction between working with forms and working with grammatical elements, for example. Grammatical elements are forms, too.

HOIJER: If I understood Newman correctly, he was distinguishing between the determination of the borders of meaning in the case of lexical items and of the borders of meaning as between the larger grammatical categories.

HOCKETT: My point is this. We do ourselves an injustice if we categorize too soon the kinds of meaning that linguistic items can have. I think that we must start our operation by assuming that meaning is a homogeneous thing, that every linguistic form has a meaning, and that it does not matter whether the form is a grammatical element, a derivational element, or any other. All have meaning, and the classification of these meanings into the meaning of stems and the meaning of derivational or inflectional elements is something which must come about in each language by virtue of the kind of language which it is. If in Chinese, for example, we can introduce after our analysis any such dichotomy, then we will have to say that number is an area of meaning which is handled by nonobligatory categories. It is therefore not a grammatical matter in the sense in which the term is being used, whereas in English it is.

In other words, we should not weight the scales in advance by assuming that we will find such a dichotomy in the language.

On the other hand, I think there is one dichotomy in Greenberg's paper that has by fiat cross-cultural relevance, that is, the distinction between intrastructurally definable privileges of occurrence of a form, and privileges of occurrence definable only by references outside of the language. Whether to say "cow" or "horse" in a particular sentence is a decision which is made independently of the structural, but when one decides and says "boys" as the plural of "boy," that is the distinction within the framework of the linguistic system as such.

GREENBERG: There are, of course, certain general classes of morpheme; Sapir, for example, distinguished several such classes. Some of these, such as derivational and inflectional morphemes, may be absent in some languages, for example, Chinese.

But where a language employs several classes of morpheme, there are important differences between them. Derivational and inflectional morphemes form closed classes of very small membership, usually, whereas the classes of root morphemes are very large, easily extendible, and more or less indefinite in number. That means that each one of the root morphemes covers a relatively definable and small area of meaning.

The problem of finding out what a certain affix means is not essentially any different from that of defining a root morpheme. But there is this practical difference, simply for quantitative reasons: if there is an inflectional class of morphemes in a language and this class has only four or five members as opposed to thousands of root morphemes, each inflectional morpheme will cover a very wide area of meaning. The result is, then, that we need a lot of text, and a great deal of experience and investigation, to discover the meanings of these inflectional morphemes.

KAPLAN: We have been talking for the most part this morning about the premises of the Whorf hypothesis, that is, about the particular features of the language from which we are going to make inferences. I would like to turn to some consideration of the conclusion, of the kind of inference that we are or are not justified in making, and I would like to begin by asking Greenberg to clarify for me some statements that he made in his initial comments, particularly those having to do with what I took to be the necessarily sentential or propositional character of metaphysics.

GREENBERG: It is sometimes stated that a language contains implicitly a metaphysics. Now, the question is, really, what one means by "language." We have to distinguish between the language and what is actually done with the language. The language itself does not contain sentences; it contains directions for making up sentences from certain units in accordance with certain rules. To make the proposition true that a language contains an implicit metaphysics, one would have to use either the word "language" or the word "metaphysics" in an unusual sense.

Someone might say to me, "Why do you exclude metaphysics from language?" The answer is that if we include metaphysics, then linguistics would include things like law, political science, economic values, religion, and so on, because those are things which are said and believed in by the people.

Let us take an imaginary situation: An explorer goes to the moon, and he has to send back a radio message as to what he saw. It is very difficult to think that he could perceive anything there that he could not express in English, however totally new it was. The only question is this: Could another explorer landing elsewhere on the moon recognize whether the particular object or situation that the first man was talking about was present where he was? In other words, could the distinguishing characteristics which are relevant for action be distinguished?

KAPLAN: What bothers me in connection with the conclusions, that is, the kind of metaphysics, is that I have the feeling that we are involving ourselves in the same danger that several people pointed out with respect to the premises, namely, that of drawing inferences from the grammar rather than from the use of the language. One might mean by "metaphysics" what corresponds to grammar, that is to say, the kind of statements that people explicitly make about the sort of world that they are in, and so on. But one might, and I think in connection with Whorf much more profitably, mean by metaphysics something quite different, which is not constituted by any sentences that are actually said but which is contained in such sentences in the sense that a careful analysis would be able to elicit it. I think one of our troubles is that we are talking about the metaphysics as though we can distinguish pretty sharply between a process of valuation, on the one hand, and a process of cognition, on the other, and then we want to put the metaphysics in terms of a set of propositions which incorporates the results of cognitions.

If one explorer reports something about the moon, and another one can identify that this is the region about which he has reported it, I would not suppose that that in itself has any bearing on the question of whether they share the same metaphysics or whether they even understand one another's metaphysics. That is, if we are going to put the problem in terms of the bearing on action, then we cannot keep isolated different values that the different individuals might have, and then fix on a constant as to what the real situation is like with respect to which they will act in terms of their individual values.

In this connection I find what Whorf says quite plausible, in contrast to what I have gathered most of your own reactions to be. One can take any X and Y, and a proposition which asserts that X and Y are similar will always be true. Nevertheless, the fact that an individual groups this Y with this X, and someone else groups a different Z with this X, seems to me to be revelatory, and revelatory not merely in valuational but also in cognitional terms.

FEARING: I was struck with Greenberg's trip to the moon. If I understand Whorf correctly, the visitor to the moon would be able to report back anything that he observed there, but the question is whether what he observes would not be wholly determined by his linguistic patterns. If another visitor with a different linguistic pattern should also arrive on the same spot, presumably he would not see it in the way the first observer did, because of the obligatory character of his particular linguistic system.

GREENBERG: My point is that they might not be able to say the same things if they spoke different languages, but that would be the result of different systems of beliefs and these are not determined by the structure of language but by the general cultural situation and the past history of the people.

For example, suppose I as an American scientist go to the moon and send back a message saying, "There are plants here of such-and-such a genus," because I have training in scientific botany. Now suppose an American Indian landed on the moon and he said, "There is something here which reminds me of a horse's saddle." I do not see that that difference in reporting has anything to do with—let us say the Indian spoke a Siouan language—the structure of the Siouan language as opposed to the structure of the English language. The two people simply have different beliefs. These are stated in language, but I believe they could be stated in any language.

LENNEBERG: I think we are now touching on something which has been mentioned time and again in the literature, namely, that language supposedly influences experience. In the case of Whorf and of many other writers, hypotheses have been formulated on the grounds of linguistic data.

Now, if the hypothesis concerns experience or cognitive processes, whatever they may be, it seems to me that verification would require material that is not linguistic. Something may be a psychological experience. We have to get out of the vicious circle of referring back to the language material.

One could think of the moon example as something like an experiment under controlled conditions, note what the persons actually see, and only then, from this data, from different types of behavior, can we actually draw conclusions, not from the reports.

LOUNSBURY: I was wondering if, in place of metaphysics, Greenberg would accept our substituting the term "perception screen" or "cognition screen." This would not be something which is embodied in propositions but, rather, would have to do with the distinctive features of a situation which a people respond to with linguistic responses.

GREENBERG: Maybe that is better, but if that is what Whorf means by "metaphysics," it seems to me it is a very unusual use of the word.

LOUNSBURY: I will just refer now to vocabulary—lexical items rather than grammatical categories. Whorf and others have put it this way: Vocabulary is a way in which a people divide up experience —a way in which people classify situations. We know that the classification of situations differs from language to language. Within a language there is a fair degree of conformity, however, among various users.

As an example, when we use the term "father" for a certain kin type, we are giving linguistic recognition to certain features which distinguish kin types, features which were brought together in a paper of Kroeber's and which have been repeated in other works on social organization. When an Iroquois uses his term "father," he is not giving linguistic recognition to precisely the same set of distinctive features. When a Crow uses the term "father," he is giving linguistic recognition to still a different bundle of distinctive semantic features. No organism responds to all features of a situation, because there is an infinity of features. He responds to selected ones to which he has learned to respond in a consistent manner, and these features might be called the crux of a situation, and that is with what our linguistic labeling has to do. It singles out different features of a situation for the purposes of a classification. The observer on the moon would report not all features of a situation that he found there but only such features as he had learned, either as a speaker of his language or as a scientist, to respond to differentially linguistically. It is in this sense we can think of a language as providing a perceptual screen in some cases, or a cognition screen, if one does not like to deal with perception.

KAPLAN: I turn now to Greenberg's earlier criticism of Whorf for ignoring the operational character of concepts, especially in connection with his notions about time among the Hopi. I am doubtful whether the kind of conclusions that we would wish to draw from linguistic and cultural data is necessarily to be restricted in that fashion, and the illustration I want to discuss is one that Lounsbury brought up. I was very much struck by the culture whose arithmetic is limited to the single proposition that one plus one equals two, the other propositions being sheer identities.

It just happens, to speak now of explicit rather than implicit metaphysics, that in the philosophy of Kant probably the most important single proposition taken as a starting point is the proposition that seven plus five equals twelve. The whole of Kant's philosophy is predicated on the assumption that this proposition is not an identity. It is not what he calls an "analytic" statement, because in the concept of twelve we do not find the concept of seven and five; so this is some kind of a synthetic connection, and he operates with this construction.

The sort of inference I would be interested in would be something like this. If arithmetical propositions present themselves as identities, I would expect that there would be less of a temptation to fall into the sort of thing which has been very prominent in Western culture since Plato: postulating the existence of certain abstract entities and giving to these abstract entities as much of a claim to independent existence as to the familiar objects of direct perception. It is then very frequently argued, at least by intellectual historians, that there is a close connection between the existence, or the belief in the existence, of such abstract entities and the support of certain types of social institutions. Specifically, the Platonic Realists argued in defense of a conception of church organization in which all power and authority were to be centralized in the Pope, who somehow was a representative of this abstract entity, The Church. Those who argued from a different metaphysic were people whose position with respect to this perfectly concrete cultural institution was just the contrary: there were not any abstract entities to which such a reality could be attached, the Church consisted in the individual communicants and the individual priests, and so on.

Now, I take it that Whorf is arguing that there is this kind of a connection between a linguistic feature of the sort that you mention, not in isolation, to be sure, but with others, and an observable pattern of cultural behavior, at least an observable set of attitudes or something of the kind.

GREENBERG: I do not see how a doctrine like that of the Platonists is based on a particular language; it could possibly have developed in any language, all other things being equal. I do not see how what is called "linguistic structure" can produce anything of the sort.

HOCKETT: I think I begin to understand what Greenberg meant when he was talking about metaphysics or beliefs being distributable in terms at the sentential level rather than at the word level, but I am not quite sure that that is true. It occurred to me in the course of this present discussion that there are certain things we could probably say about some people in any speech community regardless of the language. Some people will infer from the existence of a noun which names something the existence of the thing that it names whether the inference is correct physically, objectively, or not. We do it all the time in learning English when we reify things, and we reify a lot. We also infer from the statability of a statement the truth of the statement. I think that in any culture plenty of statements are made that nobody believes in. Perhaps from the point of view of metaphysics the habits that some people have sometimes of inferring existence from the existence of names for things is more important than inferences from the statability of a statement to the truth of the statement.

LOUNSBURY: With respect to my remark on the Bororo, I was referring, not to the possibility of reification of notions for which we have linguistic terms, like sevenness or twelveness, though there may be a great deal to that too, but rather, simply, to what we might call grammatical manipulability. A long and unwieldy expression cannot be substituted in the same grammatical frames for a simple and short one. Now, I would venture to predict that as the Bororo come to have more and more occasion to deal with numbers they will get simple grammatically manipulable terms for them. The Arawak people and others, neighboring people, have done just such a thing. They keep their own original numbers for one and two and five, but everything else they have borrowed from Portuguese.

KAPLAN: I would like to describe in a hypothetical way the sort of inference that I take it Whorf is discussing. I do not mean to be necessarily supporting this inference, but I do not think it is subject to the kind of criticism previously made.

Suppose in a given language there are a number of designations for yams in various other states, that are linguistically related to or derived from or contain in part of their construction the designation for a yam in its perfect condition. Suppose, moreover, that for a large number of other objects or situations which are important to the culture there is a similar pattern. There is a word, say, for "man," a man in the full sense, and then all the designations for inferior men or younger men, etc., are constructed from this term. Suppose, in short, there is a very marked and frequent pattern of identification in terms of the perfect condition, the fulfilled form.

Now, I would hazard an inference in such a case, and I take it that it is the sort of inference that Whorf would encourage me to hazard: here is a culture which operates in terms of fairly explicit, or at least easily recognized and verbalized, standards and norms and controls, and is constantly appraising and seeing whether things measure up and insisting on conformities and so on. It looks at the world formatively, so to speak, and contrasts with one which looks at the world descriptively and takes everything for what it is.

Whether or not the inference proved valid, it would seem to me to be perfectly reasonable and extraordinarily useful to describe the content of the inference by reference to Platonism. This is precisely how one explicitly thinking in terms of Plato's philosophy or Aristotle's, for that matter, which in this respect is very close to it, would go about looking at the world. There are certain principles of value inherent in each item, an immanent teleology as Aristotle says, and the whole business of nature is the fulfilment or the attainment of these standards. That could manifest itself in the way in which people act as well as in how they conceptualize, and a linguistic item of this kind might very well serve as a clue to that pattern.

HOCKETT: The big problem here is the hypothetical example. One might hope to find in the course of field work a nice neat system like this, and one might find it among the Hopi, but I do not think so. What one normally finds in any semantically defined family of terms, for example, words for the coconut at different stages of development, is one or more single morpheme terms and a variety of longer terms which incorporate one or another of these elements.

In a work on Ojibwa sociology the author, in discussing the different types of people of importance, says that the relatively important man of the tribelet is called by a term which means "big Indian, big person." Is this a form which her informants made up, simply translating the English of her question, "What do you call a person of importance?" Or is it actually a fixed label that is used in their own society for certain people?

Sorting out the simple and complex labels in any particular field that we might be investigating is terrifically important, but I do not think we would ever find a case that even approached the situation you described.

KROEBER: My remarks will be very much along the line of Hockett's. When Kaplan spoke, it occurred to me that this was an exceedingly pleasing picture: a language with a couple of big categories, then subdivided by making additions. Of course, it does not come that way. We do not first classify into human beings and houses and animals and then add qualifications. If there were such a language, it would be a logical reflection of the reality surrounding. It would have a little spoon and a teaspoon and a tablespoon. But all at once there is a ladle, and one starts from something else in forming that word.

Now, just how far different languages reflect with varying degrees of accuracy such a logical classification, how and why some of them are more illogical and inconsistent—incoherent it might be said—than others, is an exceedingly interesting problem. I doubt whether it has very much correlation with sophistication. I see a whole series of problems there.

Answers would be interesting, I am sure, to a very wide circle of people. The question is, Who is going to do the work? I think it is too much lexical, too much semantic, for all except a very few linguists to go in for it. It is a too "low-level" type of investigation for a trained linguist to be bothered with, and other people have a fear of being inadequate linguistically.

KAPLAN: It might be worth noting that historically this is the kind of task which classical philosophers tried to do, only they were not doing it on an empirical basis. Aristotle and others who have developed categories, as they are technically called in metaphysics, present them as classifications of the kinds of things that are meant by words which are not composite. Aristotle explicitly introduces his categories as though they were the product of an analysis of the semantics of Greek, or, I would imagine, he would suppose any other language would do as well; but there is every reason to believe that he did not get at them with anything like what we would today regard as the beginning of an acceptable methodology.

LOUNSBURY: The comment was that among linguists this sort of work is considered low level. It has been, but the time has come when all of a sudden linguists are realizing that it is not low level at all but at the highest level. The lexicon as a whole, of course, is stupendous. We could not possibly attempt to deal with all of it, yet we can deal with semantic systems within lexicons, defined, let us say, as a particular semantic field. Kinship, of course, is an obvious semantic field, as are numeral systems and color terms.

KROEBER: This sort of thing is not linguistic in your terminology.

LOUNSBURY: It is semantic, and it would require techniques for semantic investigations, but there is a mass of formalized ritual in the annual religious cycles of the Iroquois, and the terms in there just defy translation. I have tried to do something with them, and it requires a science of magic study which has not yet been developed but which would be very interesting.

One of the more obvious questions that one might begin with, for example, is: What about the extensions of kinship terms? It is "our mother, the earth"; "our elder brother, the sun"; "our grandmother, the moon"; "our grandfather, the thunder." Then we have things from social situations. They have one word, if I may introduce another one-word example, for "to give thanks" and "to greet." It is inconceivable to them how these concepts are any different, and I do not know yet what the basis for this thing is. These are just the merest hints of what we have in this religious conceptual system of theirs. It is individual systems like that which we could with profit attack now.

HOCKETT: I did want to offer one factual comment on what Kroeber said. The nineteenth-century classical philologists did not regard this kind of semantic study as beneath their dignity at all, and we have in the good dictionaries of Latin and Greek and Sanskrit all the information that anybody would want for this kind of study.

KROEBER: For twenty-five years I have been looking for a list of English verbs leaving out the Latin derivatives—common English verbs which were classified into verbs of mental action, verbs of motion, or by any system of grouping of categories at all. I have not been able to find anybody to tell me that anyone had ever even attempted a grouping. It is very easy to classify nouns into natural objects and artificial objects, etc., and to classify adjectives and adverbs, but I know of no classification of verbs in English or in any other language.

I do not see why it would not be worth doing if it can be done. Perhaps there is something in the nature of the English verb that forbids it. I do not believe it, though.

HOCKETT: I think we would find a great deal of partly cooked material, not raw material, in nineteenth-century lexicons.

GREENBERG: This nineteenth-century material is, I believe, almost all historical in nature. That is, the interest in semantics of these people was to reconstruct the lexemes or meanings which existed in the Proto-Indo-European community. It is not that the historical problems are not important, but we do not approach them in quite the same way today. Actually, I would feel that, while nineteenth-century semantics is not too sophisticated, the lexicons are often extremely good descriptive jobs of a degree of completeness which is not approached at the present time.

NEWMAN: It has often struck me that as a source for raw material linguists might begin working with something like the *Oxford English Dictionary*, where the lexemes are arranged in terms of linguistic meanings and also in terms of dates at which new meanings came in. I think the reason that we are beginning to think of working with that kind of material is that a person cannot compile such a lexicon for various languages and make sense out of it without knowing the structure of the languages. Another point is that we have, in dealing with structures, emphasized patterns or configurations, and we would be yet more inclined, if we were working with material such as is handled in the *Oxford English Dictionary*, to try to see what recurrences there were and bring these together in some way.

GREENBERG: We have here a partly practical problem in research. We are going to learn a lot about a very few languages or something about a great many languages. In principle we should know everything possible about every language but, as a practical matter, what the linguist probably should do is to get to know one language very well and to the point where he can do this kind of thing. At the same time he should get at least an elementary description of closely related languages which will give him an insight into the historical problems and material for historical reconstruction, which would interest anthropologists or archeologists who are historically oriented.

SINGER: I wanted to change the subject and come back to another point, on the problem of corroborative evidence, suggested by Greenberg's paper. Would you say that it is possible to tell whether two given languages do or do not both have, say, a subject-predicate form of proposition or sentence simply on the basis of verbal behavior, or would you also require nonverbal behavior, and, if so, what kind?

GREENBERG: I do not know if I understand this question completely. The distinction that I want to make here is not so much between verbal and nonverbal behavior as between language structure and verbal behavior. I would assume that that could be determined on the basis of language, and in language here I include always the systematic aspects of semantics. If we know the meanings of all the constructions, then we know what kind of thing is used, and it must be used at least once or we will not have it in our description.

As a matter of fact, when we study sentence types, we always find a very limited number of types to which everything said in the language has to conform. Without here entering into the empirical question as to whether there is always a subject-predicate dichotomy, a very difficult question which I would like to side-step, I would think that in every case it is at least determinable from the linguistic facts as such.

SINGER: Would you consider that an operational determination?

GREENBERG: Yes. We derive our description from verbal behavior of people—our informants. We notice certain recurrent aspects of speech and systematize them, until we can predict that, if anything else is said, it will conform to those rules. But this will not tell us what will be said.

We might say the description in the grammar of a language is oriented to a definition of one thing, namely, of a grammatical utterance in the language. Such a definition is an extremely complicated and lengthy business, but that is what we are doing, essentially.

SINGER: I was asking these questions with an ulterior motive, because it seemed to me that in your comments on Whorf and Einstein, and then in the later discussion about metaphysics and the reports on what happened on the moon, that you seemed to be imposing a grammatical doctrine or a linguistic doctrine for the analysis of metaphysics and language. One might go off, and people have gone off, in a somewhat different direction by arguing, for example, that the visual imagery, the imaginative associations of symbols, was very important even in science, and that one could therefore not reduce the so-called function of any symbol to the type of analysis which you were proposing, where it is just stripped of all associative connotation.

I think the question as to what kind of metaphysics is implicit in the language, the kind of question Kaplan was presenting, would, therefore, depend in part on what particular attitude toward the doctrine of metaphysics one had to begin with, and I think that what you are saying is that you have an analysis of language in which every sentence must be a proposition which is true or false, subject and predicate form, and the like.

It seems to me this is a doctrine with which one might argue. The history of science would not, I think, support the notion that one could reduce all symbols as they function in science, whether in equations or in the sum of surrounding scientific theory, to terms of operations defined either in specific measurements or by a doctrine of linguistic structure of the kind you are suggesting.

FEARING: I would like to raise again this question about metaphysics. I am set off by the phrase you used, the metaphysics which is *implicit* in the language. I do not know exactly what that means. How far are we justified in implying the metaphysics to another language and the culture which it represents? That is, we may examine linguistic patterns, and with our metaphysical orientation be able to say, "Well, now, this is Kantian." To what extent, however, are we justified in assuming that such an orientation is part of the mental life and mental economy of the people who use this particular language?

KAPLAN: There is really a two-step inference involved, which it would be a serious mistake to collapse into a single step. These are hypothetical or alleged inferences; I do not mean to imply that they can in fact be made. There is, first, the inference from language to some kind of metaphysical structure or system, framework, thought-world, what one will, and then, second, there is an inference as to the relation between that and the concrete behavior of particular individuals. I would suppose it to be perfectly reasonable to wish to insist on making these two inferences independently, that is, I do not see that one is necessarily committed to the second inference because he makes the first. I might say, the language that we are speaking—I mean now the particular thing that we are saying, not merely that we are saying it in English—involves the following kind of presuppositions, which I read into it, to be sure, but my reading into it is controlled by some kinds of principles of reasonable interpretation. But I will refuse to go on and, on the basis of that evidence alone, infer that our behavior is now going to be significantly patterned in that way.

Greenberg, it seems to me with complete correctness, pointed out that the fact that the sergeant barks at us does not mean that we offer him the dog biscuit. At the same time, it is worth noting that we do refer to the sergeant's voice in a term which we apply directly to the dog, and that a dog has such-and-such a status.

HOCKETT: I do not think anyone wishes to claim that the structure of the language has any metaphysics implicit in it at all. I certainly would not. I think it is a meaningless statement.

LOUNSBURY: I would like to give an example from English kinship terms and illustrate the classification inherent in them. It is basically this matter of classification to which I should apply the term "metaphysics."

When we use the English word "aunt," we are distinguishing in the first place between female and male. Among our female kinsmen we also have sister, mother, grandmother, niece, and so forth; among our male kinsmen we have so and so. So we are distinguishing this dimension of sex.

Second, we are distinguishing between first-degree collaterals and all other degrees of collaterality. In zero-degree collaterality we have father and mother, grandfather and grandmother, in other words, our lineals, son and daughter, and so forth, making a five-way distinction for generation. We have a five-way distinction in lineals.

First-degree collaterals include brother and sister, aunt and uncle, nephew and niece, and there we make only a three-way distinction for generation, unless we voluntarily specify greatuncle and grandnephew, and so forth, in which case a further five-way distinction is optional but not obligatory.

Now, we have a further component here; aunt is in the plus-one generation, and a further component yet, since this generation includes both the lineals and the consanguineals; we have the dimension of sanguinity versus affinity, and we include both here, so here we can just multiply one or take it off. Now, these are the semantic differences which we are recognizing when we use this term "aunt."

In another society they recognize quite different semantic features of one and the same genealogical situation. The reason is that these different features assume a different cultural significance in terms of other behavior. I think that is a warranted generalization.

Now, when we speak of an implicit metaphysics, what I mean by it are the features of situations which get recognized or do not get recognized in the use of linguistic terms. In other words, it is the basis for classification, the clues in situations, which are responded to. "Metaphysics" may be a bad word for it, but that is what I mean when I use that term.

HOCKETT: That would identify metaphysics with combinational analysis of meaning. I do not want to be playing tricks here. I realize that when we use the word "language" we are using a pretty technical term, and I do not mean the remark that I made a little while ago as deprecatory at all, because in this type of analysis lies the way in which we will find a connection.

But my point is that I do not believe that any of this is linguistic structure or linguistic pattern. Let me use the analogy of bridge bidding. Bridge bidding is a small signaling system which has a repertory of thirty-eight utterances in it. There are rules of bidding. The rules of bidding govern the linear sequence in which these constituent signals can be produced in a single utterance, a single utterance being one bidding for one hand. For example, one rule says, or implies, that it is not possible to say "one heart" after one spade has been said.

The stock of thirty-eight signals and the rules governing the sequence in which they can be produced are the pure pattern of the system as such, and in language I would say that only the phonemes and the rules which govern the sequences in which they occur—the stock of morphemes and the privileges of occurrence of those morphemes relative to each other—constitute the linguistic system.

In bridge bidding there is a set of conventions of bidding. Conventions of bidding are semantic. One convention of bidding, for example, is that a partner's bid of four-no-trump means one will indicate by one's next bid how many aces one has. The rules of bidding are part of the linguistic structure itself; the conventions of bidding are semantic.

Now, it is only in semantic structure, in the semantic rules for any language, that we will find the possibility of getting metaphysical content or an inherent metaphysics. But when we talk about the semantics we are already talking about something which is associated with a linguistic system, but is not itself a linguistic system as such. How can one fail to find correlations when one is looking at correlations; the semantics is the correlations. Therefore, of course, one will find it.

SECOND SESSION

THE CULTURAL CONTENT OF LANGUAGE MATERIALS

HOIJER: McQuown will begin by giving us a brief introduction to his paper.

McQUOWN: If one wanted to characterize what I have sketched in "Analysis of the Cultural Content of Language Materials," one might call it the science-fiction approach to the analysis of culture. Actually, the more general propositions everybody will subscribe to. Some of the more specific ones people may subscribe to but be unable to fill out with details. I wrote the first section having in mind what I was going to write in the second section; then I wrote the second section following the first point by point, restricting my generalizations to language (however you may define that), and filling out here because I fancy I know a little bit about what goes on in the field. In the first section I cannot get beyond some of the general propositions. Some of what is included in the second section is certainly a personal interpretation, and I hope that those portions of it which are not generally accepted will be discussed, criticized, and filled out.

In the third and following sections, I make an attempt to rationalize a methodological jump from the analysis of language to the analysis of other aspects of culture. Such a jump is frequently made without explicit statement of the steps which take place between the analysis of linguistic form, or the results of the analysis of linguistic form, and the broad cultural generalizations which we try to correlate with them.

There are a number of areas where linguists, up to the present time, have been extremely lax in working with purely linguistic materials. One of these has to do with the distribution of individual morphemes, both within short stretches and across considerably longer stretches. Harris points out in his *Methods in Structural Linguistics* (1951) that very useful data would come out of this kind of study, but I am afraid that, with present personnel and present techniques, life is too short. It is just not possible to do this kind of work except in an extremely eclectic way. We pick out the things that we happen to be interested in—but how do we know that the things in which we happen to be interested at the moment are going to turn out to be crucial when we get the full analysis of all the patterning in?

Another area, which Harris has not only spoken about but actively begun to work in, is the distribution of larger structural units across longer stretches—his discourse analysis (Harris 1952*a*, 1952*b*). This, again, has been much neglected, not deliberately, but as an almost inevitable result of the type of concentration which linguists have consciously or unconsciously brought about.

Study in either of these two directions—individual morphemes or larger structural units—requires processing of large quantities of material. This is something which Harris mentions on almost every page of his *Methods in Structural Linguistics*, but on no page does he give evidence that he has actually done so for any of his examples. One takes his word for the generalizations which he brings forth. If they sound good, then one accepts them.

Until distributional studies of intralinguistic units are correlated with similar distributional studies of extralinguistic units, we will not have approached meaning in a very satisfying fashion. There are going to be philosophers who will ask very penetrating and sometimes very annoying questions as to what a particular body of data means in some wider sense. And until we can perform distributional studies of this kind on extralinguistic as well as on linguistic data, we will not be able to make satisfying statements.

There was one other point that I wanted to make before getting back to the paper. We have all puzzled over what Whorf meant by some of his statements. The "fashions of speaking" statement is the one which is very frequently quoted, and, reading through it again in Hoijer's paper, it occurred to me that when Whorf refers to fashions of speaking that cut across all the lexical, morphological, and syntactical patterns of the language, he is not really talking about patterns of language at all, in the first instance, but about whole culture patterns, supersummative patterns, which make use of, and in some sense are limited by, the patterns of language as a medium for manifestation. If we argue about the connection between Whorf's fashions of speaking and the patterns of the rest of the culture, we are engaging in a tautology, because his fashions of speaking are in one sense the patterns of the rest of the culture. If we want to build a bridge between the strictly formal linguistic patterns and these wider patterns, we have to ascertain in what precise detail and at what precise points these larger patterns depend on some contrast within the narrow linguistic patterns as their medium of manifestation, to show us that they are really there.

One further point has to do with a typology of thought-worlds. Hoijer referred in his paper to a typology of thought-worlds, and it occurred to me that, before we would be able usefully to extend any generalizations from the patterns of language to the patterns of culture as a whole, we would need a considerably more detailed and carefully worked out and grounded typology in language itself. That area has tended to be neglected.

Returning to Harris' discourse analysis, the specific procedures which I recommend in my paper are stated much more generally than those of Harris. That is in part because I do not know what the specific substeps are going to be. Some of the substeps which Harris fills in are steps made necessary, not by any general considerations on linguistic structures as a whole and on the operations we must perform on linguistic data for the purpose of discourse analysis, but rather by certain peculiarities of English structure. Certain subheadings in his outline probably apply only to English. For that additional reason I kept extremely general my suggestions as to steps in content analysis.

VOEGELIN: You seem to use content analysis and discourse analysis synonymously. In principle do you not think there is an important difference between the two?

MCQUOWN: No. I take the stand that there is no essential difference. The difference may be important in developing precise techniques. Note that Harris says in his article (1952*a*) that he is not using meaning, yet in his conclusions he says, "These recurrences cannot be without significance, these recurrences must be meaningful in some sense on some level." I refuse to draw any sharp line between the meaningfulness of a particular sequence of phonemes, not yet constituting a morpheme, and the meaningfulness of some of the larger patterns of equivalence class sequences which he pulls out in his discourse analysis.

VOEGELIN: Harris begins with utterances irrespective of their meaning, surely.

MCQUOWN: But not with respect to their distribution.

VOEGELIN: Exactly. One could have a survey of German newspapers or English newspapers and look for the same thing irrespective of the language and certainly irrespective of its distribution, so that one begins at opposite poles with this difference: that possibly by extending ordinary linguistic procedures to discourse analysis one may arrive at meaning. Conversely, one can start with content analysis and never arrive at any structural statements.

McQuown: Up to that last sentence I agreed with everything you said. I do not accept your last sentence. But, by and large, the types of units with which the content analysts deal are units which have not been empirically established as in the minds of those who wrote the material. On the contrary, these are things that the content analysts would like to know about and which they look for. Their identification of the concept "communism" with the word "communism" and the frequency with which it occurs in a particular document may have no necessary relation to the meaning of that particular linguistic form in the minds, habits, culture, etc., of the people who wrote the document. The connection may or may not exist; the content analysts cannot really demonstrate step by step that the connection does exist. There may be other ways of demonstrating it, I will not deny that; that is why I could not accept your last sentence. One can play both ends against the middle.

Wright: Would you state that last sentence again?

Voegelin: I said, conversely, one can begin with content analysis and go as far as one wishes in the characteristic ways that such analysts work, and one will never arrive at anything structural. One may arrive, and indeed they do arrive, at statements of prediction, but not at statements of structure.

Fearing: In other words, the content analyst carries on his operations completely independently of the person who produced the material, and any effects that it may have.

Wright: And the language in which it was produced.

Voegelin: Exactly.

Hockett: A seminar in which I participated at Cornell, attended also by psychologists, medical people, anthropologists, and sociologists, examined quite a number of things called "content analysis." The conclusion we reached was that the variety of things which have been labeled "content analysis" has no common denominator of methodology or anything else which justifies using a single name for them.

McQuown: I am quite willing to replace the label "content analysis" by something else.

Kroeber: Back of analysis there remains the problem of what to call these two facets: structure and content, or form and meaning?

McQuown: I call them form and meaning, without committing myself one way or another as to the separability of the two.

HOCKETT: I tried to make a statement on that this morning. I said that we may have to use semantic evidence in order to figure out what the linguistic system of a language is, but that the system does not include the semantics. The system is abstract, it is a signaling system, and as soon as we study semantics we are no longer studying language but the semantic system associated with language.

KAPLAN: I have several times this afternoon and on previous occasions heard what sounds to me like the following statement: that beginning with an analysis which does not take any explicit account of meanings it is possible to arrive at something that would be identified as such by whoever would use that language. I would like to have that statement either corrected or explained, since it seems to me to be plainly false.

MCQUOWN: I will try to answer that. The steps in discourse analysis are pretty similar to the ones in the intralinguistic procedures of analysis, and the first one is identification. There are, of course, many ways in which one may fancy one has identified a particular item. One way is to start with a preliminary frame of the kind which I mentioned in my paper—descriptive phonetics—and try to observe within this preliminary frame, which is arbitrary—one sets it up and hopes it will get him somewhere—recurrences of items, areas of variation with cores within those areas, norms of some kind. One makes the generalization, then, that it is not due to chance that one observes certain constancies in these areas of variation. They must correlate with something. I have not used the word "meaning" so far.

One then attempts to build up a system based on these observed constancies. One groups together particular phonetic items, using the criteria of phonemic analysis, or one separates them, using the criteria of phonemic analysis which I have listed. It is really at this particular point, as a last resort, that one goes to his informant and asks him, "Do these two things sound the same to you?" It is a short cut, of course, to ask the informant this, or it is a short cut to put the informant in a situation such that he will produce a new bit of evidence which one needs to confirm or refute a hypothesis as to structure which one has set up at that particular point. One does not ask the informant about the meaning of these things; one simply asks him to produce some new material which one then manipulates.

KAPLAN: May I interrupt? What is it that you suppose yourself to have learned after you have concluded that analytic procedure?

MCQUOWN: One has, one hopes, elicited the structure of this particular bit of behavior.

KAPLAN: The critical thing is what one is including in one's structure. Perhaps I could get what I am looking for by asking you to explain what you meant by the statement that one could play both ends against the middle. And I am interested, not in the content analysis ends that you were talking about before, but in this end that you have just been discussing, and now in the middle.

MCQUOWN: I started on the lowest level—the phonetic level. There is no a priori reason why one could not start on any one of the intermediate levels. If we could devise a frame which would permit us to recognize some kind of preliminary units on another level, we could then practice operations of the same general kind and come out with morphemes, let us say, rather than with phonemes.

VOEGELIN: I am intrigued with the form of your objection—that it seems obviously false to say what we constantly say. You could say, similarly, that the general axiomatic method is obviously false, if we have to begin with undefined terms like a line or a point, and yet, beginning with such undefined terms, one can make a set of axioms and proceed from there to a modern mathematics. It seems to me that there is some analogue between the general axiomatic method and the sort of things which we are doing.

KAPLAN: That analogue is what gives me the trouble. When one has constructed a postulational system in the purely formal sense—I use the term formal as the mathematician or logician would—one cannot say that it is a system of anything at all specific. By virtue of its being purely formal it is also completely uninterpreted, and it is no more a system of geometry than it is a system of the algebraic properties of triads of real numbers, or of a vast number of other possible sorts of things. If someone were to say to me, "We are interested in formulating the systematic properties that we observe in this particular area, but we want to put it in a sufficiently formal way so that it might equally be interpreted as a quite different system," I could understand that objective, although I would be a little puzzled as to why, particularly, he should want to do it. A mathematician wants to do it because it gives him an enormous range of generalities, and he is interested in other interpretations. But I take it you are not interested in interpreting these systems so that instead of being systems of language elements they will be systems of human relations, or of chemical compounds, or something else. You are interested in language. Somehow you have got to add something to fix what in these contexts is called an interpretation of the system, for that interpretation is not something which is contained within the postulational system itself. What seemed to me to be false was the statement that somehow it never has to be added but miraculously appears out of the formal analysis.

VOEGELIN: However, your prior statement—that one does not want to use the postulates for any material other than natural language material—is not true. Many people are interested, and wondering, for example, whether some of the statements of distribution could not be applied to dots on a television screen. And one could go on to greater generalities.

SINGER: I was struck this morning, and now again, by this analogy in method and, you might say, in formal asceticism between the formal position in linguistics and the formalism at the foundations of mathematics and in symbolic logic. I think a distinction that we have made in symbolic logic in relation to logistic systems and postulate sets might be useful here.

It is true that in the development of postulate sets as formalized systems, say, a postulate set for Euclidean geometry, we have undefined terms and even uninterpreted propositions. This is with a view to its future interpretation as a physical system of geometry or as any other system that could come out of such a postulate set. When one first starts to construct a postulate set one cuts loose entirely from the interpreted system, even from the interpretation one has in mind. Generally, one has some interpretation in mind, but maintains this very saintly kind of rigorous systematic avoidance of reference to the meanings of terms and propositions. Then, when one is through constructing the formal calculus one tries to add an interpretation. Now, it seems to me that proceeding "without reference to meaning" in this sense is certainly a perfectly legitimate and fruitful device for the development of mathematics and logic.

But, there is another sense, which has grown out of that, which seems to me much more controversial, both in logic and mathematics and in linguistics. Having set up a postulate system or a logistic system in a purely formal way as an abstract calculus, is it possible to guarantee a unique interpretation, that is, can one say that, because it has this structure, it can be interpreted only in this way and in no other? This is the much narrower thesis of formalism, which asserts that one can construct a purely formal calculus and the syntactic rules which define the system are sufficient to insure a unique interpretation. Now, this thesis has proved to be slightly exaggerated. I would not say it is completely false, but it is true only for very minor and perhaps trivial parts of mathematics and logic. Thus, in these fields, semantics is needed, as well as syntactics. It was necessary, in order to insure the kind of interpretation wanted, to state semantic rules which refer to meaning.

So it seems to me that perhaps the "formal" linguist is now at a stage where he is pursuing a kind of systematic abstension from reference to meaning, in anticipation, of course, of certain interpretations. He starts with natural languages, and he hopes to end with natural languages; these have meaning. He hopes that his formalized analysis of these languages will nevertheless be useful without explicit reference to meaning. But it is highly questionable, on the basis of what has happened in mathematics and logic, that one can, merely by setting forth a system of syntactic rules, guarantee any particular and unique interpretation of the structure. Nevertheless, linguistics is still formal in the sense that it might try to describe the structure of a language without reference to its meaning, so, to use the distinction between object language and metalanguage, you are trying to give a formal, i.e., syntactical, description of the object language but in a nonformalized metalanguage.

HOCKETT: I think it ought to be made clear that a linguist, in working on a language, does not start with an abstract system. He starts with all the evidence that he can get; he pays attention to meaning differences; he finds out whether things sound the same or different to the speaker. As a matter of fact, he counts on the fact that he himself is an enculturatable individual who to some extent can acquire, has an ability to participate in, the linguistic aspect and related aspects of the culture associated with the language which he is observing. He starts with a totality which presents itself as pretty much of a hodgepodge, as it does to a newborn child. It is only by a slow process of sorting things out that he discovers the units at various levels—the phonemes, the morphemes, etc.

The reason for abstracting a phonemic system from the articulatory behavior in terms of which we observe it being manifested is that the phonemic system is not represented in the culture—in the life of the people who have it. It is represented not just by articulatory motions; it is represented by patterns of nerve impulses which are homogeneous except for their temporal and spatial arrangement. It is represented by sound waves. And in a literate community it may be represented in a completely different substance, in the form of marks on paper or some other flat surface. The point of abstraction is that a code is an abstract thing. The code has to be determined by observing actual messages, because unless we have abstracted the code and stated it in abstract terms we have not completed our job. That is the reason for abstraction.

GREENBERG: I think there are probably a number of distinct questions involved here. Partly, I think, the discussion is revolving around the fact that linguists do certain things, and we think we know what we are talking about, but the nonlinguists here perhaps are not clear on, or acquainted with, what is being done.

There is, first of all, a confusion between how one carries out his analysis and how he states his results. Now, the question that Harris raises is: Can we, by not paying any attention to the semantic side of the language—he does not say arrive at meanings, nobody could ever say that—break up an utterance and say there are eight meaningful units in this utterance. That is one question, and I would agree with everybody here that it is probably impossible to do it. But, what is more important, I do not see the point of trying to do it. Whether we can do it or not may be an interesting theoretical question, but nobody would proceed without reference to meaning. The second question is how one can state one's results. Now, from that point of view there is no doubt that any language system has a structural side and a semantic side, and it is possible to state them separately. I think that is all that is involved—the difference between making a dictionary and stating the meanings and writing the grammar.

On the other question, I think there has been some confusion as to where formal analysis and postulational systems come in. We treat either the formal side of language or the semantic side of language, but we can treat either side with or without a postulational system. In linguistics, actually, there has been practically no formal analysis in the sense in which logicians use it. We cannot find, I think, a single bona fide application of the kind of thing that was done in mathematics except, if you will pardon the reference, my own article on the analysis of kinship which is, I think, pretty completely formalized. What we have is simply occasional use of particular symbols or some of the words used in symbolic logic. There is no real formalization anyway, but what we are talking about here is whether the linguist treats the formal side of language, and that is a completely different question. To say that is the same thing would be to confuse the subject matter and the method one uses in dealing with the subject matter.

KAPLAN: I am very much content with Greenberg's last remark.

It is disappointing, I may say, since a philosopher is so very much concerned with problems of semantics and expects that the linguist will help him with them, to find that the linguist does not want to touch them either; but at least that is perfectly understandable.

I had the feeling, partially from some of the literature and partially from informal comment, that the semantic problem was looked upon as one that could be set aside, in the spirit that if we do not talk about it then the problem disappears; that the problem is occasioned only by the fact that we use shabby words, such as meaning, that do not have any definite content, and that if we talk only about these things that are quite definite and precise and easily handled, we shall have thereby done everything that anyone could reasonably want us to do.

I take it from Greenberg's last remarks that no one would really mean to say anything of the kind. I am therefore content.

HOCKETT: I think it is at this point that we return to the subject matter of McQuown's paper. When the philosopher who is interested in meaning comes to the linguist and finds that the linguist is hesitant, even though the linguist may actually, in his heart, be extremely interested in the problem of semantics, the reason for the linguist's hesitation is that, before he tackles a systematic analysis of the meaning process and ranges of meaning itself, he wants to have a very clear notion of what the units are that have the meanings. He means to know the purely internal economy of the signaling system that is being used. He wants to know the difference between a dot and a dash before he talks about the semantics. The techniques by which we can discover the units that have meaning are, I think, what McQuown was talking about in large part.

KROEBER: Greenberg's statement has not met with dissent from any of the linguists here, and part of his statement, if I understood him correctly, was that linguistics did not make use of postulates. In other words, that leaves linguistics as a natural science, operating empirically.

Speaking more or less as a layman, would it not be fair to say, in regard to this matter of content or meaning, that linguists do not want to deny meaning or divorce themselves wholly from it, but have a feeling that if one pays attention at the same time to structure and to content, indiscriminately, one will make less progress than if one differentiates? If for a time at least—and that may be a lifetime—we concentrate on structure, we will really find out more about structure than if we constantly mingle that with matters of content. Linguists have not thrown content or meaning out of the province of their science, but they are operationally using it as little as possible, for the time being. Is that an overstatement, or an understatement, perhaps?

McQuown: I would say that if linguists were uninterested in meaning they would not have struggled so long and so valiantly to set up a system of analysis which would make it possible for them to find out how the thing actually works. If they simply wanted the intellectual pleasure of playing with a nice, neat system, they would make their own system and play with it. They would not try to work with natural languages at all. They are interested, not in building in structure, but in eliciting structure. It is a natural science.

Kroeber: What I meant when I spoke of it as a natural science is that the structure is there. Linguists are trying to discover it.

Wright: I am afraid I did not understand the notion, in McQuown's paper, that the content of the language is somehow analyzable in terms of structural breakdown. Could you illustrate how this is done?

McQuown: I tried, in phrasing my references to the meaning of these segment types, to be noncommittal with respect to the precise degree of correlation. I would start out with a general statement to the effect that whatever meaning units there may be, whatever content units there may be, they will certainly not be in one-to-one correlation with the structural units of the type that are listed in my paper.

In order to do meaning analysis or content analysis, we need this particular structural analysis of the linguistic form as a starting point. We then perform certain operations on this material. And it is not from, let us say, the distribution of the plural endings in English that we come to any conclusion about the reality of the plurality concept in the culture of English speakers as a whole. It is from this plus a whole series of other distributions that we may eventually come to some conclusion. That was discussed many times this morning in connection with Whorf's pointing out certain categorical limitations in Hopi. One cannot go directly from those categorical limitations to any generalizations about the Hopi thought-world as a whole. What I tried to do here was to suggest that by taking as raw material a segmentable and structurally describable frame, such as language, one could then proceed to discover within that raw material certain patterns, which in some instances might consist of sequences of phonemes, or particular individual phonemes as they occur, or of certain tonal patterns, or of certain stress patterns, or of specific morphemes recurring here and there, or of specific sequences of constructions, etc. I would not venture to predict a priori in what particular groupings of these linguistic forms these larger patterns would be reflected. We know they are there because we read material transmitted via language, and we get the concepts out of it.

Or if language in itself is inadequate for the communication of particular patterns—if a particular sequence of morphemes, made up of particular segmented phonemes, must be uttered in conjunction with a particular integration pattern, with a particular expression on one's face, gestures, and so on, in order to get across a particular meaning —we will discover that too. The strict formal analysis of any one part of this will not give us a direct connection with the content.

KAPLAN: Would you perhaps run through an example illustrating the five steps listed in Section IV of your paper?

McQUOWN: I will do this in terms of one of the questions in my series of suggested problems. Suppose one were to discover in a series of Totonac sentences a recurrence of a particular morpheme *A* whose meaning we are trying to discover. We get this series of utterances in sequence, in a context. We observe the context and discover that morpheme *A* occurs among many other places, in the speech of women; that when it occurs in the speech of women they are talking to nonmembers of their immediate family; and that the occurrence of their husbands' names and a second linguistic form *B* do not overlap with the occurrence of the morpheme *A*.

If the linguist's wife were with him in the field and in the process of learning a little Totonac, and if she, in talking about him, did not heed this mutual exclusion between *A*, his proper name, and *B*, but mixed *A* and *B*, and if, when she mixed the two, he observed unfavorable reactions on the part of the native Totonacs listening to the conversation, he might come to the conclusion that there was some indisposition on the part of female Totonacs to refer to their husbands by means of personal names or by means of the form *B* and that they instead referred to them by means of the morpheme *A*.

What does *A* mean? *A* apparently is a sort of impersonal, used by Totonac females to refer to their husbands. I can paraphrase in English.

"Where is Mr. So-and-So today?"

"One is away."

Who is "one"? Only by putting all these things together would we gather that "one" is the husband. Without the linguistic forms all we would get in these situations, from just observing the rest of the activity, would be puzzlement. With the linguistic forms, in conjunction with the rest of the activity, we can come to some kind of tentative conclusion. The conclusion is tentative, and will remain tentative until we know some more about the culture and find out why, in terms of other activities, Totonac females refer to their husbands with the impersonal pronoun.

GREENBERG: That example struck me as a sort of garden-variety type of semantic analysis that one does ordinarily to find the meaning of a morpheme. I thought that the request was for you to illustrate the method of Harris' content or discourse analysis, whichever it is, and, as far as I can see, you gave us a very interesting exposition of how one goes about the ordinary process of finding a meaning, as it were, in a dictionary.

McQUOWN: I did mention, I think, co-occurrences of linguistic forms, and I did mention simultaneous occurrence of other activity outside. I did not make clear in the second reference that I was assuming that this outside activity had already, to some extent, been broken up into functional units. Otherwise, we cannot tell. We cannot just look at a person from the outside and be sure that we are properly interpreting his reactions.

HOCKETT: I think the proper term here is, not "content analysis" or "discourse analysis," but "distributional analysis." We can make a distributional analysis of linguistic forms purely relative to environmental linguistic forms. In so far as we can do that, no matter what tactics we use, or whether we are talking about incidents of occurrence in small environments or environments the length of whole books, we are doing pure syntactics, so to speak. If we make a distributional analysis of linguistic forms and nonlinguistic cultural forms, unit acts of one type or another, then we are, from the learning angle, studying the semantic aspect of linguistic forms.

I agree that this is a garden-variety type of analysis; in order to give an example, McQuown had to choose one which we would be able to feel. But suppose one got something much more subtle, which would require one either to live in the culture a much longer time until he could feel it or to get very extensive records and make a very thorough distributional analysis. The techniques remain fundamentally the same. I think that is the point.

KROEBER: I would like to ask McQuown a question as to the list of problems he suggests in Section VI, which, I take it, all involve culture as well as linguistics. There are eight questions there. Six of them begin with the word "Why." In general, linguists, when they are doing straight linguistics, do not ask "Why?" very much. Do you think the question arises only when one begins to consider the relation of purely linguistic structural forms to forms or patterns outside? Is it then that the "Why?" comes up legitimately, or inevitably?

McQuown: Yes. Take No. 7, the three different forms of the copula in Totonac. Does this particular trichotomy have any relationship to the rest of the Totonac cultural activities, or is this purely a linguistic matter? I do not know. I have not studied that aspect of it. But barring additional information, or without large quantities of linguistic forms which one could associate with this specific trichotomy in the hope of feeling one's way out into the rest of the culture, we could not answer this question.

Kroeber: There are possibly other languages, wholly unrelated to Totonac, that reveal similar phenomena. If so, this points to a comparative linguistics that was much discussed a hundred or so years ago, when people assumed that from some knowledge of several dozen different languages common denominators would eventuate which would give us some clue as to human language in general, or certain general principles of universal applicability even if there were no one compelling tendency.

Greenberg: Kroeber has just raised the question as to whether these "Why" questions do not arise as soon as we begin to get out of the frame of a purely descriptive approach and look at the cultural situation outside. It seems to me that when we make a synchronic descriptive study of a language there are no "Why" questions. As soon as one begins to ask how this system as we find it now arises, which is precisely the kind of question that McQuown is asking in his paper, then we have two sets of factors: one is the contemporary nonlinguistic culture; the other is previous linguistic history, which is a linguistic factor but a diachronic one. For example, McQuown's question No. 8 strikes me as one which would probably receive a historical explanation, meaning that we can understand it from regular processes in a previous state of the language.

Hockett: There is perhaps something of a jump in McQuown's paper between the description of the generalized distributional analysis and the generalized family of techniques for approaching all sorts of problems in language and culture, and the specific things that are listed in Section VI. The road from our starting point to the answer to the first query would be a very long, tortuous, and devious one if we were to do the whole thing by rigorous objective distribution analysis techniques, with computing machines doing our statistics for us. As a matter of fact, a good guess at the answer, if any good guess can be offered at all, might be reached much more quickly by intuitive means.

McQuown: I am in complete agreement, but the purpose of this paper was to suggest that it was time for us to try to extend our non-intuitive techniques to other areas. I have nothing against intuition, but I am not very comfortable with it myself, and I certainly would like to be able to get out of wider generalizations the same kind of satisfaction as is obtainable from our generalizations about linguistic structure.

Roberts: I might say that the list of questions has an astonishingly linguistic character. Would you say a word on the nonlinguistic cultural pattern side of these particular questions?

McQuown: I am not competent to do that, since that is not an area that I am trained in. The phraseology of the questions seems to be linguistic, because the problems were suggested to me by things which I observed in the linguistic forms. As to what the generalizations may be for the culture as a whole, that I can only guess at.

Singer: Here is a problem we have touched on but not tackled directly. McQuown mentions, in a number of places in his paper, that the principles of analysis and segmentation used for the analysis of language structures can be used at least as analogies for the analysis of other cultural patterns. I wonder if you would elaborate on that and indicate just the way in which they could be used. How, for example, would your scheme of segmentation be helpful for the analysis of social structures?

McQuown: I am afraid I cannot give a very satisfactory answer to that. At this particular stage of the game, this is a profession of faith more than anything else. I am sure that the general principles which I cite are of such generality that they are probably attributes of the universe and not of human beings in particular, or human culture in particular, or of the structure of language in particular.

The real problem is not just that of accepting these general principles. After all, all things have structure of some kind, and the elements within that structure contrast or complement each other, or are in free variation with each other, or show pattern congruence, or look elegant when we find out what the thing is like over-all. The real problem arises in setting up the specific hierarchy of operations which one performs in accordance with these general principles. In elaborating such a hierarchy in linguistics, we have had to spend quite a number of years. Yet, a step-by-step procedure, which can be guaranteed to give results structurally with any language we hit, is still, from the linguistic point of view, a thing of the future.

The general procedures which are followed, however, are ones for which we could construct analogues on the nonlinguistic side. I have referred to a specific attempt at constructing such analogues in the area of gesture. To date the analysis of gesture has been done only for one type of American English culture. It looks good, because I am a part of that culture and I can feel some of these things, but until the general methodology has been applied to a wide variety of such gestural systems and a wide variety of cultures, we will have no confidence that the specific methodology is of general applicability.

Now, you ask for a methodology for the analysis of social structure. I would not be surprised but what there is a fairly elaborate methodology already worked out. My interest at this point would be to attempt to state the medium through the observation of which one applies this general methodology for the analysis of social structure. I think I know the answer, but I would like to put it in that frame. I certainly have no precooked, elaborate, step-by-step methodologies for the analysis of other aspects of culture.

NEWMAN: I wonder, with respect to applying this type of approach to culture, if you feel that it is possible to identify units in culture? To my way of thinking, that is a basic difficulty.

MCQUOWN: I assume that it is possible. Otherwise I would not try to extend this methodology. It would be nice to close the door, tie language up neatly, and rest in peace.

HOCKETT: It can be demonstrated very easily that not all cultural behavior consists of arrangements of discrete units of the kind that we find in language when we analyze speech into arrangements of discrete phonemes. All we have to do is look at Western music. We have a discrete scale of pitches, but, when it comes to volume, we do not have a discrete scale. We have a continuum of different degrees of loudness and softness in symphonic music. We cannot produce a series of discrete contrasts between units. That is just as cultural as language, or as the discrete pitch scale.

KAPLAN: Apart from that question, I am puzzled as to the objective of what McQuown calls "segmentation" of cultural activity. In the earlier discussion the objective of this formal linguistic segmentation was specified, as I understand it, as an identification of the units which are the carriers of meaning. But surely one does not mean to say that the point of applying this kind of segmentation to other cultural activities is to localize units of meaning. Meaning would there have a very different sense. I am trying to stick close to what Whorf was interested in.

McQuown: I know. Unfortunately, that does not give a very adequate base from the meaning side. I would say that the purpose in extending this methodology, from my point of view, is to find what nonlinguistic units correlate with what linguistic units. Now, what you want to call that correlation, I do not care. If you want to call it "meaning," that is fine.

Suppose *L* is our linguistic system, *K* is our kinship system, *M* is another one, and *N*, another one. We have *L* completely analyzed in terms of its functional units. The same goes for *K*, *M*, and *N*. When one of the *L* functional units appears in the universe—when there is an event embodying this functional unit in the universe—we ask ourselves the question, "What functional units from areas *K*, *M*, and *N* co-occur?" Now, I do not want to expand that, because "co-occur" doesn't mean at a given time but can have time depth, etc. I cannot go into that. If we ask that question in a different way, "What is the meaning of the *L* unit when it appears?" as far as I can see the meaning of the *L* unit is the group of co-occurring units in the other areas which we can identify.

The same is the case with units from other areas—their meaning is found in the group of co-occurring units. I do not find meaning any place else. It is certainly not to be put outside all these systems as some amorphous entity to which all of them refer.

Kaplan: But are you not perhaps making the problem unnecessarily difficult for yourself by tacitly assuming that, if there are correspondences to be found, these will be, so to speak, point-by-point correspondences? I take it that Whorf does not expect to find correspondences piecemeal but, rather, by taking everything in one area, or at least cutting across a good deal of it, expects to be able to make some inferences about another.

McQuown: I have said quite a number of times that point-by-point correspondences are the exception rather than the rule. I am not sure that that is right, but I prefer to take that stand.

Lounsbury: The answer which I would give to Kaplan's question is that the method of linguistics is essentially one of classification of situations in terms of responses to them, and is applicable only to the area of sign behavior. We classify acoustic events, and thereby the articulatory means of producing them in phonemics, by means of differential responses to them. Where we do not get the differential responses to physically given acoustic events, they are thrown into a single class—an equivalence class of phonemes. I am taking the sign, now, as the situation, and responses to the sign as our basis for classification.

Let us take it the other way around. By virtue of linguistic responses to nonlinguistic situations, we effect a classification of these nonlinguistic situations. Thus, for example, from use of kin terms we effect a classification of kin types. We classify situations by virtue of differential responses to them, and it can be worked on either side of the sign relationship—whatever you want to call it.

SINGER: I have been trying to sum up in my mind the discussion about the question that McQuown himself posed, as to how this methodology for the analysis of linguistic structure could be used for the analysis of other types of cultural patterns. I find at least four different ways in which it could be used, though I think some of these were repudiated at various points in the discussion.

First, it could be used as a kind of generalized methodology of structural analysis. That is your attempt to generalize the structural principles, which, so far as I can see, is simply a branch of abstract mathematics, that is, abstract algebra. Certainly that could be used, but why call it "linguistics"?

Second, there is the discovery of similarity of structure in different parts of the culture. A structure that is revealed in the language might be repeated in, say, the kinship structure as a structure of relationships of human beings. This is ordinarily called isomorphism. Now, this may be very useful, but it need not mean that there is any real connection between language and culture, just as a particular structure which has been revealed in a particular part of the universe may have been echoed, say, in another part of the universe. The usefulness of abstract systems arises from the fact that when we abstract a system in relation to one area of the universe it might turn out to be useful in some other field. But you seemed to deny this in answer to Wright's and my questions. I do not see why you should. It might very well turn out that there may be some isomorphisms in culture.

Third, there is what you have called the language structure as a locus for the manifestation of extralinguistic patterns. I take it an example of this might be the one you were just giving of kin terms ordering kinship relations; that is, the kinship system is, so to speak, manifested in part in the kinship terminology. And there may be a lot of other cases where we would say a particular nonlinguistic phenomenon is "reflected in," or "expressed in," the structure of the language, though I would be very skeptical about there being any such unique reflection.

Finally, and perhaps this comes closest to the Whorfian thesis, is the case where there is not only a similarity of structure but an imputed identity of meaning or principle. The facts about tense and time and gender in Hopi linguistic structure are taken to imply that the Hopi have such and such a metaphysics.

Those are, it seems to me, four different ways in which structural analysis of language might be related to the structural analysis of nonlinguistic patterns.

THIRD SESSION

GESTALT THEORY AND LANGUAGE

HOIJER: The paper by Voegelin on Shawnee Laws is now open to discussion.

FEARING: I am interested in the rationale behind the equating of introversion with ground and extroversion with figure. Offhand, I do not see any compelling reason why, if you use the two categories, introversion and extroversion, one should be regarded as figure and one as ground in the Gestalt sense.

VOEGELIN: Because of the statement sometimes made that by a sort of synesthesia motion is shown by figure. Whorf was interested in that, and I think he succeeded in integrating Gestalt principles with the simple present and present progressive in English. For example, we use the simple present for "I hear you." If you say, "I am hearing you," it sounds as though you are being humorous or are a foreigner. If you say, "What are you doing?" I say, "I am working." But, if I say, "I work," it again sounds as if a foreigner is speaking. The working, the doing, would be the extroverted type of thing. The hearing would be the introverted. I think it is this: If you dichotomize personality types, extroverted can be represented as some sort of activity; introverted—ground—as nonactive.

GREENBERG: I want to say a word, in regard to Whorf's distinction between verbs in English, about the so-called present progressive "I am working." We do have here a class of, probably, perceptual verbs, but also involved in these verbs is inception of an action, or continuation. To take the rather vulgar verb, "smell," you say, "Do you smell me?" This means, "Have you begun to catch my odor?" Whereas, if you say, "Are you smelling me?" it is progressive. I am not quite sure of the analysis of the whole thing. It seems to me there is an inceptive versus progressive thing involved here. In a single verb like "smell," you get both forms. The other difference would be one of aspect. It would not be a difference if in both cases they were activities of the subject, involved perception, etc.

VOEGELIN: I did not mean to suggest that Whorf made his point. I said he succeeded in giving illustrations which integrated the thing, but I am not vouching for the success of the integration. I am certainly not suggesting that the Gestalt way of stating things, because of this very slight success of Whorf's, is to be integrated with grammar. Whorf suggested the grammatical point, and I am not arguing against it.

FEARING: I am not quite clear on the over-all argument. Would you derive from this kind of an analysis some conclusions regarding personality characteristics of a culture?

VOEGELIN: No, I have not said a word about the culture. I have simply talked of the relationship of lexical items with texts, and, of course, the texts are in the culture. I would not go further at this moment. I am asking whether anything in Gestalt can be correlated here. Whorf tried to correlate. I am trying to ascertain whether we can correlate it with something like a legal text.

HOCKETT: I am not at all sure that the approach described here can be fruitful, but I think I see in what way it would be good. We have plenty of feelings about differences among different types of discourse. These laws are very different from the autobiography in feeling, tone, etc. Now, anything of this kind may correlate with other factors in the culture. We do not know in advance what the correlation will be. If we can get a somewhat more objective technique for deciding, for example, what style or category a particular text belongs in, along the dimensions mentioned here, then we will have a more objective basis for comparison with other things we observe in culture. All the conclusions could hardly be anticipated at this time. The source of the conclusion at which we hope to arrive, we can only discuss in very general terms of possible correlation.

HOIJER: It would not be, so much, "correlation." Matters of style are in themselves cultural patterns, which would be illustrable in cultural activities of a different order. This is not a linguistic study but rather a cultural study. One would expect to find a wide variety of styles of discourse, depending upon the circumstances under which the discourse was made, the subject matter of the discourse, the particular context, and even, perhaps, the individuals involved in the discourse. I have the feeling, perhaps without understanding entirely what you are referring to when you speak of Gestalt, that this analysis is a little oversimplified. It presumes a dichotomy which you would perhaps not find.

HOCKETT: To take a flying leap at a possibility, it may be that the variety of situations in which any particular style, measurable in this way, emerged would be one of the more objective indexes that one could use in the seeking of what Opler calls "themes," which, it seems to me, he determines at present by methods at least partly obscure and highly intuitive.

FEARING: The use of the terms "introvert" and "extrovert" immediately suggests that you expect to arrive at conclusions about the personality characteristics of the people who produce the material, and I jumped a little further and said perhaps you were expecting ultimately to arrive at conclusions about the characteristic personality traits in a culture. If you use these categories "introverted" and "extroverted," you are almost obligated to talk in terms of personality traits.

I am curious to know why you selected the extroverted-introverted dichotomy. I am expressing a purely personal prejudice here. I am not at all satisfied with the introverted-extroverted dichotomy, except for its reference to rather superficial characteristics of people.

VOEGELIN: I wanted to avoid precisely the thing you asked about. If we use a definite personality characteristic, we are almost asking that whole cultures be characterized that way. I wanted to have a kind of dichotomy which could not be applied to cultures as a whole. It would be very hard to characterize cultures as being introverted or extroverted. In any given culture, there will be both. Also, within a given corpus of text material, I wanted to have both. Whorf wanted to have the languages, or some parts of the languages, correlated with Gestalt; I wanted to have both things in each given corpus. In this way you might end up by concluding that English laws are more extroverted than Shawnee laws or that funeral orations are more introverted than coyote stories.

KAPLAN: I have been troubled by the same kind of difficulties that Fearing has been expressing, but, more particularly, I am puzzled about whether the kind of objectivity you are concerned with in this description has to do with the constancy in different analysts' descriptions of the same materials, or with the constancy of perception and report on the part of members of different cultures. If it is the former, I am puzzled about why you chose this Gestalt characteristic, because, of course, there is an endless variety of specifications of style that could be made sufficiently definite so that one could expect several analysts to report the same thing. I gather from some of your discussion that you think that perhaps the Gestalt characteristic of style would be useful because one might expect, on the basis of Gestalt arguments, a certain constancy among members of the culture.

Perhaps you could make your selection clear to me, because I am puzzled as to how we can choose a style characteristic in the absence of hypotheses about the possible significance of that characteristic. Maybe you could answer my question by contrast with the sort of thing I understand various literary critics have done. They find that in Shakespeare's *Othello* there is a vast preponderance of references which deal with animals—very much greater than occurs in any other Shakespearean play. People, actions, and situations are constantly compared with animals or animal traits or situations, and this throws some light on the particular quality of, the intuitive feeling that we get out of, the play. Now, would you have been just as inclined to compare a Shawnee and an American text in terms of the proportion of references to animals as contrasted with inanimate nature or dozens of other categories that could be suggested?

Even though you cannot be expected, now, to formulate the conclusions that would be established, I wonder what anticipations led you to employ these rather unusual Gestalt categories.

Voegelin: I do not think anybody would be very happy to compare animals in cultures of the sort that Shakespeare wrote about with animals, let us say, of the Shawnee. The animals mentioned in the Shakespearean plays are largely domesticated. In the case of Shawnee, the animals, except the dog, are not domesticated, and have folkloristic connotations which make them entirely different. There would be no point in comparing references to animals in a given Shawnee text with references to animals in *Othello*. It would be impossible to do so.

If you generalized still further to say that you wanted to compare texts in which activities of humans and animals in general occurred and texts in which they did not occur—for example, if you had a particularly active story and one which was less active—there might be something to it. I do not see the possibility of making a direct comparison of *Othello* with, let us say, a coyote story.

I do think that if you could find a method, and it would work out, you could perhaps make some very general statement about the Gestalt nature of the two.

Fearing: I wanted to raise a question as to how you are using the word "absolute." Do you mean that to refer to categories which ranscend cultural boundaries completely—whole universals—and are "absolute" and "universal" equivalent terms?

Voegelin: I had thought of absolutes as being universals, but universals for a certain reason, not because of an accident of history, but perhaps by virtue of some equipment in the organism—because something is built in.

FEARING: Whorf, in general, does not argue for absolutes. He does not find much evidence for the existence of absolutes and universals.

VOEGELIN: Whorf's statement of Gestalt takes what I take from my own reading of Gestalt: the feeling that there are absolutes, and that all peoples of the world, looking up and seeing the Big Dipper, will see one shape. There will be variations in naming it, but they will perceive a single figure.

KROEBER: I was interested in Kaplan's query of why introvert and extrovert were chosen. Some years ago I found myself in the same position. I wanted to put a chapter on psychology into a general book on anthropology. I did not want to go into personality. I wanted to say something about the psychology of culture. From what angle, what concepts at hand, would I approach it? Introvert-extrovert was one thing that came up, and I gave it a few paragraphs. The fact is, in all cultural-linguistic forms, we are still groping for the psychological concepts that are best applicable.

HOCKETT: I think it is important to distinguish between universals, culturally speaking or linguistically speaking, and a cross-culturally valid frame of reference. What Whorf was seeking, and thought he had found in figure and ground, was, not a human universal, but a sort of co-ordinate, which would be valid in measuring differences from one language to another and one culture to another.

Now, language itself is a human universal. There are others. The search for a cross-culturally valid frame of reference is a different thing, and I think we can raise the question of whether it is even necessary. Some of the people who have worked the most from the point of view of cultural and linguistic patterns, such as Whorf, have found themselves impelled to search for an absolute that they could use in their wanderings—an anchor to windward. But, mathematically speaking, certainly no such point of reference is necessary. It is not necessary to have a co-ordinate system in order to have a perfectly valid geometry. It may be that we can dispense with any cross-culturally valid co-ordinate system in making these measures of linguistic and cultural differences.

NEWMAN: I want to raise a problem here. It has reference to measuring on a scale. A British psychologist conducted an experiment during which he presented folk tales to a number of people, and asked them to recall and repeat them. He found, for example, that when—I believe it was British Hindus—they repeated the stories, they put in a good deal about the internal feelings of the subject. They seemed to be much more interested in that aspect than in the actual narrative movement. I wonder if that kind of item would fit on the scale you are thinking of.

VOEGELIN: I think so, so long as they are sufficiently general so they can be compared cross-culturally.

FEARING: I think I must have misread Whorf. I have the impression that he gives little basis for any assumptions regarding absolutes. He seems to be saying that it is very difficult to make cross-cultural comparisons because of the linguistic barriers which codify the world. He does make rather oblique reference to the fact that all human beings probably perceive spatial phenomena in the same manner. It is a kind of hesitant reference, the one that I have in mind. In general, it seems to me that he is giving no aid and comfort to anyone who is seeking absolutes.

KROEBER: He is interested in differences in his comparisons, primarily, and I agree that he somewhat hesitantly concedes there may be certain absolutes. I think he is much more interested in differences between the Hopi verb and the English verb, and the effect those may have on thinking.

GREENBERG: When you use a term like "absolute," it means something tremendous is being assumed. It seems to me that scientific linguistics would be impossible, and Whorf could not have done any work on Hopi or any other language to begin with, unless in a kind of common-sense way we assume that the Hopi and we share certain aspects of experience. Translation would not be possible unless something of this kind existed. It seems to me that people can agree on certain things. Otherwise, you would never be able to learn to speak a foreign language or adjust in a foreign community.

Let us say that you are a scientific astronomer. Your idea of what the moon is differs from that of a Shawnee Indian, let us say. He has all kinds of ideas about the moon. You believe a quite different set of propositions about the moon, having to do with distance, the fact that it revolves around the earth, and so on. Nevertheless, you can agree on certain things: for example, the moon has just risen or the moon has not just risen; the moon is in the sky at the present time; the moon is directly overhead; the moon is not directly overhead.

I am not a philosopher, and I do not know what kind of assumption is involved here. Perhaps it is debatable. I know that philosophers argue about such things. As a practical matter, the linguist takes some kind of rough frame of reference for granted. I think that calling them "absolutes" stimulates a kind of shudder because the assumption of absolutes of various kinds leads to unsatisfactory conclusions.

HOCKETT: The point that ought to be made very often when Whorf is discussed underscores the linguistic aspect of what you said. He wrote in English when he described these non-European languages. He wrote it in *English.* You can do that. Some extreme forms of cultural relativism—I do not think anybody in this room subscribes to any such form—would imply an impossibility of learning another language.

KAPLAN: The feature that interests me is not the term "absolute" but the term "semantic." Greenberg was saying a moment ago there is a common world which has to be assumed, but the critical distinction to be made is that between world in the physical sense, or something like it, and what Whorf calls "thought-world." I am assuming that I am equating thought-world with some kind of semantic element here.

The specific instances of this semantic framework—let us substitute that term—that have come up in the discussion or in the paper have been these: One was purely, or at least very closely, structural —the verb-noun differentiation. The other two were both perceptual —the physiognomic perception, and the Gestalt. None of these three, so far as I can see, has the kind of characteristic which would allow it to serve for that general framework that Hockett talked about for comparison of thought-worlds.

I may have been misreading Whorf. If so, I misread him, I think, in the same way that Fearing did. I took Whorf to be insisting that you do not translate thought-worlds one into another. The term "translate" is a very loose one, from a lay viewpoint; maybe for linguistics you can attach a precise sense to it. Whorf was able to write in English and to say certain things, but, since I never did speak Hopi, I am not able to judge whether his English rendering of it has in fact succeeded in giving me that thought-world in a precise way.

The situation, as I picture it, is suggested by the following metaphoric account. Suppose that I had a shovel with which I could dig only circular holes, and suppose that you had a spade which dug only holes with straight sides. Now, there is a sense in which we could both dig in the same regions; there is no part of the earth that we could not, equally, make a hole in. But, whenever we did make holes, there would invariably be some part of the earth that my shovel would leave in and your spade would take out.

The notion of an absolute framework in terms of which we could make comparisons would then correspond to something like this: If I had a tool which dug out ever smaller portions of earth at a time, plainly I could, with that tool, approximate as closely as I liked either the circular hole or the hole with a square border. I look about for such a tool, and, supposing that I find one, I can now describe exactly the differences between my circular holes and your square ones. As long as I am operating only with that kind of tool, and the only way I can describe to you what somebody else's holes are like is by digging a hole to show you one, there is no question I will be introducing certain distortions.

Now, if I understand Whorf, his whole thesis can be summed up in the proposition that we carry different shovels so that, in fact, we do not translate. Now, if that is going to be abandoned—that is, if we are going to say that eyes are the same, and we all know the moon is now in the sky, unless we are blind—if that commonality is taken to provide us with the kind of frame that we are interested in, then, it seems to me, everything I read would disappear.

HOIJER: An analogy might be drawn in this instance to the problem of metaphor. Whereas it is not very often possible to translate a metaphor from one language to another, and, in particular, between languages as diverse as Hopi and English, we can understand and explain, paraphrase, the metaphor. Whorf, it seems to me, is not insisting on the impossibility of translation or on the uniqueness of thought-worlds. Rather, he is admitting the possibility that you can talk in English about the Hopi thought-world and make it, to a very high degree, understandable.

HOCKETT: Does this not underscore the point that I made yesterday: that the range of consideration that is important is what it is easier or more difficult to say in different languages? You can do difficult things, of course. I am sure that, however true or false Whorf's characterization of Hopi semantics may be, his writing the description he did write in English was very difficult.

FOURTH SESSION

THE WHORF HYPOTHESIS AND PSYCHOLOGICAL THEORY

HOIJER: I will ask Fearing to begin in the usual manner and give us a brief idea of what he was trying to do in his paper.

FEARING: The broad purpose was to examine some of Whorf's conceptualizations in the light of certain relevant psychological frames of reference or theory, specifically, theories of cognition or perception. When I use the word "cognition," I mean it to include perception at one end of a continuum and conceptualization at another. The word "cognition" is the generic term.

The first part of the paper is concerned with setting forth three or four major conceptions of Whorf which seem to be specifically related to the problems that the psychologist discusses under the term "cognition." I see Whorf as really presenting a theory of cognition. He is talking about the way in which the human animal sees the real world.

The second section of my paper is concerned with a problem that is discussed under the phrase "sociology of knowledge." It is inescapably one of the frames of reference within which the Whorfian theory has to be considered. Whorf is saying, in effect, that we are constrained to see the world in a certain way, and that we are unconscious of these constraints. Stated in that bald, perhaps oversimplified, way, it raises the whole question of the extent to which one can transcend these barriers and the extent to which cross-cultural comparisons may be made.

Köhler (1937) raises the same question, in a sense anticipating Whorf. He goes a bit further than does Whorf, because he says that scientific speculation and hypothesis become, in a succeeding generation, the perceptual frames of reference for a whole group of people. He speaks specifically of the physical and physiological conceptions of the nineteenth century, which have now become established as the fixed frames of reference within which reality is conceived to exist. He even questions what basis we have for assuming that these frames of reference, these perceptions, are any more valid than the perceptions of individuals who do not have this kind of cognitive background. He speculates as to whether we may not examine the perceptions of the primitive as reflections of reality on the same level as the reflections of reality that we get through particular spectacles.

There is no very satisfactory reference or system of co-ordinates that can be used to transcend some of these barriers which cognitively separate one culture from another. The closest to a satisfactory system is the kind of thinking that is implicit or stated explicitly in the work of Heinz Werner. I have summarized in my paper his attempt (1948) to set up a series of developmental constructs, in which he makes comparisons between the mental world of the child and the primitive. This course of development is in terms of what Whorf would call, I suppose, the thought-worlds of these various groups, in which there are certain parallels and consistencies. In general, the course of development is from the global undifferentiated patterns of

a Perception — *b* Conceptualization

FIG. 1.—The cognitive continuum

perception and cognition to the differentiated and abstract patterns of cognition. These two extremes are referred to by Werner as "syncretic" and "discrete." Perhaps the best example of syncretic thinking and perceiving would be the physiognomic sort of perceiving, in which the individual does not clearly distinguish between the self and the not-self. To him, the sky is threatening, the landscape is depressing. At the other extreme would be the highly sophisticated distinctions in which the external world is sharply distinguished. At this end of the continuum we would have, of course, examples of scientific analysis.

Now, this might be diagrammed, I think. (See Fig. 1.) As I interpret Werner, line *a–b* represents the cognitive continuum. At this end (*a*) is the simplest form of perceiving, figure-ground perception, in which the individual does not clearly distinguish between himself and the external world. At the other end (*b*) is the conceptualization, in which the individual observes the external world apart from himself.

At the point of conceptualization, I think symbolic processes have to come in. This kind of perceiving (at *a*) might conceivably occur in its pure form without the necessity of any intervening symbolic process. Somewhere along the continuum, symbolic techniques are utilized, and I am inclined to think that symbolic techniques and the process of conceptualization must somehow occur coincidentally. Further, I am inclined to think that symbolic techniques never arise except in the context of communication. In other words, hypothetically, we could have pure perception—the hypothetical man on a desert island. We do not have conceptualization until there is another human being present; and some kind of a relationship has to be established, which requires a symbolic process.

Now, this latter kind of analysis, this kind of cognizing, is commonly thought of as highly intellectual or abstract, as if it were qualitatively different, a wholly unique process. But *a–b* is a real continuum. It may be that not all the positions on it can be clearly described, but as I am conceiving it psychologically, it is a true continuum. We are not justified in thinking that end *b* is unique and qualitatively different.

VOEGELIN: May I ask a question? The figure and ground, you said, was on the left. How far right does it go? I would think it goes through. I do not understand why you said it was on the left.

FEARING: I do not mean to imply that people who conceptualize do not perceive in the simple global sense. All of us, regardless of our culture and our level of sophistication, conceptualize and perceive. It is a question of how frequently the patterns are used so far as the conceptual end is concerned. The figure-ground kind of perceiving is characteristic all the way through. At this end (*b*), not only do we have figure-ground perception but we also conceptualize.

GREENBERG: Does physiognomic perception necessarily involve a lack of recognition between the external world and the self? If a child thinks the moon is threatening him, he has a certain theory about the external world which is different from ours. Nevertheless, he recognizes there is some difference between the external world and himself. In the case of animals the only proof we have is how the animals behave, but it seems to me that we cannot say the dog uses symbolic processes if he behaves as though he knew the difference between himself and others. Animals that behave intelligently are making some distinctions. If that is so, how can we state that they merge themselves with the external world?

I think that is a fundamental problem. Are you stating that in order to recognize the difference between one's self, the perceiving subject, and the external world, symbolic processes are necessary?

FEARING: I am inclined to think I would say that, or approximately that. As one moves toward end *b*, one begins to distinguish one's self and the external world, and that kind of cognition requires symbolic processes.

GREENBERG: I fail to see that. The burden of proof is on those who want to show the organism does not perceive the difference between itself and the external world. In what way would one know that anyone, even an animal, does or does not distinguish himself from the external world? One cannot answer until one gets a hypothetical situation in which symbolization does not take place. We are assuming a correlation between lack of cognition and something else.

LOUNSBURY: If we allow that all primitive people have languages, and that these languages are symbol systems, and that any single individual participant in any culture has about the same magnitude of lexical content as any other individual, then what puts the primitive down at one end of the scale whereas rational man is on the other end? If it is the symbolic process, what is the necessary thing for reaching this conceptualizing end? Why are not all peoples with language at this *b* end? And why is the primitive, then, like a person with a brain injury or like an animal? Why does he indulge in so-called global thinking?

FEARING: The brain-injured individual may use language. He has to use, does use, language to express his perceptual patterns. Our difficulty is, of course—and this is the difficulty raised by Greenberg's question—to try and isolate an individual, or find examples of individuals, who has no symbolic processes. We apparently do find such examples in the case of children, but then arises the old problem of how to get at this, since our chief means of getting at anything is to use symbolic processes. So we will not get a clear-cut case. I do not think it would be possible. We will have to postulate, make some assumptions about pure perception without necessarily, at this point at least, having any empirical examples or data to establish them

LENNEBERG: May I try to interpret the continuum? I do not think that these instances are mutually exclusive. I think there is good evidence that perceptual signs continue as a substratum, whereas conceptualization may rise in degree as one moves forward. We know from experiments by psychophysicists that we can discriminate certain tones and very fine shades of colors. We do not have words for these, yet we perceive and know them.

GREENBERG: I take that for granted. The question has to do with the individual's perceiving himself as different from the external world. I fail to see why we should make that assumption.

HOCKETT: If it is dependent on the existence of communicative behavior, why not talk about communicative and symbolic behavior? What is the need for the term "conceptualization"? I think it introduces confusion.

FEARING: The term "conceptualization" refers to the fact that the individual abstracts out properties in his perceptual world and talks about them, analyzes them, constructs elaborate metaphysics, and so on. I would have no objection to changing the term and substituting some other.

There is an important point that might bear on this question. In perception the individual is closer, figuratively speaking, to the reality. Whereas, at the conceptualizing end, there are more intervening processes. So this continuum, in a very rough sense, represents the degree to which the individual is responding immediately to the given situation and the degree to which there are intervening processes in which he utilizes concepts, and these require symbolistic processes.

If we follow the Gestaltists, the most primitive kind of perceiving involves the simple differentiation between figure and ground. It is a distinction on the continuum of dominance. Incidentally, the figure-ground—I think this bears on some of the points that you were raising—is not necessarily determined by the structure of the external world. When we use the phrase "figure-ground," we do not necessarily mean that in the external world the figure and ground is given. Frequently what is figure for individual *A* is ground for individual *B*. What is figure for individuals in one cultural context might be ground for individuals in another.

KROEBER: I think Fearing is raising certain difficulties for himself with this audience due to the fact that some of his propositions are double-barreled, and some of us would accept one barrel and not the other. For instance, conceptualization depends on symbolization. I think we all accept that.

I rather liked the two terms that you mentioned but then did not continue to use, namely, "syncretic" for the one end and "discrete" for the other. I would agree wholly with your point of view: that this is a continuum and not a jump from one thing to another. We get increasing differentiation, and that is undoubtedly true even within the realm of conceptualization. There is no Hopi who would have understood this morning's discussion. He undoubtedly uses conceptualization as truly as we do, but he does not use as many concepts or as differentiated or abstract ones as we do.

But, recognizing the difference between one's self and the world I also think introduces a complication. It seems to me that it is probably based on the fact that a child first becomes aware of parts of his body at a certain age, before which he does not differentiate. And, if we call that a distinction between self and not-self, we can observe it in the human child. But, we have got perception and physiognomic recognition in animals. The puppy may go through the same stage, where he does not know what his mother's teats and his own mouth are. He certainly does not conceptualize, but he becomes aware of them.

LOUNSBURY: My question has to do with the same double-barreled hypothesis. Conceptualization depends upon symbols, and symbols depend upon communication. I cannot accept either of them, unless you are using the terms "symbol" and "symbolization" in a very wide sense, where I would use "sign" and say it depends upon sign behavior.

For instance, Pavlov's experiment with bell and food would be a case of sign behavior, but the bell would not qualify as a symbol. If so, then I cannot see that conceptualization depends upon symbols. Take a dog fight. One animal responds to incipient actions, the slightest feints, interpreting them as signs of something more to come, a completed action. In a dog fight there is a great deal of sign behavior. I cannot see where, in the interpretation on the part of one animal of incipient action on the part of another, there is anything different from conceptualization.

FEARING: Are you not bootlegging something in here when you use the word "interpretation"? The animal responds in the dog fight to the growl of the other animal. That is not conceptualization in the sense I am using it, at all.

WRIGHT: I would just like to get the full implication of this paradigm for the Whorf hypothesis. The thought-world simply does not occur until your conceptualizing stage. There is no thought-world of the physiognomic-perceiving individual.

FEARING: That is right. Whorf does not make clear at which point on such a hypothetical continuum the linguistic processes begin to operate. He says that primordially the experience of the individual is blooming confusion, kaleidoscopic. That, I think, is unsound and untrue. I do not think that the experience of the organism at any stage is a blooming confusion. There is always figure-ground differentiation. Perception in primitive types occurs preceding the development and the utilization of linguistic patterns. Whorf's discussion is wholly on the assumption that, apparently, there is no such prelinguistic stage.

HOCKETT: I begin to understand, I think, and am even willing to settle for using the word "conceptualization," but there is still one thing that disturbs me. I am unable to see that the factors can be arranged on a single scale. It seems to me it has to be expanded into several scales.

Three things have struck me as of considerable importance, if we are going to try to pin down the range in which Whorf's hypothesis belongs. The first is the very simple physiologically definable scale determined by the length and complexity of the routes followed by nervous energy from the receptors which receive the stimulus to the motor ends which give the response. I am using stimulus also in global meaning. This whole configuration would be stimulus. That is an important scale. Of course there is a wider range of possible points on that scale in a complex organism than in a simple one. The second is the degree of involvement of shared sign behavior patterns in any particular continuous stimulus response.

The third scale, which intersects both of those, in theory, is that of the complexity and the detailed character of the shared sign behavior patterns themselves. Now, I think it has been pointed out that it is only when we have shared sign behavior of that terrific degree of complexity that we call "language" that Whorf's theories come into play. The question is how to trace the effects of the Whorfian line of causality along each of these scales. How simple can a language be and still have this kind of an effect? That is a silly question because we do not know any simple language; we have no way of getting at the answers. The main point of these remarks is that I feel we try to attack too many things along a single dimension.

FEARING: I think that is sound criticism. Probably I have done that, although I had in mind that this continuum is a continuum of cognition. These other scales are related ones, and points on each of them may be correlated. I think that is possible. But I still have a feeling that there is a place here for a continuum or a dimension of cognition—a fourth in addition to the three you have given.

HOCKETT: I think the existence of the fourth scale is implied by the things that I have mentioned. It seems doubtful to me that we need a fourth scale in addition to these three.

HOIJER: We return now to our discussion of Fearing's paper. I would like to ask him to reopen the discussion with some remarks on the problem of communication.

FEARING: I put Figure 2 on the board because it illustrates how the perceiver makes a contribution to a configuration. In fact, it illustrates the perceptual process as it really works. This is actually a picture of something. As you look at it, you do of course perceive it, but you perceive it in what Werner would call "geometrical" terms, angles, or you cast about for some way of verbalizing it. You can verbalize it. Its meaning is not clear, in the sense that it is rather ambiguous. Now, if I tell you that this is a picture of a soldier going through a door with a musket on his shoulder, followed by his dog, a switch is thrown, so to speak, psychologically, and it now is perceived in wholly different terms. I do not think you are then able to perceive it in any other terms.

In the last five or ten years, the emphasis in the study of perception has shifted to the contribution of the perceiver. The idea is that

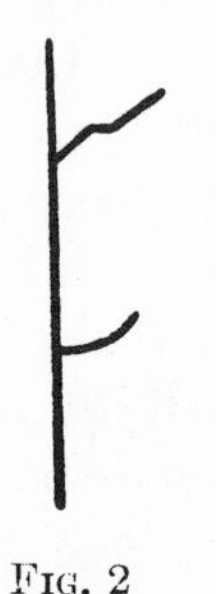

FIG. 2

perception is the resultant of a stimulus configuration, and the particular set of factors which the perceiver contributes may even include attitudes, beliefs, and biases, as well as other experience.

It was clear this morning that I am, so to speak, tying up in a single package symbolic behavior and conceptualization and communication. Assuming these are not the same, they do occur coincidentally. I do not know how. They cannot arise independently. I do not think they operate independently.

This makes it obligatory to say what I mean by communication. I mean it to include three components: communicator, interpreter or, if you prefer, communicatee, and content. The content is sign-symbol material which is produced by a communicator with the intent of bringing about certain effects in a hypothetical interpreter. The effects may be, so far as the communicator is concerned, conceived to occur with all degrees of specificity; effects may be so unspecific that the communicator may even insist that he does not care whether anybody ever listens to what he has to say or is affected by what he produces. We are not bound to accept his report. This, of course, brings up the question of the criteria for the intent. They are very difficult to establish. The word is a dangerous word; I am quite aware of it. Yet I have been unable to think about the problems of communication except as I use this term, because of its subjective mentalistic flavor. But, one thing is certain: the intent of the communicator—I do not know whether he can give you a conscious account of it or not—must be present. That means that the interpreter is psychologically or physically in his field, which is to say he must speak to somebody. On the other side of this triad of communicator-content-interpreter is the interpreter, who, in responding to content, is responding to sign-symbol material which is not just something in nature but is artifactual in the sense that he knows it is produced by a human communicator. Again, his degree of awareness of the communicator is to be conceived in all degrees of specificity. He may be conscious of the person who produced this communication, the person who wrote the letter which he is reading, as a very definite individual, or his awareness of the producer may be as vague as the very uncertain "they" in "They say." It is under these circumstances, and at the risk of making a very dogmatic statement *only* under these circumstances, that sign-symbol material is produced or utilized in a human situation.

This definition of communication excludes a great many other forms of human social interaction. We respond interpersonally in a wide range of ways, and there are important kinds of response. I am ruling out all forms of interpersonal response which do not involve the elements which I have just referred to. It seems to me to be necessary to delimit this word. Otherwise, it becomes so general as to be almost meaningless.

HOCKETT: I think it is very important to have a definition of "communication" which does not leave it coterminous with all cultural behavior on the part of human beings. I wonder, however, if there would be any serious objection to the enlargement of coverage of the term so as to provide for what goes on between certain humanly produced artifacts, e.g., a range-finder, an analogue computer, and an antiaircraft gun, which are all hooked together so that everything is automatic. We push a button and it works. Or would it not be possible to expand it to include certain types of behavior between animals? Must it be exclusively between human beings in order to attain the degree of specificity that we need to have?

FEARING: I am not sure about the first question. This machine that does all these things does not produce sign-symbol material, so I think that rules it out from my consideration. I do not know of any machine that does. Maybe that is a limitation of my knowledge.

If we can demonstrate that animals below man can produce sign-symbol material with the intent to achieve effects on other animals, I would include this as communication. But I do not think it has been demonstrated. I doubt that it will. I do not think any animal below man has the neural equipment to produce or to respond to sign-symbol material, except in a very, very rudimentary form. The gap, practically, is so great between their facilities and those of man, it seems to me, that communication, as I am defining it, is limited to human interactions.

Hockett: As far as the behavior of the human and the behavior of the gun emplacement or the electrical unit in the refrigerator is concerned, the difference might be taken to lie largely in the impulsive nature of the human being. If you look into that closer, it may be discovered that the mechanism of purpose is precisely the type of communicative informational feed-back that exists in the electric refrigerator.

Fearing: I would be willing to leave that open. I must confess great skepticism about the possibility of establishing that.

Singer: I am not going to speak specifically to the problem of communication, but to raise a more general question. I think that the program that Fearing sets out has been generalized by others in relation to the problem of cultural universals, or cross-cultural universals. He says that the approach he is taking is to consider the similarities and differences in the behavior of literates and nonliterates in the light of hypothetical developmental sequences analogous to the sequences of biological development. Then he says this might provide a set of co-ordinates, within which the uniqueness and discreteness of cultural phenomena might be recognized and at the same time ordered to constructs which might make cross-cultural comparisons possible.

Now, specifically in relation to Whorf, I think this is very important, because if you say or suggest, as Whorf does, that language has a certain impact on habitual ways of thinking and perceiving, then if someone knows independently of language some sequences of a developmental sort about perceiving and thinking, we are in a much better position, not only to appraise the Whorfian theory, but also to undertake research into the interaction of those modes of perceiving and thinking which are independent of linguistic patterns and those modes which are the result of linguistic patterns. But there are many difficulties in trying to carry out such a program. One of the difficulties is the fact that the investigation of prelinguistic modes of conception is almost always in the context of a linguistic meaning, so that all the evidence taken from children and so-called primitives is already screened through a highly sophisticated development of language. You cannot assume, without the introduction of very special criteria, that what you are getting is actually prelinguistic. Perhaps you will, then, have to go back to some sort of philogenetic theory of development or to the animals, in which case you again run into difficulties, which are well known. Therefore I would suggest that we do not have any clear-cut way of separating out from the postlinguistic context a situation which is prelinguistic.

To take an example from Fearing, Piaget finds that the child conceives of himself and perceives his world in ways that are basically and qualitatively different from those of the adult. The thinking of the child is characterized by realism, animism, and artificialism. Now, this is not unlike Whorf's characterization of the Hopi adults. Whorf seems to say, and I think many other observers of the Hopi have said, that realism and animism (in Piaget's sense) are characteristic of Hopi thought. But I am not really sure that artificialism is, although Thompson puts some emphasis on it in her characterization. The problem, therefore, is this: Has Whorf neglected a mode of perceiving and cognizing? I do not think so. He says, in effect, that the Hopi can be characterized in this way. So the issue between you and Whorf would then become, not whether he has neglected a particular mode of perceiving and thinking, but whether the mode in question is prelinguistic or postlinguistic. I wonder how we can resolve an issue like that by appeal to evidence that we would all accept.

I would just like to cite, as counterevidence to Dennis, or to the way in which Dennis is interpreted in Fearing, the findings of Havighurst and his group (Havighurst Ms.), with relation to American Indians, that a characteristic animism does not decrease with the age of the child but, rather, increases. That would seem to suggest there is something in Hopi culture that induces or retains this characteristic mode of perception. It really is not an infantile mode of perception at all but is culturally determined. I am not saying this is definitive, but I think there are other studies of Western children that have shown that certain of the characteristics which Piaget thinks are developmentally early do not decrease with age but may actually increase. If that is so, then I think we have not succeeded in isolating what is prelinguistic from what is postlinguistic. I wonder whether we have any way of making such a separation.

FEARING: With respect to this last point, I think there might be some evidence that there is a considerable amount of this kind of thinking—animism and so forth—in so-called primitive adults. Werner would say, I am sure, that in general there is more animism at all stages of development among primitives than there is among literate peoples.

In reference to this other point about the extent to which there is any empirical data that is not contaminated with symbolic material—and of course that is the sixty-four-dollar question all the way through here—there are some sketchy things. The study of Spitz (1946) referred to in my paper would come as close as any that I know about to demonstrating a prelinguistic type of perception.

LENNEBERG: I am somewhat unhappy about the kind of evidence that is sometimes drawn. I do not know whether Singer suggested that we equate evidence from child language and aboriginal language, or merely referred to it, but it seems to me that each time we make a jump from one situation to another we assume factors about which we do not know. Whatever you find in child language is probably not directly relevant to a present situation.

Now, I do not think that the case for finding a situation in which we do perceive without the help of language is hopeless, if we study instances in which we perceive, or sense, stimuli which are not expressed linguistically or in any other symbolic medium—things such as sound configurations. These need not be threshold studies, but configuration studies in a sound continuum would be perfectly suitable evidence, and also might possibly, when studied cross-culturally, shed light on some of the problems we are talking about.

NEWMAN: I get the feeling that we are trying to get at some qualitative differences between what has been termed "perception" and a kind of activity that goes on in conceptualization. But, for me at least, it is very comforting to see that in so far as we can get data on prelinguistic behavior or on the nonlinguistic behavior of animals, we do have evidence that organisms can learn to discriminate without language. I think—correct me if I am wrong on this—we also have evidence that organisms can learn to associate without language. Then language comes in at a certain point in the individual's life, and it also teaches him to discriminate and to associate sometimes in ways that appear global. For example, when the child begins to learn language, he will probably start out with some one term for all of the individuals in his environment. Then gradually he begins to discriminate, so that he has one term for "mother," one for "father," and so forth. Then after that he has to learn new kinds of associations or extensions of these terms so that, as it is pointed out, you have Mother Earth, Father Time, and so on. The generalization would be that we can get processes on a nonlinguistic level that parallel processes on the linguistic level, namely, this matter of discrimination and association.

WRIGHT: What is the significance for the Whorf hypothesis of child languages, such as the whole separate vocabulary of Japanese children for everything that they have and use up to a certain age?

HOCKETT: I think there is reasonable evidence in support of the theory that age grading in language patterns is well-nigh universal, though there may be communities where there are so few people of any one age grade that they do not have a jargon of their own. Wherever a population is dense enough so that children can be with children, adolescents with adolescents, adults with adults, there will be age-grading linguistic patterns.

I suspect that the factors which really shape the linguistic pattern in a child will stay with him throughout his life despite superficial changes in conformity with later age-grade patterns or with those which act on him when he is just past the cradle stage and first with other children. There may be factors which are transmitted through successive generations of children and not from adult members to children. This, as I say, is just a suspicion. It is one that I voiced in print, and it needs investigation.

VON GRUNEBAUM: I should like to voice a countersuspicion that children's languages are adult-imposed. We expect a child to express himself in childish language, and in certain societies this expectation is carried through and imposed more consistently than in others. Baby talk, if at all consistently practiced by a group of children, is almost always traceable to adult expectation.

HOCKETT: I do not think those two suspicions are contradictory. You are thinking of an earlier age grade than I am—the cradle and postcradle stage when the contact is with the people who take care of the child. That is the first stage in most societies. It is the stage at which, so far as I know, most of the things which have been labeled "child language" have occurred.

There is then this postcradle stage in which children are with children of about the same age. There are the terrific fires of childhood competition, conformity. It builds a different pattern. I doubt that the Japanese child language is manifested at this stage. It is primarily earlier.

KROEBER: If I may go back to what Newman and Fearing were saying, and to Figure 1, we seem to be agreed that there is a certain degree of parallelism between the undeveloped human beings and the subhumans. Animals share in most of the mental faculties that human beings have, such as perception, and also recognition and association. Some psychologists insist that animals have what we would call "insight." We could speak there of a gradual scale. Going back from animals to lower animals, we certainly find traces of those same faculties.

Associated on the human level, however, we have evidence of thinking. Behavior of children is animistically colored, and it is only with increasing conceptualization that animistic thinking or behavior is stripped off. That would seem to make this a sign of primitiveness. However, the moment we go beyond the human level, there is no trace, so far as I know, of anything we could call animistic. There is something there that is very different from perception, association, and insight.

WRIGHT: I wonder if we could not pin this down by saying that at different levels along this continuum there is certain speech behavior which, in Whorf's terminology, represents a certain segmentation of experience. Could you not work something out in such terms, using the child or primitive if you wanted to? Take your child language as a segmentation of experience, if it indeed is, and see what kind of a world view you get out of that, as contrasted with the developed world view of the adult in the same culture.

FEARING: Whorf does not do that, of course, but I do not see any reason why it cannot be done. It is a descriptive, observational, task.

GREENBERG: We have to be very careful in our use of this term "animism," because it has a very complex history and has been used in different ways in different disciplines. The anthropologist means, when he talks about animism, that a certain, particular, very specified and limited type of object, often an utterly minor part of the environment, is pervaded by some kind of a sacred being who has the possibilities of emerging from or entering it.

SINGER: I wanted to add another research job to the one that Wright suggested, and along the same lines. If we accept the generalization that Fearing has proposed—that primitives are more animistic and realistic, and have all the other qualitative characteristics in their perception that he suggests—you might try to put it alongside the characterization of so-called primitive languages, as compared with so-called civilized languages, and see if you find any clue as to the difference.

HOIJER: I am not sure that this represents a generalization that Fearing made. Perhaps he wants to correct or revise that statement.

FEARING: You mean the generalization that primitives are more animistic, more realistic, more artificial in their modes of thought, in cognizing, than civilized people. We must, of course, avoid any notion of a primitive prelogical mind.

LOUNSBURY: First, I want to deny that we accept his premise, or at least that I do. Second, this business of lumping children, psychotics, and animals together is one of the oldest bits of folklore that we have in civilized society, and I immediately tend to react against the very idea. This matter of global thinking is attributed to primitives and linked to so-called primitive languages. Primitives are supposed to have polysynthetic languages in which they can say as much in one word as I can in a sentence in English. It is assumed that this long word is just a scramble and not segmented in as many small parts as any ten-word sentence in English. The linguist has no criteria by which to call a language primitive. We have never seen a primitive language. We have studied only the languages of primitive peoples, peoples with a primitive technology and primitive science. I cannot feel there has been anything contributed to this matter of animism since Tylor.

HOIJER: I am subject to correction by Fearing here, but I do not think what he is saying is in any sense comparable to Lévy-Bruhl's notion of primitive mentality, and certainly has no relationship to the thought, which I join Lounsbury in demolishing whenever I can, that there are primitive languages in any structural sense whatsoever.

FEARING: I underscore your words. I could not accept any notion of primitive mentality, and I do not think that is implied in Werner's analysis. He is very explicit in rejecting this. These are formal categories, formal constructs with respect to the general structure of thinking, and there is global—or if you do not like that term—physiognomic perception, and so on, among literate as well as nonliterate peoples. Conception of a very high order of sophistication is found among so-called primitive, as well as literate, peoples.

But I think with Werner that there is some profit in setting up a set of constructs which will enable us to transcend cultural barriers. This all grows out of my concern about cultural relativism, the kind that seems to me to be very marked in all of Whorf that I read, and which seems to make it almost impossible to transcend cultural barriers.

Von Grunebaum: There may or may not be primitive man. But there are certainly languages which nobody would want to classify, or ever have classified, as primitive, e.g., Arabic, which definitely show a development within historical times from more primitive to less primitive. The criterion seems to be found in this: that the logical interdependence of judgments in various periods is more, or less, clearly expressed. In other words, in the more primitive stages of the development of this civilized language, the burden of the logical connection is on the communicatee; whereas in the more advanced stages, certainly toward the end of the Middle Ages, and in our period, the burden is on the speaker. He is supposed to order the main clause and the subordinate clause in such a way that the interpreter cannot go wrong.

Now, I do not know whether such a criterion would enable us to draw some sort of continuous scale from more primitive to less primitive languages. In the descriptive presentation of the history of a literary language such as Arabic, it can certainly be used to great advantage.

Hoijer: I would like to raise the question in respect to Von Grunebaum's remarks whether this is a distinction in what we call ordinary lay language or a distinction in a style of writing, or a style of exposition.

Lounsbury: It sometimes happens that when we look at another language we expect to find, for example, relative particles, subordinating particles, things like that, and, not finding them immediately, we think: How did they express subordination? How did they get a relative clause in? I had this experience with Iroquoian. It was a long time before I discovered the rules. It just happens that these depend upon features of arrangement and concord.

Von Grunebaum: What seems to me from, of course, unsystematic reading, is that in the early Arabic prose there are only two "and's." One is a real paratactic co-ordinator, which connects sentences of the same level and value: "and I came to the United States, and I visited Boston, Chicago, Los Angeles," and so forth. The other illustrates a logical progress: "I went to Boston, and then I went to New York, and then, believe it or not, to New Orleans." In the best Islamic prose, the sentences are on the whole no longer than five words, in the Arabic sense.

Then, skipping eight hundred years, we get to long unwieldy periods. They are unwieldy because Arabic has not that great mass of conjunctional material which Greek puts at the disposal of the author. But the writer makes quite clear which is the main clause—where the period ends. Whereas, in the earlier language, even in the forms expressing logical sequence, it is left very largely for the communicatee to so guess.

NEWMAN: I want to point out that we can find changes coming about in shorter periods with English. During the Elizabethan age there was a considerable use of long sentences with many subordinations. After one hundred and fifty years there are more primitive, shorter sentences. The nineteenth century is again a period of long sentences, and modern times, particularly in American literature, of short ones.

VON GRUNEBAUM: That is a question of style. The English writers of today, and those in America, could, if they would, use the conjunctional material at the disposal of English-language speakers for three or four hundred years. The Arabic writers who tried to translate Greek philosophy into Arabic had no choice. They could use only what the language provided. It was not their choice whether they would leave the burden on the interpreter or whether they wanted to take it themselves.

FEARING: This suggests the importance of the theory of communication. Whenever language is discussed, the theory of communication requires, hypothetically at least, that we recognize the operations of a communicator and a communicatee, as well as the content itself.

SINGER: I want to point out that, however legitimate this criterion of primitivity may be, it is in a context different from the three or four other contexts that we have used. We now have the usual range of ambiguity in "primitive." There is the "primitive" in the historical development of a particular culture; "primitive" as between child and adult; "primitive" in the sense of philogenetic development—subhuman to human; the last "primitive" is in the sense of contemporary primitives. Lounsbury said he had no criteria for telling whether a language is primitive in this last sense.

LOUNSBURY: I was going to ask whether we could not use the same criterion in passing, let us say, from spoken German to written German.

VON GRUNEBAUM: This is certainly so to some extent. I think it is the general experience that when we speak we cut up our sentences into smaller units because it is easier for the hearer, and even the speaker, to follow. My point is this, if I may repeat it. The modern German speaker, if he wanted to and pressed himself, could make use of all sorts of syntactical means to work out his hypertaxis in a truly Ciceronian way, whereas his ancestor a thousand years ago very likely could not have because there just was no connective material in the language of that time to do this. When one goes through Ulfilas' translation of the Bible into Gothic, one can see how hard put he was to get all of the, shall we say, sophistication of the Latin into Gothic. He could not.

HOCKETT: I think all the cases that have been cited are extremely questionable on the ground that they are based on the interpretation of written records. And written records are often incomplete; not everything need be written down.

In modern Mandarin there is a very rich system of particles and other devices for connecting clauses and indicating fine shades of difference in the relationship between clauses. In any other modern Chinese dialect that I know anything about, this is equally true. In certain modern writings you will find all these devices used. But, when Chinese writing started, it was especially under religious circumstances and with necessarily great economy of writing equipment and surfaces to write on. From that time on, for centuries, the main stylistic characteristic of written Chinese was a succinctness which put by far a greater burden on the reader rather than on the writer. So that in Confucius there are very, very few overt connectives of any kind. They will all be expressed simply by juxtaposition in a fixed order. If we were to judge anything about the history of Chinese language, in this connection, from the evidence of the dated documents, we would go very far astray.

I do not know whether this is true necessarily in the case of Arabic. We may have different kinds of records. But how can you be sure that at the time these earlier documents were produced the language which was spoken was not rich with methods of parataxis and hypertaxis, and that the people who wrote things down chose for one reason or another a style which excluded most of them?

VON GRUNEBAUM: Because we have documents, roughly of the same period, which belonged to entirely different areas. We have administrative documents, commercial documents, koranic revelations, poetry of a highly stylized kind, and we have this kind of prose. Now, it is entirely true that in these different kinds of documents the stringency of hypertactical arrangement varies. There is much more of an attempt at logical articulation in some than in others. Nevertheless, had the Koran been written four or five centuries later, a lot of ambiguities that give rise to dispute and bloodshed among the Moslems would have been avoided.

LOUNSBURY: In working with written documents, you are very likely to miss the morphemes which depend upon intonations and junctures. If you were to take an Iroquoian text, as the Indians write it, you would never be able to discover upon what relative subordination depended. There are meaningful units in language which just never get written, either by native writers or by someone who has made a complete phonetic and phonemic analysis.

VON GRUNEBAUM: This is entirely true for Arabic as well as for any other language. Do not forget that I compared written documents of the sixth century with written documents of the fourteenth century. That which was missing in the one was missing also in the other, so that a certain fairness of comparison was established.

ROBERTS: I would like to turn to the problem of the organization of thought in terms of concepts, symbols, or however you want to deal with them from the viewpoint of the people who are here, and ask if there are instruments such as cognitive maps which in your opinion ought to be discussed in this context?

FEARING: Yes. I like that phrase "cognitive maps," and think it is very useful. A cognitive map, I suppose, would be a conceptual system which is characteristic of the thought-world of the particular individual within which he perceives and thinks and otherwise operates, cognitively speaking.

ROBERTS: To what extent, do you think, can we regard speech or linguistic patterns as being models of that thought-world, and to what extent can we study cognitive maps, not divorced entirely from linguistic techniques but somewhat independently, which might permit us to compare the two?

FEARING: Is this not a reformulation of the problem we have already struggled with: To what extent can we get at the cognitive processes that are not contaminated by speech?

ROBERTS: No, I meant on a fairly empirical and practical level. I recall working with a Navaho one time, in an attempt to study the informational ranges of people through a series of cultures. I was working out a check list, debating whether I could use an actual formal questionnaire and whether the jump from agriculture to witchcraft would be sensible in one case and not in another. I wondered if there were a basic pattern of association which would make this rather lengthy questionnaire a little easier to take. Experimentally,

I worked out a series of topographical terms dealing with the map situation. I discussed them with the Navaho, in order, down through my check list. I used just principles of association which seemed reasonable to me. At the end of it I said, "How did it go, using this as a precise text?"

"It went fine," he said. "Why did you skip around so much?"

This indicated to me that he had a way of putting these things together that I did not, which could be studied and used, perhaps, in experimental procedures.

SINGER: Taking off from Roberts' question, it seems to me that a notion of a cognitive map is merely a specific example of what we have been calling a scientific construct or an ideal type, and, specifically, I think Fearing has attempted to develop a construct of primitive mentality—not in the Lévy-Bruhl sense, of course.

Parenthetically, I would like to say a word for Lévy-Bruhl. We are all familiar with the shortcomings in his theory, but he did, in some notes that were published after his death, indicate some interesting revisions in which he withdrew the theory of prelogical mentality in the sense in which he had developed it (Lévy-Bruhl 1949). He did retain the notion of *participation mystique* and developed it in such a way that it seems to me to be quite similar to Fearing's and Piaget's.

As another example of the same thing, Redfield, in his recent attempt (1953) to characterize, or at least develop an ideal construct of, the primitive world view, has, it seems to me, hit upon exactly the same characteristic, that is, the lack of sharpness of separation of self and the rest of the world.

So I think we should not be too critical of Lévy-Bruhl. You are developing a construct here of something that presumably can be applied to most primitive groups, a cultural characteristic or habitual mode in thinking and perceiving.

Now, I think that we are perhaps mistaken also in being so determined to find data that are not contaminated by the postlinguistic situation. Some of us might go on studying monkeys and children before they are contaminated by adults, but on the whole the kind of evidence we will get is going to be very meager and very suspect. We have to get the evidence for so-called prelinguistic or primitive mentalities from material that has been "contaminated" by the postlinguistic development, and work out criteria that we can apply within that situation. It seems to me that Von Grunebaum's proposed criterion is of that type. It can be applied within a postlinguistic situation, although, if it were valid, it would give us some sort of scale for grading from the least primitive to the more primitive.

Finally, judging from the spirited resistance here, not only to the notion that there are primitive languages, but to the notion that there may be criteria by which some languages might be judged more primitive than others, I would at least draw this conclusion, as a challenge to the linguists. On the one hand, we have accepted a constructed primitive *mentality*, and, on the other hand, everybody very stoutly insists there is no such thing as primitive *language; ergo*, we have discovered a characteristic of primitive mentality which is extralinguistic!

HOCKETT: I have been feeling for the last half-hour that we are just about ready to formulate a program for investigation along certain of these lines. We have at least one definable area for investigation. We know that if we perform psychological experimentation on animals, or on a child before that child has begun to learn a language, the result will be the kind of stimulus response sequences that you have when language is not playing a part. At any time after that, as soon as the human being has begun to acquire a language, any kind of psychological test you perform on the child may get results which are contaminated by language. You cannot tell. Of course, psychologists have sometimes distinguished between verbal and nonverbal tests, but that is a rather superficial thing. If the response is to push a button, rather than to write something down, you do not know whether the integration of the stimulus to which the subject is responding is governed by the internalized linguistic system or whether it is not.

It is precisely in this field that we could construct some experiments. They would have to be performed cross-culturally to get conclusions along this line. We might be able to determine the level of complexity of reaction in an individual at which linguistic factors do develop and play a part in causing differential responses from one person to another.

I have one specific such experiment, or series of experiments, in mind. It is in connection with the ways in which most people associate the words "high" and "low" in English, by a certain assignment to the scale of heights, physically, and to the scale of pitches. We all know what we mean by a "high pitch" and by a "high position," also by a "high number." Now, in Chinese, the same pair of adjectives which we can translate as "high" and "low" applies to all three of these scales and in the same way. But Greenberg tells me that among the classical Greeks the word that meant low in altitude meant what we mean by high in pitch. It seems to me that we can perform some experiments on this sort of thing which would tell us whether there is a cultural common denominator—the result of an early association which is spread throughout the human race—or whether the explanation lies with the subcultural and biological, in some more fundamental sense.

FEARING: There is quite a literature on synesthesia which I think bears on this.

HOCKETT: I know a good deal of experimentation has been done by the psychologists, and the first step in any program of this kind would be to make a very careful examination of the reports of these experiments to see the extent to which possible linguistic factors were taken into consideration in the interpretation. It may be that would settle the matter and there would be no further need for further experimentation. I sort of doubt it.

WRIGHT: I wondered if the cross-cultural Rorschach tests would provide useful data to the linguist in this connection?

HOCKETT: Someone at Cornell attempted some Rorschach run-offs with some of the Chinese students there a few years ago. The results, as I remember, were not susceptible of any particular interpretation.

MCQUOWN: I just want to add a word to this. I do not want to leave it at this particular point, because this is one instance in which we can multiply, add up to a couple of dozen, situations in which we can concretely bring together linguistic data with psychological techniques for measuring perception in one way and another and check them off against one another. With spatial perceptions one can do the same thing.

Color, of course, is an old story, which I think needs to be reworked very carefully. There is a recent article by Verne Ray on color perception, which does not mention what goes on from the point of view of language. I will not quarrel at all with his technique for flashing the cards and getting reactions. I would like to see some correlation of linguistic data with the kind of data one gets by this technique.

NEWMAN: I think we do very often load the experiment by using artificial symbols, or by using them in very special situations. I read a description of one nineteenth-century experiment in which the experimenter tried to ascertain to what degree a group of subjects could discriminate nine very similar shades of gray. He gave the shades sequential numbers from one to nine, and had the subjects learn these and see whether they could discriminate the shades better. The result was that they could do it much better.

LENNEBERG: I did some work on color terminology, trying to define the range of colors that would fit certain color words, and made a prediction of what would happen on tests. We worked not arbitrarily, but on recognition of colors in standardized tests. It so happened that the prediction that the names which had fairly unambiguous references would be much more easily remembered and recognized than names without such references was borne out. For instance, red had a better chance of being picked out of a group of colors than something which one subject might call "aqua," and another, "turquoise."

FEARING: I wonder if the study of art products of various cultures might be profitable, on the hypothesis that they reflected perceptual habits or patterns of the individuals in the different cultures? There is a little such study which uses as examples some analyses of Chinese paintings in which shadows, as I recall, were omitted and the method of depicting perspective was quite different from our own. I am a little hazy about the details. Of course, there are a great many steps in such a chain of reasoning that would need to be checked. I do not know how valid it is.

ROBERTS: We have been conducting a series of studies with the Navaho, in folklore, music, and in graphic arts. Unfortunately the results are not in yet.

We do have the negative results of one small study. Someone noticed that many of the figures in Navaho art are open; the circles are not entirely closed, and the squares have the corners off. He wondered if this would be reflected in perception. A number of figures were presented; one, for illustration, was a circle with a break in it. If it is flashed on the screen very rapidly, people see it as a closed circle. His hypothesis was that, since the Navaho are used to open circles, they might perceive more quickly than the control group. It did not work out. The perceptual level of the Navaho and that of the control group were exactly the same.

KAPLAN: Would it not be important to recognize that, in dealing with materials like those provided by the arts, your analogue is not to language but to speech. If that is the term you use for the contrast, then your analogue is not to the resources made available but rather to the resources actually being taken advantage of. In so far as relating these kinds of inferences to the Whorfian thesis is concerned, I should not suppose that they would have any bearing on it. It would be comparable to making our inferences in the kind of cases discussed earlier—not from the features of the language but from the characteristics of the style of a particular person using the language for a particular subject matter and purpose.

HOCKETT: A painting from a given culture might be comparable to a bit of speech, but a tradition, a style, or a technique in one of the arts comparable to language is a stock of possibilities. It is possible to make a comparison in various ways.

KAPLAN: Well, just consider whether, aside from any other factors, the rate of change and the degree of innovation and variation, for example in painting, are comparable to the rather broad and fundamental kind of cultural change that is involved in the change of language. I am puzzled by this reaction on the part of the linguists who, in the case of the Arabic manuscripts, put all the emphasis on the fact that these people were doing philosophy, and we have no way of knowing whether everybody also spoke that way.

I should be interested in comparing ways of painting, but these do, in fact, occupy different roles in different cultures, and no doubt Navaho react to a Navaho painting very differently from the way most Europeans would react to a Picasso painting. Factors in this area would be so critical that I should think one could more profitably investigate other types of symbolization.

ROBERTS: I just wanted to comment that Dave McAllester, who is an anthropologist and a musicologist, has been analyzing Navaho music structurally. This is quite intuitive, and he has not completed his analysis, but he sees congruence between the structure of Navaho music and the kind of formulation that was made by Kluckhohn in the Northrop volume on the Navaho world view.

FIFTH SESSION

IDENTIFYING THE DOMINANT CONCEPTUAL CATEGORIES IN A LANGUAGE

HOIJER: The discussion this morning will begin with the paper by Newman on the problem of identifying dominant conceptual categories in a language.

NEWMAN: Essentially this paper is an attempt to tackle the problem of meaning, or, perhaps, what Greenberg has called "systematic semantics," in two different ways: first, by trying to get at the meaning categories through grammatical form; and, second, through lexical form. In both cases, and I suppose this is a postulate of method for linguists, we will want to proceed from some kind of formal base.

In the first part of the paper, I attempt to see what kind of grammatical evidence there is in Yokuts for some of the conclusions reached intuitively when I dealt with the problem of style in Yokuts. My main point is simply that grammar, since it is a system and has parts, can be dealt with analytically, and we ought to be able to arrive at some kind of statement of the system of meanings on an inductive basis. The attempt I previously made with this sort of problem aimed more toward some kind of core of meaning; my impression is that Whorf, too, tried to get at meaning by picking out some kind of central characteristic of meaning in a language. I feel that this approach needs correction, in the recognition that the parts of a grammatical system have all kinds of relationships and are not merely related to a core concept as appendages. I make the more specific point that the describing of a grammatical system in terms of its meanings can be started by simply making an inventory of the large number of concepts expressed, and the problem can be pursued by trying to find which of these component concepts or conceptual categories are the more important in the particular language that you are dealing with.

The latter, of course, poses a problem of method, and I suggested three different criteria that might be used for measuring the degree of dominance. One is obligatoriness. I am not sure whether it is possible to say that one of two obligatory categories in a language is more obligatory than the other, although this strikes me as perhaps being true. But at least we do have the opposition between obligatory and optional. Certain categories are obligatory, and those can be assumed to have more importance than the categories that are expressed in optional ways. Another criterion is range. There is a category expressed in a language, e.g., tense. Does it go through all the morphological classes or word classes of the language? Do both noun and verb express tense, or is it only the verb that expresses tense? The third criterion is what I call the "selective frequency" of certain optional features. Given an optional feature, does it occur with high frequency in a sampling of the language, or very rarely?

In the second part of the paper, I deal with lexemic form as a point of departure, that is, using lexemes as units. I do not know whether one can, or to what degree one can, speak of a semantic system. The present stage of my work is highly exploratory, but I have been trying, starting from lexemes and, generally, lexemes within certain vocabulary classes, to study how the concepts show segmentation or interrelationship. Incidentally, I noticed that similar ideas were brought up in several papers. Greenberg spoke about discrimination and similarity, and I think we were speaking about the same sort of thing yesterday on a psychological level, in terms of perception increasing discrimination.

HOIJER: May I add one point to your discussion of the measures of dominance of grammatical and other categories in a language? This is in reference to the kind of text material collected. A completely false notion of frequencies of occurrence of particular categories may be gained if the texts collected are all of one kind. Many of us have depended too heavily on ritual texts of a formal character and neglected the collection of casual conversational data. The latter, if acquired in sufficient amounts, might well affect seriously our frequency counts.

GREENBERG: I was especially interested in Newman's remarks on the richness of the resources of the Yokuts verb as compared to the relatively slender use of those resources. I, and others, have made counts of the relative frequency of certain structural units—the ratio of morphemes to words in text material. This, as I call it, "index of analysis" gives a rough average for Yokuts of 2.2 morphemes per word in the verb only. As it turns out, this is just about the same as for all the other languages (to be sure, a relatively small group) that I have examined. In this respect, then, Yokuts is normal.

KAPLAN: I would like some further clarification of the notion of a conceptual category. We have two things which we can comparatively easily identify by form in some sense—the limits within which conceptual categories are to be localized. There is at the one extreme a formal specification, that is, a specification in some kind of structural or linguistic terms. If I understand them rightly, Newman's criteria are really criteria for the selection of those forms, or formal features, that can reasonably be expected to be significant with respect to conceptual categories. At the other extreme there is what might be called an "empirical class," to use the term "class" as distinct from category, which is simply the limitation in a culture of an aggregate of items as belonging to a particular class. I would not expect that we would normally have any difficulty in finding those specifications. In fact, it comes to nothing other than recognizing which words in the language name general properties. But now I am at a loss for any clear idea of what, as between these two, constitutes a conceptual category.

If I work from the first end, I run the danger of tautologizing. Last year, in a group concerned with a similar problem, much fuss was occasioned in the minds of the nonlinguists when Hoijer reported that the Navaho category of round objects includes items such as "news"; none of the philosophers and other people present could begin to understand why "news" is a round object. And, of course, if you just identify a form class as "round object," then that "news" is a round object is a tautological consequence of its formal characteristics. Something, then, has to be done with that notion of round object before it can be usable for our purposes as a conceptual category.

The trouble with working from the other end, as I see it, is this: it is simply an ordering, in terms of increasing generality, of the classes that a language provides for. Your so-called conceptual categories would simply be the most general classes, and I would not expect those to be either significant for culture patterns or of particular philosophic or any other interest.

A third alternative, which is for me a kind of model of what we have in mind, is this: Apparently, we mean by a conceptual category that kind of general empirical class which we would fall back on if we were playing "Twenty Questions." That is, it is the scheme in terms of which every particular item that is considered is given some kind of localization. We have plenty of classes available to English speakers other than living or dead; animal, vegetable, or mineral; male or female; but the chances are that if we were to play "Twenty Questions" these would be the sorts of things that would be picked out to make the localization.

Now, I do not know if those are conceptual categories, or what conceptual categories are. Supposing I have decided on the basis of your criteria which of the formal features are important, how do I get from the purely linguistic level to a concept level with respect to them?

HOCKETT: The term "conceptual category" is no necessary part of the machinery, either for our purely formal task of finding out the structure of a language, the pattern of a language, or for handling semantic patterns. Therefore, we should not use it, and such questions would not arise.

MCQUOWN: I do not want to level the guns on conceptual categories right away, because I myself use the term very loosely, and Whorf uses it not only loosely but with considerable grace and facility, but I agree entirely with Hockett. If we set up a priori a contrast of this kind, then we have created a needless difficulty.

I was trying in my paper to build a bridge between the formal categories which we can get out of language, by techniques which have been elaborated with a considerable amount of effort over a hundred-year period, and the conceptual categories on the other end of the continuum. These categories we can intuit out, but we cannot at the present time show them to all comers as we can linguistic forms. I was careful to point out that I do not naïvely assume that we can, at one end of this continuum, equate particular linguistic forms to particular conceptual categories at the other end. On the contrary, the thing is much more complex than that, and we have to go step by step. We have to bring in, not only the forms of language, but the forms of all other cultural activities, and find out how these things in the final analysis add up to particular large, general categories which determine the thought-world and our activities.

KAPLAN: But the procedure that you mentioned seems to me to be the tautological one that you, among others, very properly warned us against. If you are going to identify your conceptual category in terms which rest not just on your analysis of language but also, in an essential way, on your analysis of all the other culture patterns—if you are finally going to say, "Yes, Whorf is right; it turns out that language is very closely associated with these other culture patterns"—this will simply be a restatement of what you have done in order to identify the pattern.

McQuown: That does not frighten me in the least, because I do not think there is any other way.

Let me take another approach. Suppose a particular philosopher has worked out within the framework which God and his environment gave him a particular system of categories with which he operates, classifies the universe with a reasonable amount of satisfaction, and so on. Suppose we want to work out the ontogeny of these categories. The method which I have suggested for working out general cultural categories could be applied to the particular subculture of this philosopher, and explain the various factors and their interrelationships that brought about his particular categorization. Questions as to the generality of this categorization—the ways it is shared by all of his society, what portions are shared by him and a small group of people, and so on—come after the determination of the ontogeny and the inner make-up, and they are very important questions. I do not want to rule them out at all.

Hockett: I want to express agreement with this last by paraphrasing it. What the linguists together with the anthropologists can do in the case of the term "conceptual category" is, first, not use it except in quotation marks, and, second, do a lexicographical job with it. If somebody uses it, find out under what conditions, how it fits into the system of terminology and other behavior that person manifests—exactly as you would with the Algonquian word *manitou*, or any other word. It is not part of the linguist's metalanguage.

Greenberg: That was almost what I was going to say. People using this term seem to have meant by it roughly the following: A conceptual category is the meaning segment, if any, common to all the members of a single formally defined class of morphemes. Now, it is a hypothesis, actually, that all the meanings which are found in a formally defined class of morphemes have a common element. Very common in the history of the Western world, among philosophers particularly, has been the assumption that all morpheme classes do have such a common meaning. If it cannot be defined grammatically, on the basis of actual experience, then you make up some word, which means that you might as well use the grammatical word because that is how it has been arrived at anyway. So, for example, substance becomes related to substantive, if you want to say what is common to all the meanings of root morphemes for nouns in English.

Lounsbury: I would like to comment on two parts of your definition: "common to all the members of the form class" and "if any."

If we assume that a form class is defined by means of formal criteria, then it is a form class, and we would not necessarily expect that there be semantic features common to all the members of the class. It may very well be that there is a semantic feature common to a large number, a majority even, of the members of the class, and it may even be that you can get evidence that a people using the language continue to generalize and analogize from this. If you can catch them in the act of so analogizing, I would be willing to admit that a certain form class represents a conceptual category, even though this is not common to all the members of the class.

Now, I have caught English speakers and Portuguese speakers analogizing in this way. Portuguese has quite a number of pairs of words which have the same root but have masculine and feminine endings, such as *mato,* which is masculine, and denotes the sparse, dry-area scrub forest, as opposed to *mata,* which is feminine, and denotes the dense tropical rain forest. Then there are *copo,* which is an ordinary glass that one drinks liquid out of, and *copa,* which is a large goblet or loving cup, such as is awarded for athletic skill; *sapato,* which is a shoe, and *sapata,* which is a large heavier peasant boot; and many others. This is just an example, and nothing can ever be proved by examples. But I draw from such phenomena the suggestion that a certain form class may have a meaning, or denote a conceptual category, let us say, which is common to a large number of the members of a class but not to all.

HOIJER: I might add that form classes in the same language and at a given period in its history will vary in the degree to which content may be found of the kind that you have described. An interesting point that Sapir used to refer to as a dynamic factor in the growth of language is the passing out of existence of certain formal categorizations, at least in their semantic usefulness, within the lifetime of a language or within a particular period of a language.

KAPLAN: I want to comment on a suggestion made by Greenberg. Incidentally, with respect to the instance of substance and substantive, I should have supposed that the relationship was the other way around—that the substantive was indicated by the grammarian as that which designates substances rather than that the metaphysician took a grammarian's category. I do not deny that the metaphysician was operating with a grammatical category, but that is different from the grammarian's category, and it is the grammatical category, I assume, that we are trying to track down.

I would like to get a reaction from Newman as to the feeling expressed by Hockett and Greenberg concerning conceptual categories. I cannot quite reconcile that standpoint with what I take to be the standpoint in his paper, and it is the latter which seems to me to follow Whorf.

NEWMAN: When I was using the term "grammatical categories," I was not sure myself what I meant, and I think one important feature of tackling problems of this kind is that we may come to a better understanding of what the things are that we subsume under the term. For example, I would like to know, in connection with the discussion of Lounsbury, to just what extent in a given language you will find meaning common to the members of a class. Are there some languages where you have classes in which, say, 60 per cent of your forms fit into a meaning class and the others scatter, and other languages in which 90 per cent clearly have a common meaning and the rest scatter? Is this a differential feature of language? If you have, let us say, a two-sided formal category such as singular and plural, will you get more of this scatter, or less, than if you have a three- or four-sided system? These are all parts of the problem of finding out the nature of the phenomenon that we are dealing with. I feel that at the stage in which we do not know what we are talking about we can use any term and frankly say that we do not know its content.

HOCKETT: I still think that linguists have to learn to speak more clearly than they do when they use a term so redolent with metaphysic connotations as "conceptual category." We should have a different terminology to discuss possible common meanings of some of the forms which are of a single grammatical class.

Now, that is a very real problem for linguistic and semantic investigation, and it is one we can tackle. We have enough data to say some things in a number of cases. We can say some things about gender in French, gender in German, and the two gender systems of Russian; we can say some things about the animate versus inanimate gender classification in Algonquian; we can say things about a number of categories of English, even. I think if you will examine any such grammatical categorization you will find—particularly if you look at what happens to innovations or new formations— that there are in every case some classifications which, so far as you can tell, are purely arbitrary and some which are not purely arbitrary.

Take the Algonquian animate and inanimate, for example. All nouns referring to people or animals or spirits are animate, and those nouns remain animate no matter how they may be used in a transferred sense. For example, if you use the animate noun meaning *person* in a transferred sense meaning *doll*, it is still animate. On the other hand, if you use an inanimate noun in a transferred sense to refer to a person or animal or spirit, it becomes animate. If an inanimate noun occurs in a context in which the thing named by it is assigned animate properties, such as speaking or understanding speech, it becomes animate in that context, as is shown by what happens to an adjacent word or by what happens to the inflection of a particular word. You can go along for quite a time stating what Bloomfield in his unpublished grammar calls "definable gender," but then you have to add a list of nouns which are, as a matter of fact, animate, although none of the general statements that you have made up to that time could possibly be taken as covering them.

I think that in every case of the kind you will find two factors involved: a purely arbitrary inherited factor, and certain semantic guiding principles. We do not need "conceptual category" as a term in this, and linguists should learn to speak more clearly than to use such words.

LOUNSBURY: I agree that it would be better to use a different term, but I would like to point out that, whatever we call it, this particular thing is not given by formal methods of linguistic analysis. It is only hinted at, foreshadowed. And our formal classes, in turn, are not defined by any such semantic features. They are defined in formal terms. It is really the task of language-and-culture studies to see what correspondence, if any, there may be between them.

KAPLAN: We are concerned somehow or other with a relation between language and something else involved in culture, which is variously describable as conceptual categories, thought-worlds—all the rest. Now, concededly, all these terms are vague, but I do not see how we can even begin to go on if we refuse to clarify them.

But one of the difficulties that I am still confronted with is the justification for the notion that certain connections are arbitrary and some are not. I can see how in certain cases you would be justified in saying something is arbitrary if you were able to show through analogy of sounds, or something of the kind, that one word had been treated as though it were a different word. But otherwise, what appears to you to be arbitrariness may simply be the reflection of a fundamental difference in the conceptual categories of the culture using that language and those of your own.

I would like to propose a specific example, very closely allied and possibly identical with one which Whorf discussed, which might provide a focal point. One of the basic divisions that is made among explicit philosophies, and I would suppose it expresses a basic division also among thought-worlds or conceptual categories that people themselves employ, is that between the Heraclitean schools and the Parmenidean, that is, those for whom the world is fundamentally a matter of processes and events and happenings and those for whom the world is fundamentally a matter of objects or things or substances. Now, I would like to hear you discuss these two categories of conceptualization in relation to linguistic forms such as verbs or tenses. Surely we are not going to say that the mere fact that one language has a great many tenses and a great many verbs indicates that the conceptual categories that it includes are close to the Heraclitean pattern, whereas if the language goes easy on number of tenses and discriminations in them and verbs, that it involves the other kind of conceptual categories. I am very distrustful of that sort of thing, and it looks as though that is what Whorf is doing. I wonder whether Newman is attempting to do something similar but wishing to set down certain constraints so as to make what he is doing more probable, or whether he is trying to do something different.

NEWMAN: I suppose all linguists are familiar with the fact that, in setting up a difference between nouns and verbs, the distinction in some cases is clear and in other cases is not clear. There are overlappings. In many cases languages will be built up in such a way that the word class in which events are described seems to be the central one; you start with that, and when you try to make up references to entities you derive from the verb class. I do not know just what that means, but I would like to see how it fits in with other facts of the grammatical categories and their meaning contents. I think it might be possible to say that certain languages are, to put it very flatly, event-dominated, and my impression is that there are fewer languages that are substance- or thing-dominated.

VOEGELIN: One study, much neglected, may serve to focus the problem. What happens to grammatical categories, and the conceptual categories, if any, that are associated with them, when a language begins to break down? This breakdown is taking place in many American Indian communities, and it may account, at least in part, for the seeming arbitrariness of their categories.

HOIJER: I would like to add a point on the question of the arbitrariness of classifications. There is a classification of verbs in Navaho, whereby verbs having to do with movement are classified in terms of what sorts of things are being moved. If a person speaks of the movement of a boulder, for example, he uses one verb form; if he speaks of a movement of something that is slender, like a stick, he uses another verb form, and so on through something like sixteen or seventeen classifications. It is not too difficult to define these classes, at least in a rough way; they correspond in large part to semantic realities. But the round-object class in Navaho, while it is not infrequently used in reference to round solid objects, is also used of many concepts, like "news," which have no such characteristics. This comes about, it seems, because of acculturational factors—nearly all the new concepts that have entered Navaho culture in recent times are put into the round-object class. Arbitrariness in this instance, then, is due largely to historical circumstance.

McQuown: I want to point out that any linguistic category, that is, any formal category, is inevitably the result of history, although the original extralinguistic reasons for assigning certain things to this category may have been lost in the dim and distant past. It is not only the result of history, it is a part of history, and at the present time may have its previous orientation completely skewed by having something new come into it.

My other point is on the morpheme. I want to generalize morpheme from language to culture. If this particular definition for a linguistic formal unit were generalized to the whole of culture, then the problem of meaning would vanish. You can speak of meaning only when you limit yourself to one part; then you can say that that part has meaning in terms of the rest.

With respect to the Parmenidean and Heraclitean schools, I might make the somewhat facetious suggestion that they developed these two particular ways of looking at the universe—this is not a new idea at all—because the language which they both spoke happened to contain a major subject-predicate dichotomy, and one of them decided to concentrate on the predicate and explain the whole universe in terms of that, while the other decided to take the subject and explain the whole universe in terms of that. Supposing they had spoken a language where there were three or four or five possibilities? There might have been that many schools arising.

Greenberg: Let me try to clarify my earlier remarks on ascertaining the meanings of morpheme classes and the arbitrary nature of these. First of all, the membership of a morpheme class, say, the animate versus inanimate classes in the Algonquian languages, is determined by linguistic procedures alone. That means only one type of behavior, linguistic behavior, is being observed.

Once this is done, the obvious question arises: Can we find parallels in other aspects of behavior? Thus many animate nouns in Algonquian have reference to things we should normally call animate, and so also with the inanimate nouns. In both classes, however, we find a residue: nouns which are linguistically classed as animate or inanimate but which refer to things that cannot be so classified. So we say, provisionally, that these inclusions are arbitrary.

Of course it may be that some of these so-called arbitrary inclusions are not really so; the people may behave, let us say, as if tobacco were animate, and not the inanimate thing we hold it to be. But we avoid the tautology of saying that Algonquian speakers believe tobacco to be animate because they classify the term, linguistically, as an animate noun. We can justify their regarding tobacco as animate only if nonlinguistic behavior toward tobacco corroborates the linguistic.

KAPLAN: I want to make a statement with respect to one that McQuown made earlier on Heraclitus and Parmenides. The statement that the philosophy derives from the grammar of Greek has been very frequently made. I ran across it in Charles Peirce, who attributed it to the linguist Sayce. I remember reading Sayce's two volumes and finding nothing more than the one sentence quoted by Peirce that if Aristotle had been a Mexican his logic would have been different.

Now, when such a statement is made, is there anything to be said other than that Greek has a subject and predicate and that the subjective formal category relates to substances and the predicate formal category relates to predicates? Most philosophers would be utterly unimpressed merely by that fact. Have any of the many people who have made this kind of connection, linguists or others, done anything to fill in the gaps and make that conclusion more acceptable?

MCQUOWN: Not to my knowledge. I threw it out semifacetiously, because I make all sorts of qualifications. After all, all the Indo-European-speaking peoples have this particular subject-predicate dichotomy. I am sure that this kind of distinction in the Indo-European languages is not responsible for these two schools of philosophers in Greece. After all, they did not arise elsewhere throughout the Indo-European-speaking territory, and there are many languages throughout the world that have this subject-predicate dichotomy. But if you put this area of optionality, of choice, together with the other factors in the culture of the time, then you can explain the limits within which the linguistic and cultural operated and make plausible some kind of a connection between this linguistic fact and the other facts in the culture.

SINGER: I am struck by the all-or-none approach we are taking to the problem. We are fascinated by the Whorf hypothesis, or "hunch" as you call it, but every time we try to break the problem down in terms of some kind of methodology whereby we can investigate it, the result seems to be completely negative and skeptical. I wonder whether that is psychological, or whether it merely reflects the state of the problem. One of the things that interests me about papers like Newman's, Greenberg's, and Hockett's is that they make some effort to break down the problem in terms of the kind of inferences that might be made, and I wonder whether it would not be profitable to stick to that level of discussion.

Coming back to the last comment that Greenberg made, I would certainly agree that one cannot tell a priori, at least from the structure of the language, which of the conceptual categories are dominant, nor could one tell very much about them without examining verbal and other behavior. I wonder, however, whether the linguist is not being overmodest. Is that all one can tell about the matter on the basis of language? Many of us nonlinguists were more or less seduced into an interest in language, because we were after methods for ascertaining the conceptual system and the value system and the orientational system of a culture, and linguists led us to believe that they had a fairly precise and controlled method available through a study of language.

Now, take a problem of determining, not a whole system but, say, the dominance of a conceptual category. (I would not argue about the definition of "conceptual category." On the common-sense level I think we all know what it means.) Take a category like "time": obviously "time" is handled in the morphology of language, in different ways in different languages, and Newman has suggested some criteria for determining whether or not "time" is a dominant category. To stay at the grammatical level obviously is not enough. But suppose we go into semantics and ask the question: How many and what kind of "time" words are there? That is still not verbal behavior. Suppose we find a language in which there is an elaborate tense distinction, but very few time words. Are the distinctions made grammatically and not made semantically, or vice versa? Then is "time" a dominant category or not? Now, can we pursue the problem along those lines and say, even before we get to verbal behavior, whether there is a way of deciding which categories are dominant at the level of semantics and grammar?

NEWMAN: I do not know how to handle the matter of dominance in lexical studies. The only way of trying to come to any conclusions on this kind of problem that I can see is a purely indefinite one.

I am perfectly willing to go at problems of this sort by taking specific languages and seeing what we can do with setting up methods. I suppose one way would be to see, if there is a tense system, whether the formal grammatical features having to do with tense occur in the same utterances with the lexemes having to do with tense. There is a great deal of one and not of the other, perhaps. Do we very often get them joined?

I do not think we would want to set up a distinction between what you referred to as empirical classes and grammatical, or conceptual, categories. We know enough to say, I think, that will not work out.

LOUNSBURY: One way of getting at dominance in lexical items involves text analysis plus ethnography. I had always been very skeptical of this notion of themes in culture when I read about it, yet I find that it is sort of inescapable if we do text analysis, say, with Iroquoian religious texts. We find the theme of giving thanks coming up over and over again, in numerous lexical items. We also observe that this type of discourse comes up, not only at religious gatherings, but at every possible gathering—social, political, or what-not. One just about has to conclude that it is a major theme in Iroquoian thought, but it is reflected in lexical items.

I feel that we have approached this problem from the more difficult end, namely, the things that get wrapped up in morphological apparatus. If we would approach it from the other end—the analysis of lexical items, of important lexical sets, and so on—we would not be anywhere nearly so confused and discouraged. To be sure, the results would not get the spectacular type of phrasing which has seduced nonlinguists into the field, and our activity would look much more like that of old-time philologists except that we would be collecting our own documents from living languages. It would look like the work anthropologists have been doing all along, and it would look, to some extent, like the work of literary critics. It seems to me that is the easy end of this whole problem, and it is the one which I would have the courage to tackle.

GREENBERG: This is more or less to back up Lounsbury and also to refer to something that came up the first day. It seems to me that there is no difference in principle between what we call lexical and grammatical or morphological. The problem is the meaning of morphemes. Certain morphemes are root morphemes, and certain ones are inflectional or derivational morphemes. In principle there is no difference between testing whether certain distinctions in kin terms are correlated with differences in behavior and testing whether the distinction between past tense and future tense in a language is so correlated.

Now, we can easily ascertain when it is appropriate to a situation to distinguish between cousin and brother, and how often this comes up in daily life. But when we get into things like the meanings of morphemes in inflectional categories, the class itself is usually a very small one. If it is compulsory, it is almost bound to be something which is quite important in the life of people in general, e.g., all people constantly react relevantly to time.

KENNARD: The point has been made several times, and sort of passed over, that we take for granted that the dictionary, or lexicography, is a rough index of the emphasis on the items in the culture. But lexical items alone are not enough. They are combined within a particular structure, and there are a variety of ways within any linguistic system and in any cultural context to convey a certain kind of meaning.

GREENBERG: It was to deal with precisely this kind of problem that I set up what might have looked like this unnecessary business of elementary meaning units in my paper. The idea was to put together in one category all those meanings which could not be resolved into other meanings.

NEWMAN: I wonder, too, in relation to what you said on the matter of method here, whether it is not best to deal with lexemes. I am talking about these all the time, and I find that seems to be the best way of tackling this problem of meanings outside of the grammatical system. The way I have been operating is to take some term, usually a word, and get a number of English words translating it. Usually, the informant will give me a one-word translation to begin with. That seems to be a standard convention for translating, but we know, of course, that it is not very good. Then he will start giving me other words, that is, adding, and then he will begin qualifying or subtracting from each one. Now, my feeling is that, if we can do that enough, we can at least approximate meanings. We will never get the full meaning of any term, but the more we can add and subtract, the closer we can come to the full content of the term given.

SINGER: While it is true that, in principle, there may be no difference between a lexical and grammatical analysis, at least to a nonlinguist, all sorts of psychological and other practical differences arise. Here, again, I think it is the linguists who have more or less led us to believe that speakers are largely unconscious of *grammatical* categories like number or tense, whereas they are not unconscious of number and time and sex differentiations when lexically expressed. I wonder whether, at least in that sense, there still is not a very important difference to be made.

Second, should we not develop some fairly precise technique to describe linguistically how a language deals with a category, not only in grammar, not only in the lexicon, but in all the ways the language as an instrument provides? If English does not have the dominance attached to gender in grammar that some of the European languages have, there are obviously many other ways in which English handles sex distinctions or the sex categories. So you would have to have some summarizing description of the ways in which English deals with sex differences, and then make a comparison with another language which may deal with them in some other way, including a fairly systematic allowance for it in the case of something like gender.

Finally, I would suggest the following distinction, which is also suggested in Hockett's paper: you have, on the one hand, the purely systemic aspects of the language, whether they be in syntax or semantics, and then you have verbal or nonverbal behavior, either uses of the language or concrete manifestations of the particular attitudes, values, and categories involved. Now, it seems to me that in cultural analysis and in kinship analysis there is an intermediate level which might be useful to consider, that is, what Kluckhohn and Bateson called cultural structure, "ethos" and "eidos," which, I take it, would correspond roughly to what Whorf calls the "habitual" modes of perceiving, thinking, and, I would add, feeling. Cultural structure is neither verbal behavior, necessarily, nor nonverbal behavior, but is deduced and abstracted from verbal and nonverbal behavior. In the case of kinship analysis, of course, you have social structure abstracted from verbal and nonverbal behavior, so that language, as your set of habits, is to verbal behavior as cultural structure is to cultural behavior and as social structure is to social usage. Perhaps if we try to compare the systemic aspects of language and the ways in which these categories appear in them as, say, an attempt to describe cultural structure or total culture pattern, we might have another way of checking the type of theories suggested by Whorf.

GREENBERG: Your last point is implicit in what has already been said. When someone says there is a distinction in the behavior of a paternal aunt and a maternal aunt which corresponds with the fact that they are addressed by different terms, he is saying in effect that he finds, with far more than chance frequency, that certain behavior is followed with one relative and certain other behavior, with the second relative. We can set up many such hypotheses on the basis of linguistic facts; the problem is how to test them. In certain areas of culture, like kinship, there appears to be a high correlation of terms and behavior, but my guess is that we should get only a negative result from an examination of tense, for example, in its relationship to behavior.

SINGER: Let me give you just one example of the kind of thing that bothers me. I happen to be interested in the classification of cultures into "shame" cultures and "guilt" cultures. I am told that some cultures, like the Hopi, do not have a word for guilt, they use chiefly a word which means to us shame. On the other hand we know that our culture uses excessively the word for guilt and related words. Are we to conclude from that, that the Hopi do not feel as much guilt as we do? It seems to me that if you followed some of the preliminary suggestions of inferring from language to behavior and to culture, that would certainly be the inference to be drawn. Yet we find cases where Hopi feel guilt, cases where people in our culture call "guilt" feelings something that is obviously shame, and cases in our culture where we have a very self-conscious ethic of guilt. We are not so sure, then, that we can make such an inference. We would have to have some way of testing the extent to which we feel guilt and shame and Hopi feel guilt and shame. In addition to knowing the language and the words for shame and guilt in both cases, we should have to know something about the cultural norms and the ethics of both cultures on this question of guilt and shame, because that, in turn, would help us to interpret whatever statistical observations we make of behavior.

HOIJER: With one qualification that I should like to add. The base in your Hopi example is too narrow; you would not be justified in drawing any inferences at all. This is only a clue to a kind of inference that might be drawn providing you got additional semantic, grammatical, or whatever other kind of linguistic material might be necessary. In other words, fashions of speaking are in a sense lines of similarity which connect a large number of meaning categories that you find in a language, rather than specific items of meaning contrast.

The method involves what I like to call "total immersion" in the language. The meaning categories of a language, when you take the trouble to pay as close attention to them analytically as we customarily do to the structural features of language, are cumulative in their effect, so that you gain an intuitive knowledge of these lines of similarity or fashions of speaking that pervade, or appear to pervade, the language. At least intuitively, you know that they are different from those lines of similarity or fashions of speaking which are in other languages that you may know about. The question of defining the difference, of expressing the contrast, is an exceedingly difficult one, because you must do it in a language, with an apparatus which was not constructed for this purpose and which you have to twist about to do so.

SIXTH SESSION

THE PROBLEM OF THE WHORF HYPOTHESIS

HOIJER: I have asked Kaplan to review briefly, and in his own terms, our progress to date.

KAPLAN: I took it that the general problem with which this conference was to be concerned was the predictive relations, if any, of language, not merely to other patterns of culture but, in Whorf's terms, to some kind of cultural configuration or theme or thought-world. Even in connection with that very first formulation of the problem we have certainly had some disagreements, though they have been more tacit than overt. On the few occasions on which any reference has been made to something like cultural themes or general configurations, I have caught as many expressions of doubt and distrust of any such notion as of warm approval of it, so that we have to leave the problem equivocal in that respect even in its initial formulation.

The first thing that has struck me about the general character of all the discussion is that it has been very largely concerned with the premise of this inference—the first term in this predictive relation—rather than with the second, or the conclusion. It has been, that is to say, linguistic rather than cultural.

We began with a discussion of the ways in which we ought to specify the first term of our relationship, that is, language, the particular features of language, or the modes of description of those features which might plausibly be regarded as providing premises for such inferences. There was one point—one of the very, very few that I have registered—on which there seems to have been a considerable area of agreement, namely, that these characteristics of language have to be treated in terms of probabilities, frequencies, degrees, and various other kinds of quantitative or semiquantitative specifications, rather than in terms of the larger, looser qualitative descriptions that Whorf and others seem to operate with. There have been problems, even there, that we sometimes skirted and in a few instances went into a little further—problems having to do with the contrast between language and verbal behavior or, perhaps, for a sharper contrast, between language and style. If we are going to be characterizing the relevant features of language in terms of frequencies and probabilities, then we are discussing, as Hockett said, what in fact is said in a language or, at any rate, the ease with which certain things could be said, which I suppose will relate itself to the probability or frequency of their occurrence.

Another problem that we have been struggling with, in connection with the specification of language, is that of the formalism of the specifications. I mean, not the formalism of the linguist's own language, not the formalism of the metalanguage of the systematic description, but the formalism of what is being described in the object language concerned. We have spoken many times of systematic abstention from the nonformal aspects of the language being considered, but I have not felt any clear-cut statement of just what the positions of various people here are on that point, as it relates to theses like Whorf's. Partly we have been confused, I think, by a question of an intellectual division of labor: whose business is it to study meaning? But there have been also some principal questions, for in places where we have come closest to directly facing the nonformal science of the object language, it has been suggested by a number of people that there is really no way in which a study of the semantic features of language can be truthfully separated from a study of the culture as a whole. This arose again and again in questions concerning whether the interest in lexicon is merely an appendix to grammar, and this was qualified only in the respect that, after all, the lexicon may be important for establishing certain structural features of the language, or, possibly, its history. But what of the lexicon which may be critically important in allowing us to make the kind of inference or bridge that constitutes the posing of the original problem?

I think it is also worth mentioning, in connection with the linguistic emphasis, that McQuown's paper suggested an extension of the methods and concepts that are employed for the specification of language to a specification of culture. I do not know whether there was explicit disagreement with respect to this. There was no explicit agreement among us, nor much discussion at all of the characteristics of culture which may be inferred from a knowledge of various features of language.

Now, in spite of this linguistic emphasis there has been a considerable interest in the semantic side of the picture, but here there really has been a whole complex of problems and disagreements.

Voegelin's discussion of the first part of his paper was concerned, as Hockett afterward formulated it in terms of its bearing on our general problem, with the possibilities of some kind of universal frame of reference or, at least, some kind of frame of reference which transcended the particular culture or language in the community being considered. Others suggested that, not only may there not be such a frame, but it might also be quite dispensable. It might be possible to operate in terms of direct comparisons from culture to culture or language to language rather than by first relating each of them to some single co-ordinate system, frame, calibrating instrument, or what you will. Among the frames of reference possible, there was still considerable doubt as to whether these were going to be looked for in perceptual terms, particularly the Gestalt or physiognomic phenomena that we considered, or whether there was some kind of semantic absolute that could be developed and fruitfully applied in this area.

A second range of problems dealing with the semantic side was those brought up in the discussion of Fearing's paper on the perception-conceptualization continuum. One of the difficulties which that got us into might be labeled the problem of linguistic self-sufficiency, since one of the points that Fearing was urging was that Whorf had failed to take account of prelinguistic experience, or whatever information we might have about characteristics of the reacting organism that are not closely dependent upon linguistic phenomena. Fearing was inclined to formulate Whorf's hypotheses, or consider investigation into them, in terms of possible relations between languages and perceptual processes, whereas others here thought of them primarily in terms of relationships between language and, if I may say so, possible perceptual or cultural kinds of phenomena.

We also had the problem there, rather a fundamental one I think, of whether we are involved in unnecessary and perhaps confusing thinking in psychologizing the linguistic process and discussing conceptualization, rather than contenting ourselves with putting the matter solely in terms of the manipulation of symbols. There is, on the other hand, the possibility that we may be deluding ourselves into supposing that we can deal with linguistic phenomena from the relevant standpoints without relating them to a theory of communication.

We were also involved with the problem concerning the relevance to our main inference of developmental states, both of the individual and, if possible, with respect to language. This was focused around our discussion of primitiveness, everyone apparently being quite willing to talk about the primitiveness of a culture but most people being quite unwilling to talk about the primitiveness of language, although some attention was given to the possible specification of traits—perhaps stylistic traits, perhaps linguistic ones—which might reasonably be related to various developmental states localized elsewhere.

And, finally, in connection with semantic frames and contents, we did discuss, I think for the first time this morning with Newman's paper, something which comes closest to the conclusion of the Whorfian inference, namely, conceptual categories or various other such notions. Two rather basic questions arose. First, is it meaningful to talk about anything of this kind, and, second, even if so, is it necessary to bring anything of this kind into the picture in order to do something with our basic inference? That, I think, we virtually left in terms of the question.

A third set of problems is that where we pursued directly the content of the inference by trying to break it down, as Singer pointed out this morning, into problems of the middle range—neither the vast Whorfian or older type of flat statement of connection nor the rather detailed and specific and restricted linguistic considerations. Those matters arose largely in connection with Greenberg's and Newman's papers. Here I think there were two main problems.

One is the question of whether one can fruitfully operate in terms of some kind of dichotomy—I am not going to try to label it further—of the sort that has been posed in terms of a contrast between meaning and structure. For instance, Greenberg suggested this morning that all we have is a specification of elementary meaning units in a language; they will have different structural characteristics but all of them equally will have meanings, and if we are going to be interested in what these meanings will allow us to infer about culture, it is not going to be useful for us to try to impose on these meanings a dichotomization of this sort.

The other problem that arose, and was already prefigured in a number of statements in several papers, is this: once we do go into this mid-range semantic analysis with respect to the Whorfian inference, then we find that there is no way in which we can satisfactorily carry out that analysis without making full use of ethnological materials. But if we are going to do that, then the inference reduces itself to a tautology; it would thereby certainly acquire truth. It would not necessarily lose its value or interest, but it would certainly be radically transformed in character from what I would imagine Whorf and most of his readers suppose him to have been saying. I do not know that we have even suggested some way of getting out of this impasse of either being unable to get at the contents of language or getting at them by way of those very cultural materials to which we would like to infer on the basis of a knowledge of the contents.

SINGER: Your report hits at all the problems, but it seems to me to hit a little too hard at the basic problem. That reference to ethnographic and ethnological materials lands us in tautology is something that I am not at all convinced about. I think that perhaps the tautology arises only if you define the problem in very general terms: if you get down to specific cases, it need not be a tautology. For example, if you have the statement, which you might call a "linguistic proposition," about a language, that certain categories are dominant in this language—presumably that is a proposition which linguistic analysis can establish—that is the premise. The conclusion or the inference drawn from that might be, right or wrong, that users of that language habitually are led to perceive or think about a certain area of experience that is related to this category. If it happens to be "time," say that they habitually attach a good deal of importance to time. Now, I called it a conclusion, but that could be an independent proposition established by cultural analysis and ethnological observation.

I do not see why the two propositions are merely two ways of saying the same thing. You say that, because a particular category of time is dominant in a language, you are led to expect that the users of that language habitually perceive or think about time in a certain way. That does not sound like a tautology at all. In fact, in most cases it seems to me it was argued that it was false. I wonder whether we could elaborate that, because if your intimations are correct, then it does seem to me that we are wasting our time—that we are led into this by a series of mistakes.

KAPLAN: Not only do I not intend to defend the accuracy of my account as to what happened, but I certainly do not mean to defend as conclusive, or even as my temporary position, a kind of difficulty which I stated. That is, I do not think that, in fact, this inference is tautologous, but this seems to me to be a focus of difficulty.

With respect to your specific example, as I recall the way the problem arose in discussion, if you are going to talk about the way people habitually think, you are going to be very hard put to it to find specifications of how they think that are other than specifications of how they speak. But only in so far as you do it in terms of nonlinguistic behavior do you get out of the danger of tautology. This is one area of difficulty.

The second sort of difficulty is, to disagree with you and put the matter the other way around, that as long as you speak in general terms it does not look so bad, but when you get down to specifics it becomes tough. If you label that category a time category, in general terms, no one is going to have any difficulties because, roughly speaking, we know that these tenses have something to do with time or this set of lexical items specifies time. But when someone asks you to detail with what justification you are interpreting these specific features of the language, structural or semantic, as having the given meaning content, the chances are that in supporting your interpretation of these linguistic features you will again be making use of those cultural features to which subsequently you make an inference.

SINGER: That seems to me much too general. First of all, you may be able to establish the cultural propositions without reference to verbal behavior It is very difficult, but a priori there is no reason to argue that you have to establish them only with reference to the verbal behavior; they might be established with reference to nonverbal behavior. Second, even if you established the cultural propositions with reference to verbal behavior, I see no reason why it should be exactly the same verbal behavior that is involved in establishing the linguistic propositions, and if it is not the same verbal behavior, then, again, I do not see your difficulty.

The difficulty arises only when you say—in general—that you have to establish it with reference to verbal or linguistic behavior, but you also establish the linguistic propositions with reference to verbal behavior, and, therefore, you are just looking at the same thing from two different points of view. If you pin down the verbal data from which the characterization of the language is drawn and pin down the verbal data from which the characterization of the culture is drawn, there may be two entirely different kinds of things. As Kennard pointed out this morning, you have to refer to numerous different kinds of situations, and those situations may not be the same for establishing linguistic propositions and for establishing cultural propositions. Even if it were granted that most cultural propositions had to refer to verbal behavior, for a noncoincidence of the verbal data involved, I cannot see how, logically, you can say that they would be exactly the same data, and if they are not the same data then there is no tautology.

FEARING: I would like some further discussion on this question of the difficulties of the observation of nonlinguistic behavior. Those difficulties are probably very great, but it is also easy to exaggerate them, and I think we tended to do so when we discussed this earlier. There are examples of this in Whorf; one follows his discussion of time (1952: 41):

> It is clear how the emphasis on "saving time" which goes with all the above and is very obvious objectification of time, leads to a high valuation of "speed," which shows itself in a great deal of our behavior.
>
> Still another behavioral effect is that the character of monotony and regularity possessed by our image of time as an evenly scaled limitless tape measure persuades us to behave as if that monotony were more true of events than it really is. That is, it helps to routinize us. We tend to select and favor whatever bears out this view, to "play up to" the routine aspects of existence.

What he is doing here is, in a rough and general way, describing nonlinguistic behavior as correlated with linguistic analysis.

Now, the descriptions which he uses are not, perhaps, too precise, but he is talking about something that certainly is perfectly possible to do. Since linguistic behavior plays such a dominant role, it might be thought of as a series of indexes which tells us in general where we might look in a cultural setup for certain kinds of behavior. From the point of view of the anthropologist, this would be extremely useful.

REDFIELD: I have been much encouraged and stimulated by the trend of remarks in the last few minutes, since Kaplan's report, for I think that his recent remarks have brought us again to the course of discussion that was suggested in the recommendation that went out. If I recall that invitation, it was suggested that some, or possibly even all, of four things might be in some degree accomplished by this conference, and one of the last of these four was the consideration of particular research plans. I would imagine that these research plans would involve acceptance in some form of the formulation which Kaplan gave to the matter, when he spoke of our general question as one of prediction as to some cultural fact from propositions derived from a more strictly linguistic analysis.

At this point there was discussion as to whether such predictions involve tautology or not. I was myself on this matter persuaded by Singer's remarks, and whether or not all of us are now persuaded that there are no necessary tautologies involved, I would venture to express the hope that if that matter should be more fully discussed among us we would come to a form of words in which we would find ourselves in substantial agreement that the inference drawn from the propositions enunciated from the linguistic analysis says something additional, that we did not fully know from the mere enunciation of the linguistic propositions. Some such form of words would get us around this argument about tautology.

Assuming that that is surpassable, then I would like to add that I would agree also with Singer's suggestion that the second half of this proposition in two parts which premises an inference has a manner of verification, both from nonlinguistic and also from linguistic behavior, that is not a matter of formal linguistics.

Now, at last, I come to what was in my mind before this conference began and still is. I would imagine that there was a great range of kinds of inferences, propositions, which might be derived if you began at the end of the language and considered the linguistic analysis only. The abstractness, the apparent scope of the proposition you utter from the linguistic analysis with regard to the people who are the speakers of the language, might in the one case be very wide indeed, and in the other case quite restricted, with cases a little less restricted and a little less wide in between.

For example, if you studied Trobriand language alone and had no knowledge of Malinowski, I suppose the fact that there are so many words for yams of various kinds would be the basis for an inference that among these people yams were important, and that would be the proposition that I suppose it would be fairly easy to confirm by examining both linguistic and nonlinguistic behavior in the Trobriand Islands.

From the linguistic analysis, you would not be able to predict that people would often say with deep feeling, "Oh, what a beautiful yam!" in situations of social and ritual importance, but you would be able to go and see that happen if you began at the other end. In that instance I find it difficult to separate the nonlinguistic from the linguistic behavior that would confirm the inference you would draw from the merely linguistic fact, in this case, chiefly lexical. At the other extreme I have in mind a proposition such as you find in some of the papers by Dorothy Lee, particularly that paper in which she speaks about the conception of the self in certain Indian-speaking groups and draws from the linguistic fact alone the inference that these people, and I am almost quoting her verbatim, are unable to, and do not, separate themselves from society. That is the kind of proposition which I find it very hard to set up as a research enterprise. I would set that at the other end of the range that I am conceiving. Somewhere near the one from Dorothy Lee and farther away from the one about the yams is the kind of proposition that Whorf has in his papers on Hopi, particularly illustrated by the proposition with regard to the disposition of Hopi thinking to be concerned with preparatory action or some such thing, and he gets that from a linguistic analysis of the verbal forms of the language, as I recall it. Then he says we can see this is true, because the Hopi spend a very great deal of time getting ready for ceremonies and getting ready for this and getting ready for that. If that is so, I should suppose that that which is really an offhand inference and an offhand statement is confirmable from something outside of the purely linguistic analysis and represents something between these two extremes. It would illustrate the kind of proposition which I would hope that someone who knows language and culture somewhere in the world would put before us, before the week is out, for examination to see whether, indeed, these two aspects, the proposition from a linguistic analysis and the partial confirmation from a nonlinguistic action and linguistic behavior, could be worked out by precise examination of materials, both linguistic and nonlinguistic.

GREENBERG: It seems to me that one very important point of agreement—I assume it is agreement, since almost no voice has been raised against it—is the proposition that we must make a distinction between language and verbal behavior. On its account it is quite legitimate, as Redfield was just saying, to set up what would be nontautologous possible agreements between linguistic facts and facts of either verbal or nonverbal behavior; we do not have to go entirely to nonverbal behavior at all. In fact, some of the things that Whorf mentions in regard to time, like keeping records, we obviously get from verbal behavior of people, and in these cases we have statable propositions which can be empirically confirmed or disproved by observation of verbal and nonverbal behavior of people.

NEWMAN: I think the matter of tautology comes into the methodological strategy we use. That is, I can make certain inferences or statements from the data I get in dealing with Zuni words and phrases, that I believe to be true about Zuni culture. Now, where I think I might get into a tautology is if I assume, then, that these must be true of the culture as it is described by the ethnologist, or even go further in some cases and say that if the ethnologist does not find what I find through my study of words, he is wrong. In other words, what we have got to do is to try to find what we can infer about culture from our language data, both linguistic in a strict sense and lexical as well, and then see to what extent they are related to the kind of data independently arrived at by ethnologists.

HOCKETT: It is perhaps unfortunate that we feel constrained to take as a point of departure in our work Whorf's discussion of the relationships between language and the rest of the culture. It is a stimulating point of departure, but it is also misleading in certain ways.

Whorf's concern is at a very high level of abstraction—in a sense he is up in the clouds. He is doing, in a way which uses linguistic data, the sort of thing that Opler does in his thematic analysis, or that other anthropologists have done in connection with culture and personality. It is a very, very long series of complex successive abstractions from the level of people moving around the village, tying their shoes, dancing, gathering food, etc.

Now, the linguistic aspect of human behavior in connection with gathering wild rice or getting married or building houses or decorating moccasins is just as important to me as the linguistic aspect of these high-flown ultimate abstractions of a thematic account, and I think it is important to get down to this level of more simple, directly observable behavior, and more immediately deducible patterns of behavior, both nonlinguistic and linguistic. If we get down to these, then we can see that in a certain sense the difference between what the linguist would do in a semantic study, if he did it well, and what the ethnographer would do in a study of a particular field of behavior, reduces to zero. If the ethnographer is taking language into account, then he gets the words and the patterns of speaking that accompany practices, and if the linguist is studying the vocabulary connected with the particular range of behavior, then he takes note of the practices and objects to which the utterances refer.

The real difference, then, is not between these two things but between two things that can be done: ethnographic analysis which pays no attention to language, and ethnographic analysis which does. In this connection I will state a fundamental belief of mine in a form which exaggerates only in one way. The form in which I shall make the statement does not imply that there is any matter of degree in it —actually, there is. Ethnography without linguistics is blind. Linguistics without ethnography is sterile.

LOUNSBURY: I agree wholeheartedly with Hockett. I have heard a number of expressions of discouragement with the linguistic approach to understanding of thought-worlds. Yet I have never felt discouraged about this because the things that I have had anything to do with have been of this more basic sort just mentioned.

For example, in all the ethnography of the Iroquois, I have never seen a reference to anything more than the political prerogatives of the members of the noble lineages. I have never seen anything about the supernatural endowments of members of the noble lineages, the supernaturally imposed responsibilities which are incumbent upon them, and the terrible things that happen if they do not fulfil these. I would never have gotten onto this except through dealing with linguistic materials.

Words came up which had to be translated, and in the process of tracking them down I got all sorts of ethnographic case material which would have completely escaped notice otherwise. If you are working at the bottom level like this, combining ethnography with linguistics, there is just no cause at all to be discouraged with the linguistic approach to the conceptual system of the people.

LENNEBERG: I certainly agree with Lounsbury that linguistic material, whatever it may be, can and should be of great interest to many of the problems we have discussed. It has been pointed out in the discussion that the general method of going from language to something else need not be tautologous, and I agree with that.

But two other pitfalls, I think, might be mentioned. For one, an inference from linguistic data toward something else can be so broad that it can be meaningless. To give an example that has been often quoted, someone in the last century mentioned that some Indian language has very many different words for eating—eating with people and eating alone and eating this and eating that. From that somebody might infer that probably these Indians eat with people, that they eat in this way and eat in that way. This certainly would be true. You can verify it and the inference will be borne out, yet it is perfectly useless because everybody eats, and you cannot do anything with this kind of inference.

This is somewhat reminiscent of the preparatory work observed by Whorf. He studied a language and induced from it that the Hopi engage in preparatory work. I challenge anybody to establish that they do that more than we do. You might find one instance where they do something that we might not do, but on the whole you cannot quantify this. The same thing is true with the time business. The inferences made were certainly borne out by reference to the behavior, but I am sure you will find among people who speak our languages behavior just like that of the Hopi.

HOIJER: I feel that I must enter some objection to Lenneberg's characterization of Whorf's generalization of Hopi preparing activities. His conclusion was not that the Hopi spends time in preparation, which certainly is a useless conclusion, since we all spend time in preparation; his conclusion was relative to the nature of Hopi preparing activities—a highly specific thing, very different from anything in our culture, and extremely different even from anything in the neighboring Navaho culture.

SINGER: I think that, while Whorf made careless descriptions in many respects, he has proved his worth as a gadfly; he has fascinated many of us, linguists and nonlinguists alike. He has posed problems which we want to try to pin down and sharpen, and I think that, while some of the inferences may be tautological, and it is important to recognize which ones, we are agreed that there is a range of possible nontautological inferences. The next problem would be to try to systematize these and determine the hypotheses on which they might be based, and, it seems to me, most of us are also agreed that causal hypotheses which attempt to connect language with other features of cultural behavior are pretty dubious, at least in any straight determinist form. I think we should pursue the problem as to what kind of hypotheses, then, would enable us to draw inferences, especially in this middle range, from language to culture.

Here I would like to suggest a type of hypothesis, broached in many of the papers, which is in general instrumental in character. Roughly, the assumption seems to be that language is an instrument and that it has certain features which facilitate our noticing or perceiving or thinking about certain things. I think that is certainly one step in the right direction, but it would require much more psychological and theoretical investigation to establish the validity of these hypotheses about the senses in which language does or does not facilitate certain modes of perception or thinking and the like.

Specifically, I was somewhat disturbed by a too easy assumption of presence and absence—that because a language has a certain linguistic feature it therefore facilitates our noticing or our thinking about the things which that linguistic feature perhaps is connected with semantically—though I think Greenberg's paper and some of the others did withhold assent to that. Now, in a general way that is common sense. On the other hand, do we know enough about language, and its relationship to what it enables us to do in perceiving and thinking, to assert it with any great probability?

I think that it is possible to say, for example, that certain features of the language have an inhibiting influence; certainly we know that there are many features of languages, and particularly of symbolic and mathematical languages, where we have certain devices to keep us from thinking about the things that are designated by the symbols. In ordinary language there are all sorts of conventional phrases, like "How do you do," which would occasion surprise if people really took notice of their literal meaning, and perhaps there is a whole area in language which, for better or worse, has inhibiting, and various kinds of distorting, influences.

Conversely, the absence of certain features or words from a language would not need to mean that the people who use that language do not pay attention to those things; in the obvious case of taboos and sacred works the absence of certain words or features becomes very, very significant, because what is designated by such absences has some extraordinary psychological value.

I am just throwing these out as suggestions. The idea of language as an instrument which facilitates modes of perception and cognition is a very fruitful kind of hypothesis, but we have as yet nothing more than the crudest kind of common-sense notion about this. If we could empirically establish the instrumental and facilitating and inhibiting properties of a language for a group of people, then we would have some hypotheses on which to base this idea in a controlled way.

VON GRUNEBAUM: I should like to call your attention to an example which seems to me to show, at the same time, the usefulness of this approach and its limitations.

In the fourth century of our era one Marius Victorinus tried to translate Plotinus into Latin. He had very great difficulties because there was no abstract terminology to render the many very subtle terms of Plotinus into contemporary Latin. Benz has put together the terms he used, and they are really rather grotesque six- and seven-syllable words which explain to a certain extent why the Latin verbs of Plotinus never gained great currency. Now, this clumsiness of Latin in providing for this type of terminology certainly was an inhibiting factor in the spread of Neo-Platonic philosophy in that period.

So far, Singer's position that language is an instrument which helps or inhibits certain developments would be proved true. But then, when we jump six or eight centuries into the high tide of scholasticism, we find that St. Thomas or St. Bonaventure had terms, also in Latin, also theologisms—of course, not theologisms of their period but gradually evolved theologisms—that in subtlety and precision and syntactical maneuverability equal the Greek terms of the Greek Fathers. In other words, since the drive of the culture within which St. Thomas and St. Bonaventure wrote was so strong, since dominant experience impelled them and their contemporaries so strongly to abstract and philosophize their religious experience in just that type of terminology, there was enough of a will, enough of a collective drive, to hammer out of the somewhat recalcitrant Latin language material terms with which this could be done—an impulse which had not been there when Marius Victorinus made his attempts.

So language is an instrument that inhibits or helps, but the dominant experience of a culture, the ardent wish to get one's religious experience ordered in a specific type of scholastic or philosophical system, helps to overcome what inhibitions the language system as such might contain.

EGGAN: I was just going to say that I do not like to see Whorf sold so short in these statements. I think if Lenneberg went out to the Hopi country for two or three weeks he would see this preparing; they not only prepare for things, but when they get through they take them all apart, and next time they start all over again. We would not do that. We would store them away, bring them out again, and save all that valuable time.

The amazing thing about Whorf is that he did a sort of an intellectual ethnography without being in the Hopi country. I think he was there only two or three weeks, and undoubtedly read some literature, but he has more good insight into the Hopi culture than any linguist I know who has talked about culture except, perhaps, Sapir on the Navaho.

GREENBERG: It may be that Whorf had a fine intuition for ethnography and made excellent ethnographic observations. It may be true that he was a very good linguist and isolated a morpheme meaning "future." But, on the other hand, there is no real correlation between the two things, and he said there is. Finding there is a separate morpheme meaning the expective in a language does not enable one to predict what kind of expective or preparational activity will take place. How could one possibly decide from the mere existence of such a morpheme that someone is going to pull out things, rescrape them, and do things of that sort.

All people are surely prepared for the future, and, what is more, they must deal with it linguistically. Now, how would one be able to predict from the fact that there is a morpheme in Hopi which is translated as the expective, and a unit in English which means "I am going to," that the Hopi type of preparation would be one kind of thing, specifically, and the English type of preparation another kind of thing?

HOIJER: I must enter again an objection to what I consider to be a vulgarization of Whorf's work, and I refer you to his material. Whorf made no such inference from the expective particle nor would he, indeed, make one from the phrase "I am going to." This issue is of no great significance as a matter of methodology or theory, but I think that the example is well drawn, and you cannot deny the existence of the example simply by vulgarizing it.

The point has been made, not only by me but by Eggan, who has worked with Hopi for several years, and by a number of other people who have had actual experience with the Hopi, that in this particular instance Whorf drew a connection from certain classes of linguistic phenomena widespread and significant throughout the language, and expressible in a variety of ways, semantic and grammatical, to a peculiar aspect of Hopi culture which in its totality is uniquely Hopi, though it has certain resemblances in broader aspects to other Puebloan cultural activities. This aspect of Hopi culture is certainly not one of these activities like eating, sleeping, and preparing that is characteristic of the human animal as a species. The accuracy of Whorf's connection might be doubted by people who would examine the totality of the culture, but it cannot be doubted on the basis of saying that he made a prediction on the strength of a single morpheme or that he made a prediction about a characteristic of behavior which is found in every human society.

HOCKETT: I am disturbed by the implication here that we are concerned with the making of inferences from linguistic data to other matters. Let us look at the Whorfian case very closely for a moment.

Whorf sat in New York for many, many hours and worked with a native speaker of Hopi, who was a native of Hopi culture. Whorf talked with him in English, got Hopi words, got Hopi texts, asked all sorts of questions about the meanings of these words, asked how to say this, that, and the other. He was presumably aiming toward a linguistic description of the Hopi language, but he got all sorts of other reactions from his informant. This underscores the point that I was trying to make earlier—that linguists and ethnologists actually go through many of the same operations, ask the same kind of questions, and watch for the same subtle clues on the part of their informants.

HOIJER: This point I think is a very good one. Whorf did not make his inferences simply from a consideration of language as a linguist understands it. He was building, or attempting to build, a bridge between language and the rest of culture, by carefully defining certain aspects or categories of the structure of the language. This involved him, not only in linguistic field research, but also in ethnographic field research.

HOCKETT: So far as method is concerned, it is possible to define a linguistic system, a language, in such narrow nonsemantic terms that nobody can make any inferences whatsoever from the system. I can write a grammar that will say absolutely nothing about meanings, although I had to use meaning in getting the information. I can put it purely in terms of a list of elements and statements as to their privileges of occurrence relative to each other in utterances. Nobody could make any cultural deductions from that, so let us be careful about what we are making deductions from. We are making the deductions from a body of information that contains the basis for those deductions, namely, information about the culture, not just about the language as pure system.

KROEBER: It seems to me that Whorf tried to find a set of superpatterns of the Hopi culture or language—what Sapir might have called a trend or slope—which was generic and ran through all the patterns of Hopi culture and Hopi language. Once you get on that high level, or very generalized basis, then it is almost inevitable that you look to see whether the slope of the language and the slope of the culture are not the same. If you have imagination, as Whorf certainly did, and a genuine insight and a touch of genius, you will see certain similarities. He has long seemed to me very much like Spengler, who is interested in the largest patterns that can possibly be developed. In his characterization of Western civilization, Spengler connected such diverse elements as counterpoint in music, double-entry bookkeeping, clocks, and Gothic architecture as having certain qualities resembling each other.

Now, are those connections real or do they exist essentially in some gift of perception which he has, possibly aesthetic—in the sense that the words are tied together in a superpattern—but entirely nonintellectual and unverifiable? Frankly, I do not know. My guess would be that there is something in these formulations of Spengler, but that there is not nearly as much in them as he thinks there is. And it seems to me you have something of the same sort of quality of mind in Whorf. In these so-called metalinguistic papers he is freeing himself from the ordinary business of a linguist and trying to deal with patterns and qualities and interrelations of patterns and qualities of a necessarily less substantial but larger kind than we ordinarily deal with. They are in a sense, therefore, forecasts. Perhaps they are true insights. Perhaps they are true insights that can be verified. Perhaps they are true insights that can never be verified. Perhaps they are just verbal aberrations. I personally have always found them very interesting and very stimulating, but I do think they will be hard to prove.

NEWMAN: I wonder whether we could not all agree that what we are trying to do is to diminish, as far as possible, the intuitive aspect of Whorf's approach. I do not think there is an absolute dichotomy between 100 per cent verifiability and 100 per cent intuitive approach, but I think the trend of the discussion has been to see both techniques in the methodology and logical features of the approach and to find a methodology which would give us a better basis for at least defining what we are talking about.

One other point I want to make is that in characterizing the culture or thought-world of a people, we will have to be careful to avoid the kind of emphasis that sometimes turns up in a cultural relativity approach, that is, looking only for the distinctive characteristics of a given culture. I think it is important that we find linguistic evidence in every language, so far as I know, that males are distinguished from females, and that this is revealed not only in relationship terms but that your informants will tell you that women say this, men do not say this, etc. Certain very broad general features that do not distinguish cultures but are found in all cultures come out of both linguistic data and ethnological data.

LOUNSBURY: Are we to conclude that the so-called Whorf hypothesis, or Whorf's position, does not include making inferences from language to culture but simply involves making inferences from ethnographic data connected incidentally to linguistic work? Many readers simply equate with the Whorfian position a position such as was taken by Dorothy Lee in the introduction to one of her papers, and there she says in so many words that she assumes that the basic premises underlying cultural patterns and the basic premises underlying linguistic patterns are one and the same, or are derived from one and the same set of premises. Now, this is making inferences from linguistic data to cultural data.

HOCKETT: It seems to me that the point of departure for inferences may be, on the one hand, purely ethnographic information gathered with very slight, if any, attention to the verbal behavior associated with practices that are being asked about or observed, or, on the other hand, may make extremely full use of the way in which the people who do the behaving speak about it and speak as they are behaving.

Whorf was obviously utilizing the second, because his aim, at least at first, was to describe the linguistic system. The difference between the Whorfian approach and a nonlinguistic, non-Whorfian approach would be the difference between doing ethnography solely in terms of translation, and going out under ideal field conditions and first working for seven years to learn the language so you could take it down and then going ahead to fill in more details. That makes for constant awareness of the linguistic organizations that are given to all the different cultural practices that you observe and hear about.

SINGER: I think Lounsbury's question can be answered by saying that most of us do not think of this as a problem of making an inference, blind, from linguistic data. I think Hockett's position is certainly the sensible one—that even in setting up the linguistic characterization you are using some nonlinguistic material, probably. But I think Kroeber's remarks suggest the kind of interpretation that is congenial at least to me—that you have emerging on the basis of the linguistic analysis some over-all pattern, and then you find a pattern emerging from the cultural material, including some verbal material, and there seems to be some correlation. Then the question is: What is the meaning of the correlation; is it causal, is it tautological, or what? To ask for a series of mechanical steps of inference from one to the other probably is not quite the way to put it, if you conceive of it as a problem of correlation or congruence.

LOUNSBURY: If you conceive of it as a problem of causality, however, you need the mechanical steps. And if you conceive of it as a problem of correlation, you need more than a single case of a single language in a single culture to establish the correlation.

SINGER: Yes, you have to compare, and on that point Kroeber's remarks suggested a question. One thing that strikes me about Whorf is that the type of over-all pattern that he kept picking out was the kind of pattern that a physicist who had read Whitehead might have been interested in, that is, concepts of time, of space, of matter—in short, the pattern of physics.

Now, Northrop and, I think, Kluckhohn to a lesser extent explicitly take the position that an over-all characterization of a cultural pattern must ultimately rest on physics, or at least on that culture's physics, and something like that seems to be in back of Whorf's mind too. I wonder whether that has any merit. One misses in Whorf concepts of self, of social relations, interpersonal relations, and a lot of others which physicists ordinarily are not interested in, yet which most of us suspect the various people in these different, even exotic, cultures are very much interested in. Whose system is Whorf really describing—the Hopi system or the kind of system that a physicist would have been interested in finding?

SEVENTH SESSION

THE SAPIR-WHORF HYPOTHESIS

FEARING: Our discussion will center around Hoijer's paper on the Sapir-Whorf hypothesis. Hoijer will begin by introducing his paper.

HOIJER: My paper is an attempt both to clarify, and perhaps to interpret, the Whorf hypothesis and to illustrate it by reference to materials on Navaho language and culture. It seems to me that I can find a theme of Navaho culture as a whole, which is reflected not only in the religious patterns I have described but as well in certain language patterns. I offer this illustration, admittedly brief and incomplete, for your criticism.

KROEBER: I think Hoijer's paper brings us considerably nearer to the center of thought implicit from the beginning in our deliberations here. I see three steps in what he is doing and wanting to do. First of all, we have the ordinary formal linguistic analysis of Navaho and the grammar in the ordinary sense of the word. Second, we have as an example this peculiar class of stems where verbal action and an object class are wrapped up together in the one package, which you can no longer subdivide. If you got only one such verbal stem it would not mean very much, but when you have Navaho verbs classifying themselves according to principles of this sort, you are evidently faced with an important phenomenon. Third comes a matter of the ideology of the Navaho as expressed in their culture, and the degree of correspondence between that and the second feature, the verb semantics. If Hoijer can establish that correspondence so as to convince others who do not know the Navaho, that would be in line with the suggestions that Whorf threw out. It certainly would be important and interesting.

We have a great deal on record on Navaho ideology, and much of it is widely known. I suppose the grammar is pretty well known by now. Where we need more information, however, is precisely on these semantic classes. I realize it would be a tough and wearisome job to work them out. But that is certainly the third member and the middle member through which the connection would take place. If your example is, as I think it is, typical, it means that it is not language as a whole, speech as a whole, that we are trying to correlate with culture, but the semantic aspects, which we have been seeing increasingly for three days the straight linguists are trying to throw out of their pure form linguistics.

We need more work in semantics if this whole area that we are discussing here is to be developed, and I think that work will have to be done by the linguists. I think the trouble with Dorothy Lee's effort has perhaps been that she did not control the material appropriately, and consequently she could advance her constructs without being able to prove or disprove them. But you can prove something about Navaho semantics, or at least give us evidence which convinces you. The next step would be to see whether we agree with you as to how far that semantic classification corresponds with the structure of the culture.

I think the drift away from semantics, the throwing of meaning out of linguistic study, was a necessary step. Until that happened linguistic study had been a kind of mishmash of form and meaning and would not have got to where it is now. It was this refinement, this narrowing of linguistic interest, that has again by counterbalance revived the problem, and I think the problem is a perfectly legitimate one. Now, before we talk about the interactions or interrelations of cultural and linguistic structure, we have to have more interest shown in semantics and a tangible body of results from work done in it.

HOCKETT: A thesis of this kind is extremely tempting. But to me it resembles very much the thematic analysis that I mentioned before, and whenever I read about theme analysis I have to remind myself over and over of one thing, before it can make sense. It is not a matter of correlation; it is not a matter of causal relation. It is simply a matter of a consistent coexistence, a nondirect coexistence. Themes are not a set of consistent logical postulates, in terms of which the behavior of people is logical, predictable. Themes are the bases for analogies, often conflicting, in terms of which the actual behavior conforms in this, that, and the other context.

KAPLAN: I want to talk about this in terms of the logic of what we might call the "consonant" relations. This might be a happier term than "consistency," which has a narrower technical sense. The question is this: What kind of a relationship are we trying to establish between the inferences we draw from language and from other culture patterns, since it is not stated to be a causal relationship. In fact, that is often explicitly denied.

It seems to me that the relationship has a perfectly straightforward logical structure, in predictive terms which I will systematize as follows. This is a schematization and an obvious simplification. Suppose we forget that we are talking about culture or anything else and just consider some kind of a complex—a complex that plainly is analyzable in terms of, for instance, your procedures of investigation into a set of different kinds of features which I will call "traits." I am schematizing it as a single proposition, which is related to these sets of propositions or traits in the following way: from any combination of several traits as premises, we induce a proposition which is of such a kind that with high probability we can derive from that single proposition and the initial conditions the other members of the set of traits.

Now, notice that you do not just take some one trait and get at a proposition and then expect within a reasonable probability to get to the other traits, but you work configurationally. It is like the idea of an individual belonging to a certain family, not because he has the Hapsburg chin, or some other distinctive feature like a nose, but because of the whole cast of features. Sometimes it is the chin and the nose. Sometimes it is the eyes, mouth, and ears. Sometimes it is the complexion and the hair. Various sets of these features will allow you to identify the family membership with a high probability of accuracy. If members of a family look quite different from one another, then we would simply say this is one of those structures that does not cohere very much, and this whole pattern of inference would break down because the fundamental assumption with respect to it would not be true.

In the present case, to speak concretely in cultural terms, it seems to me that one thing at least has to be recognized. That is the underlying empirical assumption for the whole procedure, namely, that a culture, like an individual, has a distinctive character. In fact, the logic of characterology seems to be the one involved here. Normally, we expect to find that the things an individual does, his behavior, are all of a piece. So, if the elements of a culture are similarly related, you might expect that its aspects relate to each other in some similar fashion, without, of course, suggesting an identity between individual character and culture.

What I suppose would be of particular interest to this conference is simply the fact that emphasis has in recent years been given to the possibility of making good use of the particular linguistic traits in a culture in conjunction with some of these others in order to make such inferences, but without necessarily attaching to the linguistic ones any distinctive position among all of these. The mere fact that they are linguistic and are going to have something to do with conceptions or world views is, so to speak, an unfortunate accident that might be misleading. I did not gather from Hoijer that anyone would wish to say that, because his data are linguistic, they directly and immediately reflect this single character in a way in which the other parts of culture do not. It is rather that they provide another, and apparently a useful, element to combine with others.

This sort of logic, it seems to me, is quite acceptable. The fruitfulness as well as accuracy of the analysis in the given case are testable in terms of the kind of inferences you can get about other sorts of behavior and how, conversely, you can get back to that type from these others.

NEWMAN: I just wanted to mention one point on the indefensibility of arriving at a world view by inferences from some one aspect of culture. In anthropology this has turned up in studies of folk literature. The first notion was that you could, by studying the literature, infer the culture. As anthropologists have worked more and more with literary material, they have come to see that there are all kinds of special historical and formal stylistic features which make that kind of inferring undesirable. You can get a cultural picture or a world view from the literature alone, but it will not be the same kind that you will get from other cultural material.

There are, of course, explanations for this—mainly historical. Literature may be borrowed, and so reflect a world view of the culture from which it came, or it may, because of its age in a society, reflect something of an earlier stage of the culture. This suggests that it might be fruitful to make separate inferences from different aspects of the culture, and then see whether any explanation might be found for the lack of correspondence among them. Is there some way of dealing with different kinds of material, in the realization that they will have their own nature, so to speak, and using this as a kind of test of inferences?

ROBERTS: Several things have struck me. First, we are not in agreement on what culture is. Second, to be a little bit constructive I feel I have to introduce a term "values," although, having sat through a number of values conferences, I know that this is every bit as controversial an area as the one we have been discussing here. But we have been doing work on values of the Navaho, and it strikes me that Hoijer is essentially making a values statement, at least one which we could include under our rubric of "values," and one which is essentially a dominant value because it is easy to think of.

As far as I know, this view of nature which Hoijer has given has been supported by every Navaho specialist and is supported to a considerable extent by the work the Values Study team led by Florence Kluckhohn has been doing in the area. Nonetheless, there are underlying contradictory or variant values which do not concord with this. One of the orientations on a cross-cultural questionnaire we gave to samples drawn from Mormon, Spanish-American, Zuni, and Texan communities was the relationship between man and nature. We presented a trichotomy: "man versus nature," "man in nature," and "man subjugated to nature." I am not quite sure precisely where this view of nature expressed by Hoijer would fit, but presumably it would be "in nature" or "subjugated to nature," "in nature" being essentially involved in this harmonic notion.

The Spanish-American group tended to be the most subjugated to nature of any of the groups. This questionnaire forced a choice—first, second, and third—so that maybe their views, if collected some other way, would be at variance with this, but they were strikingly subjugated to nature. The Navaho and Zuni tended to be more in nature. We had a diagram of probabilities ranging out from the center, and the Navaho tended to be between "in nature" and "subjugated to nature." The Mormons and the Texans tended to be strongly versus nature, but the Mormons were a little more in nature than the Texans.

We had the same thing on a time dimension. Here we had the imaginative trichotomy, which will strike most of you as novel, dividing people into past-oriented, present-oriented, or future-oriented. In this case, once again giving the range of questions, the Navaho, Zuni, and Spanish-Americans were all present-oriented. The Mormons and Texans were future-oriented. I could go on. There were other orientations and diverse results.

Furthermore, in terms of these orientations there was a great deal of variation in subjects within any single community, and what we were dealing with were statistical findings, or a preponderant or a quantitative kind of thing. I think that if we are to approach profitably the general problem of the conference here, we cannot think in terms of—and this is probably unfortunate—mechanical models, but must deal with statistical models.

These more or less random examples are taken simply to indicate that the problem of working out the world view of a group of people is indeed a complicated one. When we reach a point of talking about actual research design, I think that we can talk profitably about the kind of examination which we can make of these linguistic notions and parallel developments going on in studies of child socialization, projective systems, folklore, art, and so on. The main point is that one-to-one correspondence between this feature of culture and that feature of language cannot be made. We will eventually have to make a statistical kind of formulation, and perhaps we will have to work out the values. It strikes me this is essentially an area of values inquiry. Perhaps we should work out independently our notions of values, using these various approaches, and then put them together again.

KROEBER: I am in agreement with Roberts. I think values perhaps are part of the area of consonance that Kaplan spoke about, and I see an interrelation between this subsuming consonance and values. I think in each case the subsuming structure and the values are only partly in the consciousness of the people to whose language and culture reference is being made.

I would like to say that I do not see very clearly this area or unit of consonance. What kind of a structure is it? Is it a construct? Is it an operational tool, and only that, which allows us to predict? Is it merely a construct in the mind of the scholar and scientist or is it something that, however implicitly or unconsciously, influences the people in the culture or the language?

KAPLAN: I should suppose it to be both. It would not exist in the culture in the explicit and crystallized form that at any stage of inquiry the cultural anthropologist would attach to it; it would have to be localized in whatever patterns he identifies as the carriers of the culture, that is, those factors which impose constraints and which provide for persistence of ways of doing things. Some of these would undoubtedly just be immediate interpersonal relations. Some of them would be, I suppose, practices of child-rearing and so on—all the familiar sorts of things.

I take it that the hypothesis is that the culture has character. I only know the Ruth Benedict kind of formulation: that the particular practice is subject to, if not a single, at least a small set of principles which are convenient formulations of the kind of constraints that keeps it going along those channels.

FEARING: Whorf makes quite a point that language does not only express ideas but somehow also constrains ideas. I would like to see the linguists and others present discuss this aspect of Whorf more explicitly and, if possible, clarify it and the related idea that these constraints operating in the individual, in which language plays a dominant role, are for the individual unconscious. This may bear on what Kaplan is saying.

GREENBERG: It seems to me language is a part of culture and shares with the rest of culture this compulsory aspect, which is an unconscious aspect to a considerable extent. You do not realize your behavior falls within a certain range, although you might say you are constrained: "I can't do it differently." I think that the constraint is precisely on the kind of thing that the linguist describes in his grammar. I am under constraint when I speak English to follow the rules of English, the structural part of the language. For example, I cannot have certain sequences of consonants. Those are against the rules. I am unconscious of this. Only the linguist, when he makes his analysis, is able to bring it to consciousness.

With respect to language inhibiting ideas, the tenor of the discussion here has been to more or less discard any very drastic hypothesis in that direction. The feeling seems to be that if a certain scientific view of the world does not arise in a particular culture, or does, that the language plays no very large role in the matter, though it might create certain temporary difficulties because in every language it is a bit easier to say certain things than others. You recall Von Grunebaum's remarks on the translation of Plotinus. I believe the general answer that I would give is "No," but at the same time language is not so different from the rest of the culture that constraint does not operate in a different sphere.

FEARING: Is it not true that Whorf is actually saying something less than that—that at least he is imposing yet more difficulties on the possibility that you can have ideas (I use a very loose phrase here), which are inconsistent with the world view which language imposes upon you? This is a point that is relevant to the whole question of bridging the cultural boundaries.

KENNARD: If I may speak to that point, I think he uses two phrases: the "suggestive" kind and, the counterpart, the "inhibitory." Certain frequently recurring arrangements tend to make people who are speakers of a language unconsciously project this kind of arrangement into the things they are talking about. These arrangements have a suggestive value.

Now, we do have a whole history for the fact that in the development of science people have succeeded in escaping these limitations, which is the point that Von Grunebaum was making yesterday. But

I think we also have to recognize that in many of the societies that we are dealing with we do not have a differentiation of specialists anything like that which has developed in the Western world since the period of the classical civilization.

KAPLAN: I want to add something to my reply to Kroeber's previous question, which also bears on your remark.

Without in the least minimizing the empirical difficulties that are involved in this area, there are certain artificial difficulties that I think could be and should be completely set aside. These are in my mind especially because of Kroeber's mention of Spengler as having been one who apparently entertained similar ideas. The artificial difficulties, as I am calling them, are those which arise from attempting to attach to this character of the culture a status at least logically independent of its localization in specific practices in the culture. Then one begins to have the idea of constraints somehow being externally imposed.

I would take the kind of statement that Whorf makes about language not expressing ideas to be more clearly rendered by saying that verbal behavior does not express ideas, but having ideas consists in the verbal behavior. Similarly, one would not see the various patterns in the culture express, let us call it, its central principle; they constitute it. Our formulation of the principle is only an indirect way of saying something about these other practices.

Now, you still have the specific empirical questions of the precise form in which these constraints manifest themselves. Let me illustrate with a hypothetical case relating to another aspect of culture. Such an instance, of course, introduces additional difficulties because it may not be so close as language to the central principle of the culture.

Suppose you had a culture in which the family expressed and inculcated into the child patterns of extreme assertiveness and competitiveness with his siblings, and this was from the beginning built into his orientation toward the other members of the family. I can imagine that someone might then say that this early family life imposes constraints on the kind of recreational activities the child will engage in: he will be much happier in, will much prefer, or be more inclined, to play games that do not involve co-operating teams but, rather, marked competition between individuals. Indeed we might even say that he could not imagine a game participated in spontaneously for enjoyment, in a playful spirit; he could not imagine a game in which people co-operate with one another.

But one who is particularly imaginative might formulate such a pastime, and he might under special conditions induce other people to engage in it with him, although we would not expect that they would feel happy about it. They would feel it to be pointless, or something of the sort. Here I do not sense any difficulties in principle. I wonder whether this pattern is not substantially the kind of pattern we are considering in the Whorfian case.

FEARING: The competitiveness here would be a fragment of the world view, and presumably no person in this hypothetical family would necessarily be in a position, unless he were an unusual person, to express this world view in any kind of abstract assertion or proposition.

KAPLAN: It might be carried as far as this: A philosopher in such a culture might very well agree with Plato or Peirce in analyzing existence as what Peirce called "reacting against"; to exist is to react against. Consequently, he would not even conceive of competitiveness as a world view, because for him it would be identical with simply existing.

HOCKETT: In the life of the community, what counts is those ideas which are transmitted from one person to another. From that you can eliminate the term "idea" and talk simply about communication.

Now, language is not our only communicative system. It is not the only one in any culture. Among human beings it is certainly the one which is most persuasive and flexible and complete. If you want to consider the impact of the semantic structure of a language on the life of a community, then I think you can see how it will have an impact, not via ideas, but directly, in that any report which a person brings in from an observation post will be largely verbal. Therefore it will be strained through the semantic categories which the language affords. Any language we know anything about is an extremely flexible instrument, and there are a great many personal differences in individual handling of it. One person would make a very poor report, because he does not control the instrument very well.

What normally happens when something new is introduced into the life of a community is that the language adapts in a reasonable length of time to take care of new needs and situations. The delay is not great. Occasionally, before the adaptation has become complete, you have a stage during which the pattern of the language inherited from the earlier stage can confuse the issues and lead to difficulties in handling the items that are being introduced. Occasionally the length of time that it takes for adaptation is rather surprisingly great. I think this is very rare. Of course, the language that could not adapt fairly quickly would have been eliminated half a million years ago by the process of selection.

FEARING: Would you accept, then, that the language might function to direct the attention of the individual to certain aspects of his physical environment? You mentioned the word "report." He comes back and makes a report, verbally of course. Should it not be added that linguistic patterns have a dynamic function in determining to a large extent—and this seems to be implicit in Whorf—what the individual will actually see?

HOCKETT: This is true of the given individual making the report at the given time, or making the observations at the given time, because his linguistic system is that which structures the world for him. However, for the community as a whole this will change, and even for an individual this will change, usually very rapidly, as it needs change.

WRIGHT: It occurs to me that a great many bilingual Chinese, in the United States because they have nowhere else to go at the moment, are accessible as a group to study. Perhaps they would afford good subjects for a study of the question of bilingualism and its pertinence to the Whorf hypothesis.

VOEGELIN: In the context of Wright's remark about bilingualism, could you have two cultures interiorized and in that sense become bicultural?

ROBERTS: I have checked bilinguals on about ten thousand items each, to find out the things that they knew personally; that they thought they knew well enough to teach to other people; and that they did not know themselves but knew people who did. My impression is that the not radically acculturated bilingual, say, a Zuni who knows English but who, on the behavior level, seems to interact much like every other Zuni, tends to have the personal knowledge, but to be Zuni in character. He has a greater range of the instrumental control—banks, loan agencies—and he has heard about a great many things that I think the nonbilingual would not have heard of. I think this character of knowledge is different precisely in its quality and that the internalization of it in the psychological sense is also different.

Now, returning to the Whorf hypothesis, one wonders when fashions of thinking, to the extent that they are conditionally determined by language, become settled or fixed. Perhaps this occurs at eight or nine years of age. What you are interested in is not the language as it is represented in the lexicon but the language as controlled by an eight- or nine-year-old child; this may be the area that would tell us more psychologically. I think one avenue into this is to assess the linguistic control of individuals in different situations and different stages of maturation and then to match this against other avenues of inquiry, psychological perhaps, which would tend to give evidence as to fashions of thought or thought-world.

GREENBERG: There is an imaginative experiment which has occurred to me, which, if it could be carried out, would be a perfect test of the Whorf hypothesis. Suppose, for example, we took a people like the Baganda in East Africa and transported them to the Arctic area. Their culture will now become completely Eskimo, with Eskimo technology, interaction on the basis of kinship, religious beliefs, and so on, and the only thing we will keep constant is the Baganda language. What would happen?

It would take a lot longer to say things, and maybe when somebody wanted persons to come out and help kill a walrus, the walrus would get away. Obviously there would be certain changes. There would be incongruity. There would be no word for seal, no word for walrus, and a great many words for different kinds of desires which would be useless. Everybody would see that right away. Everyone admits there is a certain degree of congruence between the meanings of specific lexical elements and the cultural environment of the people.

Let us say you go up there, now, and record Eskimo culture and study the Eskimo-Baganda language. Would that situation strike you as incongruous? One does not know. It seems to me this would be the perfect experiment if you could do it.

HOIJER: You do not have to go to all that trouble and expense. There are situations in America, some of them right outside our door, where you can do the same sort of experimenting on people speaking the European languages, American Indian languages, and any other language you can think of.

SINGER: In relation to Greenberg's imaginary experiment, it seems to me that, before that or even some of these other kinds of experiments could really be made profitable in terms of the results you would get, you would have to have—I think several people have suggested this at different points in the conference—some kind of typology of languages, on the one hand, and a typology of world views, or at least a typology of total cultural patterns, on the other. Otherwise, you do not really know what you are looking for.

Now, you might get something that way and you might not. I think Hoijer's suggestion of these comparisons at the end of his paper begin to give us material that would build up some kind of typology. They need not be absolute. They can be comparative in scale, more of this-and-this type and more of that-and-that type.

FEARING: Would the Benedict sort of thing be typology?

SINGER: That is, of course, a very crude one—a typology of configurations, based chiefly on a psychological interpretation. But certainly something like that, or more sophisticated and refined, would have to come in.

HOCKETT: I am not sure we need a general typology as a frame of reference for this. That is something we are apt to seek sometimes when we do not need it. One can construct a geometry without a co-ordinate system. Here you might want a typology but not a typology which would serve as a co-ordinate system for comparative statements of result.

EIGHTH SESSION

CHINESE VERSUS ENGLISH: AN EXPLORATION OF THE WHORFIAN THESES

HOIJER: Our discussion in this session will center about Hockett's paper, "Chinese versus English: An Exploration of the Whorfian Theses." Hockett will begin.

HOCKETT: I am going to make the most of this opportunity to open my mouth for a slightly longer period of time at once to say some things which could or could not be interpreted as an introduction to this paper, because I think they need to be said.

Several times in the last few days I have tried to make the point that we should not concentrate our fire so far up in the clouds—that we should work more with folk dances, and kinship systems, and not so much with thought-worlds as yet. The tendency to deal more with high-level matters such as thought-worlds is very strong today in the field of anthropology. It has not always been so. I happen to regret it, not because it is an addition to the problems which anthropologists deal with, but because to such a great extent it tends to replace the lower-level problems. I think we can safely arrive at higher-level abstractions only by going through a great deal of laborious detailed work on the lower levels, in terms of what we really see and what we find out by first questions when we go to the field.

Now, I think that our discussion so far has been aimed at too high a level of abstraction, on the one hand, and I also think that it has been too specific, on the other. In order to show what I mean by that criticism of all of us, including myself, I should like to offer an outline of the points of contact of linguistics and ethnology, as I have been able to see them, in terms of which we can show just where the Whorfian thesis and matters akin to it might fall. The existence of an outline with headings and subheadings does not necessarily imply there is some positive contribution made at each point. But at least it indicates what kind of questions can be asked. Whorf's questions fall at one place in this outline and not all over it.

The first division I make of the whole matter of points of contact between linguistics and exolinguistics is the division I shall call existential versus methodological. I am referring to points of contact between language and other acts of human behavior which are there, whether they are observed and analyzed by us or not. The existential point of contact I divide into two subdivisions.

In the first place, there are certain questions we can ask which concern the human race as a whole. Language is a human universal; it is exclusively a human possession or attribute. There are other exclusively human patterns and institutions, some of them universal as is language, some of them not. So from this we get a synchronic problem, or a contrastive problem if you will, and a historical problem. The synchronic or contrastive problem is: What are the correlations between the fact that a man is a speaking animal and alone of all known biological species possesses speech and the fact that he has developed other exclusively human institutions, whether they be widespread or universal? There are several lines of attack that have to be taken to answer this, and some of them call for a great deal of gathering of data which I do not think has been done. For one thing, we need more comparative study of primate behavior, communicative and otherwise, in order to see what language does for human beings which nothing does for nonhuman primates. Human beings are also social animals, so that a similar behavior study needs to be made, contrasting what human beings do with language with what ants, bees, or any other such social group does without language. Third, human beings are domesticated animals, and there are domesticated animals that do not have languages. An analysis needs to be made in this direction. That is all in a sense a synchronic aspect of this very general problem. The diachronic problem is how in all human history—the history of man's emergence from something not yet a human being to what he is now—language has interrelated, causally or otherwise, with other developing institutions.

So much for this human-race aspect of the existential point of contact. The other aspect of the existential point of contact is the examination of the way in which communities differentiated in culture and in language compare with each other. What differences may there be between the kind of impact that one linguistic system in one community has on the rest of the culture of that community and the kind that another has in another community? Probably one of the most significant things that can be said along this line will turn out necessarily to involve some historical depth. That was hinted at this morning in my remark that a language will accommodate to new introductions in time, but there may be an interim during which fashions of speech appropriate to an earlier time have not adapted. I think it is in this second subdivision of the existential points of connection that the Whorfian investigation fundamentally belongs.

Now, about the methodological point of contact, there are three obvious rubrics. The first is the use of general ethnographic materials in seeking linguistic data. I will say no more about this. It is something that any linguist has to do in some kinds of problems at least. The second is the reverse of that—the use of linguistic materials in a search for cultural conclusions, historical or otherwise. In this connection, we should not lose sight of the use of linguistic time perspective in the attempt to reconstruct aboriginal history, for example, in North America. Relatively little has been done along this line, but the data are being gathered. We can push back some aspects of the aboriginal history of this continent, if we make use of the comparative method wherever and whenever it applies, and in so doing we can sort out what words are probably old words and tell from what direction they came, and so on. It is a vast and extremely fertile field, in which linguistics can make a material contribution to one range of ethnological investigation.

The third methodological interconnection is one which I always feel a little hesitant about stating, and yet I think it must be stated. There are people who believe that we have attained some rather greater degree of success in finding the rhyme and reason in that facet of human behavior called language than we have for any other facet of human life above the purely biological level. That is to say, we certainly know more about language than we do about culture as a whole—possibly more about language than we do about any other namable facet of culture. If this is true, or to the extent that it is true, the reason is very obvious. Of all the complex phenomena that make up cultural behavior, language is the easiest to get at. To the extent that it is true that we have achieved methods for the analysis of linguistic structure somewhat more coherent and more productive than many of the methods yet available for study of other phases of culture, I think it follows that we may reasonably expect to benefit by trying to extrapolate from the methods of the linguist toward methods for use on culture as a whole or on other facets of culture.

That is my outline. I would not guarantee there is a place in that outline for every specific instance you can cite, but I think it does indicate that the field is rather larger than has been suggested by any of the points that came up this week. As a matter of fact, we have not stuck closely to the Whorfian theses as I see them. We have made forays toward these other matters that I have mentioned here, and so I thought it would be a good idea to give this outline as a justification. We have said things about these other matters, and I think we should see the relations between the different kinds of connections there are.

Now, as for my paper, I tried in the first short section to define a couple of terms. Then I started with the most obvious kinds of differences between Chinese and English, some of them of the kind that you would find between any two languages, analyzed a number of examples, and listed any slightly more complicated ones that I could find, until I ran out. That is what I did. It is raw material for discussion of matters of this kind. I would make only one general point about it. I would not consider that a particular difference between Chinese and English makes a difference in the behavior pattern of the two peoples. I would say that the difference is a difference worthy of consideration in its own right.

GREENBERG: There is one question which is raised for me in the introductory section of your paper. You seem to exclude systematic semantics from language, or at least from linguistics. Those who are present now are wholeheartedly willing to include the systematic aspect of semantics in language study. Is this a question of terminology?

HOCKETT: I think so. I am in agreement with you and the rest of us here that it had better be the linguists who work on this systematic end of semantics.

SINGER: What do you call your study? Semantics? You are not being a linguist when you do this?

HOCKETT: Yes. The question was whether, in doing this, I am going beyond the linguistic analysis. I am getting into the relationships between Chinese forms and the circumstances and environment in which they occur.

LOUNSBURY: In regard to Singer's question, it might help if one of us linguists stated that linguistic methodology depends upon questions of meaning at only three points. Some would narrow this down to two points. Whether it is three, two, or one, at all these points we ask, not what is the meaning, but only: Are the meanings of two forms the same or different? When we do more than that and go into language, that is semantics. If you want to say linguistics includes both of these, since linguists do both, that is perfectly all right. Then we will need a new term for the former type of formal analysis, which at present goes under the name of linguistics.

McQuown: Getting back to this semantics argument, where does form leave off and meaning begin? I have settled this for myself with the generalization that there is nothing but form, and if you put yourself in any one part of the form and look at the rest of the stuff, the rest of the stuff is the semantics. When you look out from language to some adjacent behavioral system, and ask yourself in what co-occurrences of linguistic forms do I perceive the reflection of this adjacent behavioral system, you are in a sense doing preformal analysis of that system. If you look at it from the point of view of one of the functions of the linguistic system, you are doing the semantics as a part of the linguistic system. The whole argument is a waste of time. The only answer that you are ever going to get is one which will derive from a controlled working-out one by one of all the systems, and a careful statement, system by system, of the consonances between the individual systems. So much for the question of form and content, whatever you want to call it.

Fearing: Hockett's introductory statement raised a question in my mind. He appears to be dubious about the higher-order type of abstracting. Yet, I take it you do not feel that it should be ruled out?

Hockett: That is right.

Fearing: Then, at what point would the investigator be justified in moving from the study of declarations on moccasins to some kind of higher abstraction?

Hockett: I have no idea how one would know when the time has come. My feeling is that too many people are trying to go to the higher-order abstractions without studying the lower, or are concentrating their interest on the lower only on a pro tempore basis in order to get to the higher.

Fearing: I can understand that, and it seems to me to be sound. But what will determine what lower-order phenomena you are going to study? Do you start out assembling a lot of separate bits of observations? Would there not be a danger here that you might observe phenomena which at that level seem to you real, but which are really not significant in the higher order? I know there is no simple answer to this.

Hockett: I think the answer for most of us lies in the experience people have in doing actual ethnographic field work. They find that, no matter what problem they have in their heads in advance, they are led by what is going on.

Fearing: Does that not mean that they really have adopted, consciously or unconsciously, some higher-order abstraction as the organizing principle behind their observations? You say they are led when they go into the field.

HOCKETT: They are led by what is going on there—what the people are doing.

FEARING: But they make no distinction methodologically as to whether this which is going on is more significant than that which is going on.

HOCKETT: Obviously they do, on the basis of their own previous experience. In the case of the very simple part of linguistic analysis, we know what happens. We know that the worker goes into the field with the conviction that the language of these people has a phonemic system. We know that, when he listens to the forms in the language, he misses some distinctions between sounds and he hears some that are not in the system, because of his previous experience. Then he has a procedure, which is largely empathy, enculturation, learning to react as the people who speak this language react, by which he adjusts his perhaps very accurate hearing, in a phonetic sense, to the phonemic hearing that these people have. So far as I can see, there is no kind of ethnographic or linguistic field work which does not rely on this process.

GREENBERG: I want to return to this business of consonance. It would be very neat if this conference could agree by adopting the word "agreement." The general semanticist is always talking about differences in meaning, interpretations; there is also the opposite thing. We agree on a word, such as happens in a diplomatic conference, and everybody is happy. Then some day a border incident occurs, and each one says he is keeping the treaty and the other man in breaking it. What do we mean by consonance, or whatever you want to call it?

Kaplan's exposition this morning still left certain questions in my mind. In general, he was apparently suggesting a kind of physiognomic method, parallel to that of the physical anthropologist when he sets up rational types—types of faces and figures within a particular social group.

Now, to recognize whether something belongs to one group rather than another—to a type—you must set up the type, and for every type you must have a cluster of characteristics. Thus a given something may lack some of the characteristics but will have enough of the others so that we can assign it to the type. This is not the same thing as setting up a single diagnostic criterion. It is rather the setting-up of a cluster of characteristics which occur together with more than chance correlation. Such correlation is absolutely necessary, for, if it is lacking, you have nothing at all.

The matter of fashions of speaking still bothers me. What are these things that cut across all kinds of linguistic lines and different aspects of the language? I must confess that all the attempts made up to now to get at them have seemed to me very unsatisfactory and no more than the vaguest analogies. I think a close examination of the data in the case of the one elaborate attempt, by Whorf, to show the so-called objective differences in time as between English and Hopi, makes the whole thing evaporate on the basis of empirical facts from the languages. The instrumental nature of language is the important thing. Language is not a philosophical instrument, basically. It contains a classification—it has to, in order to deal with the universe. But the people using it are interacting in very specific ways and quite different areas. There was an eighteenth-century German philosopher and folklorist who said that language was invented by wise priests who wanted a system of symbolism in order to teach certain truths about the nature of the universe. I am afraid that in Whorf's approach there is a good deal of this wise-priest approach.

WRIGHT: It struck me that Hockett was not too happy about having to do this paper, and it struck me also that there is a great deal that one can learn on the Chinese world view from other materials. For example, the Chinese themselves have said a great deal about the relation of language to thought, language to ideas, and vice versa. I would think that in a developed civilization such as this, with a four-thousand-year-old history, it is in a sense relevant for our purpose. The case is quite different from that of the Zuni or others like them who probably have never been worried about the relation of their ideas to their medium of expression or to the possible effect of their medium of expression on their ideas. Furthermore, much Chinese literature is folkloristic and bears a very close relation to ordinary customs. A good deal of the drama, for instance, is a reflection of the vernacular of its time. All this suggests that a division of labor should continue. Hockett should go on analyzing structure, while the rest of us try to develop constructs about the world view; then, eventually, we should look for connections. Is that sensible?

HOCKETT: I reject any notion that I am trying to get a Chinese world view here. I am talking about things at a far lower level. I am talking about the explicit differences in the way in which speakers of Chinese and speakers of English are led to handle things by the nature of the semantic category they inherit from those from whom they learn the language. That is the only exception, and that is the one I am extremely skeptical about. It is true I made the statement too general. Possibly there is a connection, but I am extremely dubious about it.

On the division-of-labor business, I think that has to be allowed, not primarily along lines prescribed in terms of angle of approach, but along lines of the personal interests of the participants. That will not follow the simple dichotomy that you propose.

KAPLAN: Pursuing Greenberg's diplomatic metaphor, I would like to enter in the record a plea, which I do not expect for one moment will find acceptance, but which I will feel better for having said. I am quite sure that I speak for many people in areas like philosophy or social philosophy, and I suspect perhaps also anthropology, if I invite linguists and other persons who are very properly hardheadedly approaching these areas not to be too reluctant to enter upon investigations, and even formulate hunches, which are without adequate scientific backing. I invite this, not merely because these matters are of such considerable interest to others, but also because numbers of other people in other disciplines are necessarily confronted with these questions in the kinds of problems they are faced with. I am myself extremely suspicious of the idea, both in diplomacy and in the higher strategy of scientific enterprise, that we should first do one thing and, after we have taken care of that to our satisfaction, then go on and do this other thing. Nobody consciously and deliberately lays out programs for a lifetime even for his own personal work, to say nothing of the whole state of a science. But in so far as this conference has any impact on our individual attitudes or on those of others interested in these questions, I did want it to register that it is not so bad to let yourself go in this direction. You may be doing some others a lot of good, and, at the very least, you will be taking steps toward preventing a lot of future reworking of ground, just to correct all the misapprehensions that became crystallized and hardened because the scientific worker did not want to touch it.

HOIJER: I would like to second that as an anthropologist and as a linguist. If you have no clouds, your bread-and-butter facts may not be worth much. It would be a lucky "chance," as Greenberg is so fond of saying, if they were worth anything at all, and the chance is it will be nothing. We keep both of these objectives in mind so that they may fructify each other. I agree with Hockett when he says we must not eliminate the ordinary everyday things, but I do not think we need to wait until we have finished these before we go on to the "higher" things. If we do wait until that happens, we will never get to the higher things.

WRIGHT: I would like to underscore that from my own field. The traditional Sinologue was concerned through successive generations that every fact about China should be known and annotated. He would not generalize at all. He scarcely analyzed. He accumulated facts and, by doing this, abdicated from making sense to people who did not know anything about the field.

HOCKETT: Would it sound completely contradictory if I were to say at this point that I agree with the point that has been made? What I am saying is: let us be sure that we keep our card files enlarged and not lose sight of them in the more abstract field.

I suppose one reason that I want to emphasize keeping the card file straight is that one of the problems that confronts us is not a matter of how abstract we are going to get but the matter of trying to work linguistics in with nonlinguistics. It is precisely in this context that I think it is necessary that we do harder work at the lower levels.

KENNARD: I was speculating about the point that was made and discussed outside of the meeting by members of the group. There was a long period in anthropology of gathering data in the most minute detail, and there seems to have been a period of reaction against this. In other words, we had large quantities of data, and nobody knew what to do with the material to make it meaningful in terms of a scientific problem or an intellectual interest. There are people who are concerned solely with theoretical structure and others who are concerned more with the empirical facts.

One of the things that happens in the course of a gathering like this is that we learn, informally, a great deal about the field experience and the impressions of our fellow field workers which they do not produce in their monographs. They will say, "My impression, having lived with these people for two years, . . ." and give a whole series of anecdotes which illustrate quite well the characterization. But, in accordance with some canon of what are scientific data, they choose to leave it out of the printed material.

SINGER: I just want to qualify the interpretation Greenberg suggested. I do not believe there are many people, even among philosophers, who think of language as a consciously devised instrument of priests, or even of linguists. The sense in which I was using the notion of instrumentality is, I think, very much the same as the sense in which it has been used here: it is easier to say some things in a language than others, and harder to say some things in a language than others. That is, there is an instrumental efficacy of the language in relation to saying certain things, and, I still think, in perceiving or in thinking about certain things. I think ethnolinguistics in this sense can investigate such questions empirically, just as Lenneberg investigated which codable colors are more easily discriminated than other codable colors.

HOCKETT: I wonder whether we could not add a generalization that in the normal case it is easier to say those things which it is more often necessary to say, and harder to say those things which it is less often necessary to say. The abnormal case is the one which arises from time to time due to specific factors of culture history—for example, the case of Swedish. Sweden has become pretty thoroughly democratized; it is the kind of country in which you can approach a stranger on the street. But this happens to be very difficult, because they have inherited from the predemocratic days a highly undemocratic set of forms of personal address, by virtue of which it is very difficult to speak with normal politeness to a person until you know a great deal about his status relative to yours, and this no longer is symbolized by the clothes he wears. Therefore you have an impasse.

There are at least two examples of this kind of lag, due to specific circumstances, in English. Lounsbury reminds me that we have no proper way to address a waiter. We also do not have any appropriate form of reference for a woman who comes to clean our house for us. We call her the "cleaning lady," or something of that kind.

There is, too, the case of terms of reference to matters that are sectional in our culture. For most things that one would talk about, one can choose among numerous style levels. One can talk in an elevated style, the ordinary style we are using here, or one can talk at a very low level. When it comes to sectional matters, the vocabulary is still split. With medical terminology, you can talk up here, or you can talk down here; there is no ordinary level.

KAPLAN: I would like to ask for clarification on the orders of difference discussed in your paper. I did not quite get that. It is especially summarized in your diagram [p. 112], as zero-order, first-order, and higher-order differences.

HOCKETT: Suppose we have the word *A* in Chinese and the word *B* in English. Word *A* and word *B* cover similar, but not identical, ranges of meaning. There is a zero-order difference, because you cannot find a word in Chinese, or in any other language, that covers the same meaning as word *B*. Suppose we have words *A* and *C* in

Chinese, words *B* and *D* in English. The statement that I made first is true of *A* and *B* and is also true of *C* and *D*, and, furthermore, the difference in the semantic coverage of *A* versus *B* is the same as the difference in the semantic coverage of *C* and *D*, in some indefinable sense.

KAPLAN: What do you mean by the difference being the same in the two cases?

HOCKETT: Take the example of motion and locus. There are examples of motion in Chinese and English. In English you use almost any one of these versions of motion, not only for motion from one place to another, but also for growth, from one coverage to a larger coverage, or for static extension into the contour. None of the equivalent Chinese vocabulary of words for motion covers those same extended senses. That, it seems to me, is not the same as the difference between the English word "rise" and the Chinese word equivalent to it. It is a systematic difference in what happened in the whole array of words in English and Chinese.

KAPLAN: This seems to be of considerable interest for our own conceptualization, if I dare say so, because the problem we were discussing earlier of how to get up to this higher region would by you be answered. This is your Jacob's ladder, in other words.

Could you also give some instances of a third- or fourth-order difference? I suspect you would be saying exactly the kind of thing that Whorf says, or that you uneasily allowed yourself to say in the paragraph.

HOCKETT: The difference between a zero-order and the differences of some higher order, I think I can see. But stratifying these higher orders escapes me as yet, or even trying to say whether a particular difference should be classified as third or fourth order. Perhaps this is the Jacob's ladder, but you can see only the first rung.

KAPLAN: It seemed to me that what Hoijer was describing in Navaho belongs squarely on your ladder. I should suppose that we can now focus quite specifically on a strategy for at least one kind of research, if you or anyone else could say something about the procedures by which the student of this subject might surmount it.

HOCKETT: Get to work on a bilingual dictionary. That is how it happened to me—by working on a Chinese-English dictionary.

VOEGELIN: Another way would be to translate a text.

WRIGHT: Philologists have been doing that for years.

KAPLAN: I obviously did not express myself clearly, because that does not at all get off what I had in mind. When you make your bilingual dictionary, you are getting in the first instance your zero-order differences; we are presumably not interested in the zero-order differences except in so far as they give us a point of departure for the other.

Can some clarification be given of what it is that we are looking for? I can give a hypothetical one, not because I like this answer, but because it will specify what kind of an answer I would take to be an appropriate one. Consider what you have within a single language as given by something like Roget's thesaurus. I do not know what the actual history of that particular book is, but presumably it would be correct to say that it is, more or less, an a priori systemization. Someone has in mind a set of categories coming out of our philosophical traditions, and you fit all the words into it.

One might imagine constructing an inductive Roget. One might imagine that words are grouped together as belonging to the same semantic area in a degree of closeness which is specified by the frequency with which, when one of the words is given to a native speaker as a stimulus and he is invited to explain it by other words, the other words enter into his explanation. In this fashion one would, in principle, be building up a semantic system, a set of clusters of the semantic contents in the language, and, in fact, they are clustered by the speakers of the language.

This is one conceivable possibility of what one might be looking for in mounting from order to order. There may be a totally different way to describe it, and I invite your description.

HOCKETT: If you will agree that certain of the examples in my paper do merit classification as an order higher than zero, I would say that perhaps you are asking for a process which is not durable. What you have to do is look around until you find a range where they are higher, and formulate a hypothesis on the basis of what it may be.

GREENBERG: We have actually been doing something of this kind for a long time in certain areas of the lexicon which a priori we expect to be higher order, on the basis of what the reference is to in our own experience. We simply examine common elements which enter into the definition of a fairly large number of terms, whether they are systematically related or not.

I remember in my own paper I used the term "generic meaning" and gave an example from kinship. I said that in English there is a common specification—male—which enters into the definition of the terms "brother," "uncle," "father," "grandfather." Whereas there are many languages where this does not enter in, in the same way.

KAPLAN: Suppose you have some other terminological system which hangs together fairly well, e.g., a numeral system. Have there been, to any extent, studies for which systems themselves are the data—studies which are interested in trying to uncover, if possible, differences of the next higher order? I do not mean a study only of the kinship vocabulary or the numeral vocabulary, but of both of these, perhaps with some others, in the attempt to see what characterizes this whole set of vocabularies in one language as compared to the whole set of vocabularies in some other language. I would suppose that follows from the procedure you described.

WRIGHT: I would suppose it to be very difficult to get at the steps beyond the first order of difference. What would you envision the top order to be? I have just been dealing with European efforts to translate the Bible into vernacular and classical Chinese, and they get to the top of the ladder and go off into space. There is no conceivable equivalent, so they render the Hebrew sounds into Chinese. The Chinese then translate the Hebrew sounds into Chinese. What do you have? You have no communication, nothing.

HOCKETT: I think it is legitimate to ask what happens to orders that may be actually very high. Perhaps there are only one, two, or maybe three, rungs on the ladder, and you stop short of ever reaching any single attainment. The diversity of human behavior suggests that, so far as meanings incorporated in language are concerned, that might be true.

KAPLAN: I do not know whether it is in the sequence of orders, but I would venture to say that the answer to Wright's question is nothing other than this old friend, or enemy, the thought-world. Some of us have been trying to steer away from it, because we could not see how to provide anchorage for it.

SINGER: In the history of attempts to axiomatize branches of knowledge, we have found this kind of thing happening. This is one answer to your question of a method for determining systematic clusterings of meanings, especially if you follow a procedure, something like you suggested, of trying to find elementary units which are contained in various complex meaning units. Obviously, if you just take ordinary speech, or some texts of ordinary language, and try to analyze them in these terms, you will find it very difficult to construct an axiom system that would fit your text. On the other hand, you can introduce at a number of points a certain arbitrariness by way of the definitions, and then it is possible to get something like a systematic ordering of the terms in relation to one another. But you would obviously find that in many of those cases you have ruled out a good many of the usages that most people would think important.

Now, that has actually happened in fields like psychology. In the attempts to axiomatize the terms of psychology, and its propositions, you can say that something of a ladder has been achieved. A certain area of psychological terminology has been systematized. But I think most people, including many psychologists, would say that it has been narrowed down to such an extent, and so many definitions that are arbitrary have been introduced, that it may be regarded as a premature axiomatization.

In other words, the question of whether or not you can order a language system accurately in this way is not at all a theoretical question. Of course you can always do it. It depends in part on what your ultimate standards for an adequate systemization are and on how many shades of meaning you want to catch in your system. If you are content with a fairly narrow thing, which is very simple and restricted but may still have some reference to actual usage, you can do it.

McQuown: Whether or not Harris says so in print, or admits it to himself in his less formal moments, one of the things which he is trying to do is to create a methodology whereby one can go up the rungs of this ladder. This is precisely what I indicated in my four or five points, without making any attempt to fill in the framework because I do not know what the framework would be until it reveals itself as you investigate the materials that could occur in the language.

What you need, aside from simply assuming there is a ladder and that the ladder does have rungs, is the assurance that you are going to come out with some kind of a categorization and not simply an amplification—which is to start with a system and reduce the raw data to the system. That can be done. Or you can make a dichotomy, putting all the forms of the language in two classes, and perhaps find some correlation. There may be sixty other ways to cut the cake that have not been investigated. What you need is a method which will make it possible for you to investigate all the possible relationships that occur in the material and build them up empirically, step by step and level by level, until finally you do arrive at these general patterns. Let me hasten to add I believe in playing both ends against the middle. I think this process of going up the ladder, even if you have a good methodology, can be greatly facilitated by having some inkling of what you are looking for so that you can elicit the proper data to help you find your way up.

KAPLAN: Greenberg's particularly apt illustration of the difficulties suggests a type of investigation which appears to be promising and by no means impracticable. If you were to consider kinship system vocabularies with vocabularies of behavior quite closely related to kinship systems, for instance, other interpersonal relations, and find in various languages the distinctive patterns by which terms like "brother" are extended beyond the specific kinship meaning to particular other senses, you would have something of the adjoining step and something which could equally be extended in terms of connections that you already know from your cultural anthropology in fact exist and operate in the culture.

When I raised the question about comparisons between kinship and numeral vocabularies, Greenberg asked me, in a note, what we could expect to find in common between a mathematical vocabulary and others. That may be a perfectly good question. One could expect to find important elements of commonality between those language features that relate to closely connected aspects of the culture. This, I should think, is something both workable and promising in connection with our general interest.

HOCKETT: In connection with McQuown's point, and in the specific case of Chinese, it seems to me that although you can get a great many more zero-order and low-order differences just considering words and sentences as I have, mounting the ladder higher is probably going to depend on determining regularities of recurrences and associations over stretches of speech longer than single utterances, which would be precisely what McQuown said. I do not think you can go far upward on the ladder.

NEWMAN: One of the reasons why I started working with the relationship system in Zuni was that I began to get peculiar things about other terms referring to interpersonal relations on the general level. When I tried to elicit a term with a given English term, the informant would in most cases very quickly give me something more or less equivalent in his language. Then as I would go into it more, it would seem to me very unequivalent.

When I elicited the Zuni equivalent of "friend," for example, the informant, having defined it as the Zuni counterpart of friend, told me that one does not use it in a Zuni village except to kid somebody. If one calls someone one's friend, people will laugh. Several kin terms, similarly extended, produce the same reaction. Here we have, of course, a further definition in terms of group behavior and ethnological study.

HOCKETT: I think this indicates that even zero-order differences can be of extreme importance; that is, linguistically ascertained zero-order differences can be extremely important in cultures as a whole. Compare the meanings associated with the words "friend" and "acquaintance" in American English and in British English. Need I say more?

NINTH SESSION

THE STRATEGY OF RESEARCH IN THE INTER-RELATIONS OF LANGUAGE AND OTHER ASPECTS OF CULTURE

HOIJER: Our purpose this morning is to consider some practical proposals for testing the Whorf hypothesis or any derivations therefrom. I have asked Kennard if he would give us the benefit of his experiences with the Hopi, and let us in on any plans for research among the Hopi, along these lines, that he may have in mind.

KENNARD: In looking through the material I have available on the Hopi language, with an eye to its relevance for the Whorf hypothesis, I found data of two types. One of these suggests a confirmation of Whorf's hypothesis, or at least the possibility of such confirmation, while the other seems to be irrelevant.

The first type may be illustrated by reference to a premorpheme that means, roughly, a superlative intensity of effort. Added to a phrase "a man runs," it gives us "a man runs as fast as he can"; to the phrase "wrap a bundle," "wrap a bundle as tightly as possible"; to "think," "think hard, concentrate." All this is suggestive of non-linguistic facets of Hopi behavior—their emphasis on persistence. Whorf has made a good deal of this parallelism.

On the other hand, we find the so-called validity forms of the Hopi verb. These are modal particles, used with every verb utterance to denote speaking from inference or from hearsay or from firsthand knowledge, etc. One could speculate that, in terms of the kind of criteria which are insisted on in our legal system, this would be beautifully adapted to laws of evidence. But, in fact, it does not seem to have any connection at all with what is believed or accepted, regardless of the fact that formally these distinctions must be made.

WRIGHT: You mean that these particles are used, but do not provide any gradation of credibility?

KENNARD: If none of them is used, the man is speaking from firsthand knowledge. Wherever the knowledge of the speaker is inferred rather than firsthand, this, in general, is what is indicated by these elements. As I said, this is a formal distinction that must be made, but, because of a whole series of other factors, the responses of listeners are not to any extent affected by the presence of the degree of credibility which can be expressed by this series of elements.

KROEBER: I have been working over a Luiseño grammar and dictionary in the last couple of years. Luiseño, of course, is an Uto-Aztecan language—not too close to Hopi, not too different from it. I was interested in seeing whether I could discover any parallels to, especially, the kind of verb classes Whorf reports in Hopi. I could not, and I have come to the conclusion that, on the whole, the semantic range of most stems is fairly close to what you would get among nonliterary people in most European languages. Where the culture is simple, the total range of verbs is smaller, and the total range of meaning is narrow.

The only class of verbs in any way distinctive of Luiseño is a class of which the core meaning seems to be a vivid visual description of an action, which might be by a person or by an animal, or might be inanimate movement. From that core, there are extensions out to what you might call more specifically cultural senses. For instance, there is a word which is used in the sense of marking or striping something. It is not, as I remember, the stem for the adjective "striping"; it does not mean *to be striped.* It means *to stripe something* or, by extension, *to mark something.* Perhaps the most concrete meaning is what a deer does in fighting; in defending itself, it comes down with both feet and cuts two gashes. From that we get a number of other meanings, such as *to irrigate.* When you irrigate, you stripe the fields.

Now, when we think in terms of that meaning, we think of the use of the effect—its social function. We think of irrigating, agriculture, or leading water. But the Luiseño apparently chose to extend this verb metaphorically to irrigating, because he thought of the act of making more or less parallel ditches in the ground. It is more dynamic. He does not think of the purpose; he thinks of the act.

That tendency is exemplified again and again, and sometimes the action is conceived very vividly. For instance, there is one stem which in the intransitive is applied to a woman's dress draggling; the skirt is a little long behind, and, as a woman walks, it trails over the ground. In the transitive form the stem is used of a chicken hawk. The hawk swoops down and strikes a bird or chicken; before it can rise from the ground it flies more or less horizontally while it is gaining elevation with its new load, the struggling victim flaps about more and more, and that particular thing is denoted by the transitive form.

Of the two meanings, I think that referring to the chicken hawk preceded the reference to draggling of the dress. Aboriginally, the Luiseño wore a back and front apron, really, which did not reach the ground. The meaning of the woman's dress dragging like a train must, then, be much more recent.

There is quite a group of these verbs, and they have a certain picturesqueness and stand out. But apart from those there was nothing I could see that was in any way specially distinctive, as compared either with the European languages or possibly with the Yokuts. As against the reality or validity of Whorfian classes, the Hopi and Luiseño are sufficiently distinct that one might easily have such a class in Hopi and not have it represented in Luiseño, but at any rate I could find no corroboration in this language.

FEARING: I would be interested in knowing what problems of research design would be involved in observing along linguistic behaviors to these hypotheses regarding presumed relationships between the linguistic patterns and nonlinguistic behavior, e.g., what kind of units of behavior you would look for, under what conditions, and so on.

KENNARD: I think one of the most difficult factors in designing is that any linguistic system is a partial or selective system of reference to all other acts, processes, and events, that take place in all the other cultural systems. How much is supplied or formally referred to, and what is recreated in the world of experience by people who share a common experience and a common series of assumptions, we can formally analyze in linguistic terms. The extent to which we can do it, in terms of control over meanings and over classes of events or types of experience which can be assumed, is the problem which is the most difficult one to formulate. What has constantly cropped up in our discussions is that in the development of linguistic methodology we have, in order to delineate the elements, excluded the whole realm of meaning and function, and have limited ourselves to the occurrence and distribution of particular forms. Now we are trying to move from this side of the problem, and the question of how we are going to handle the semantic side is probably the most difficult part of our formulation.

FEARING: Just how, concretely, would you envisage setting out on this enterprise? Would you set up hypotheses, based upon linguistic analysis, that such-and-such kinds of behavior are likely to be found in the community? How would you go about testing the hypotheses in terms of observation? Let us imagine, for example, that your hypotheses assert that on the basis of linguistic analysis there is a concern with shame or guilt. We would have a problem, then, of the units of behavior, or the criteria for guilt behavior—independent of linguistic behavior.

VOEGELIN: The problem you suggest is perhaps too difficult to start with. It is probably better to begin on problems similar to that suggested by Kroeber's Luiseño examples. Here it is not difficult to see the relation between the movement along the ground of the chicken hawk and its prey and the draggling of a woman's dress. The latter meaning, made presumably when the Luiseño were first introduced to long dresses, is an understandable extension of the former.

There is much material of this sort in American Indian dictionaries. One can search out meanings which we know must be the results of acculturation and find out how the language expresses them. There are three obvious possibilities: the new meaning may be denoted by a European borrowing, by a native descriptive phrase or compound, or by extending metaphorically the meaning of a native term.

The third possibility suggests an intriguing experiment to test the Whorf hypothesis. Let Hopi speakers, for example, be presented with carefully drawn diagrams suggestive of movement and other similar concepts in physics and asked to describe these in Hopi. Would their responses follow the fashions of speaking Whorf has suggested? Or would the Hopi find other linguistic resources not predicted by Whorf?

FEARING: At a slightly more complex level you might present them with motion pictures in which a certain idea is enacted—for example, shame might be depicted in our terms—and see how they handle it.

LENNEBERG: I would like to comment on a few of the difficulties in these experimental setups. You try to get performances that can be compared, and then to find out whether or not the difference in performance is significant in general terms. Now, suppose the performances that are to be compared are those of Indians and English-speaking people, in short, speakers of one language and speakers of another. One of the greatest traps here is that you get verbal responses in two different languages, and this is all you have to compare. There is no extralinguistic check on your experiment.

This is not, I think, an insuperable difficulty; we can provide extralinguistic checks on our material. Suppose, for example, that we subject English speakers to a set of physical stimuli and record their linguistic responses. To some of these stimuli the responses are fairly uniform; to others there is greater or less variation in linguistic response as between individual speakers. Once you have these results, the experiment may be repeated with Hopi speakers, and so furnish a common base for comparing the two cultures.

WRIGHT: What is the performance? Give an example.

LENNEBERG: Well, the work on color that I spoke of earlier would be one case in point. There the stimuli are colors and, presumably, not all colors are dealt with in the same way and with the same ease in one language as in others.

LOUNSBURY: I would just like to ask Lenneberg whether he has done cross-cultural work in his color experiments, and whether he has done such cross-cultural work within our own society? For example, I feel quite sure that a woman's color vocabulary is quite a bit greater than a man's.

LENNEBERG: Yes. I have data on the sex difference, and some colors are unanimously called by girls something and by men something else. I have not tried different cultural strata in our society.

SINGER: I am a bit bothered by the trend of discussion, because it seems to me there are at least two very different kinds of uses for these experiments.

One use would serve, simply, as a kind of appendage to the linguistic analysis, that is, the discovery of what certain terms or expressions in the language mean, of what kind of situations they are used in, and of something about the language and variety of usage. But it seemed to me that, in talking about correlations and congruences, we were interested in something a little different. For example, the question asked in your color experiment—if you have terms for certain colors and not for certain others what is the effect on fineness of discrimination as between the two sets—seems to me to be a psycholinguistic problem. But the first is not, in the ordinary sense.

LENNEBERG: Precisely. You have to do in all such research two things. First, you have to do a piece of linguistic research. By "linguistic" I include, in this case, semantic. This, which has nothing to do with psychology, and has nothing to do with the congruence problem at all, is basic. It is descriptive; there is no prediction involved and no hypothesis. After you do the linguistic research, then you can try to make predictions of nonlinguistic behavior on the basis of what you know of the linguistic situation of your speakers. But you do not have your subjects speak or use the terms, because that would be somewhat of a circularity.

Obviously, whatever you do in this type of experimentation will always be on a much lower level than the Whorfian thesis. It is something like an anchoring point, if you wish, from which, if you have enough data, you eventually may, perhaps inferentially, go up to a higher, more complex situation or problem.

VOEGELIN: I think that the appendix-like sort of thing that I referred to also has bearing on the Whorfian kind of suggestions, for two reasons. First, it could test a suggestion independently arrived at by Whorf. You could see whether the verbs and the other suffixes in Hopi that Whorf says would be so good for use in modern mechanics were actually used, or whether the Hopi, rather perversely, would use others.

Second, if you did not have a Whorf hypothesis for another language, and that is the situation we find ourselves in for most languages, it might provide one. Hoijer's on Navaho looks very promising, but I do not know many that look promising.

LOUNSBURY: I have a fairly simple-minded suggestion. This has to do with a kind of psychological test of a hypothesis in which I do not believe, but on which I would be willing to be shown wrong. One of the things which I object to in the Whorfian papers is the ingenious little drawings of how the Shawnee, say, clean a gun, or something like that, which things are based simply upon etymology, faded metaphors if you will, linguistic constructions which I have supposed have a cultural significance only in the historical sense of a given place in a given time.

There is a possibility for testing this sort of thing in the Iroquoian languages. Some of the eastern Iroquoians call a horse, for example, "one rides on its back," and the western ones call it, "it pulls logs." Now, I would say that this has cultural significance only in a historical sense, and that what was important at the time that the horse was named has no importance today for conceptualization of the horse—their conceptualization of the horse is no different from ours.

Now, this would be my hypothesis. To test it, suppose we took, in the nature of a projective test, ink blots one of which would be purposely designed to suggest something pulling something like a log, provided you wanted to read that sort of thing into it, and another which would suggest, if you wanted to so read into it, someone riding on a four-footed thing. These would be as blurred and hazy, of course, as ink blots. Suppose it should turn out that speakers of Oneida and Mohawk, seeing the one of these, would respond with their word for "horse" while the others would not, but that the others, seeing the second, would respond with their word for "horse," whereas the former would not. Or suppose it did not work out perfectly, but that at least there was a statistical preponderance if you did this with a large number of speakers of the different languages. Then my hypothesis of no connection, of no life in this metaphor, would be proved wrong, and Whorf's illustrations would be justified.

FEARING: The projective techniques are extremely useful, but I am not sure that they would test your hypothesis. By the very nature of the projective stimuli, the ambiguity is such that if you put in the structuring of a stimulus too definitely, you are loading the dice to get the subject response. If you make it more ambiguous, then you give him an opportunity to react with other structurizations, and he might not perceive your horse.

SINGER: It seems to me that experiments of this kind are useful, but very limited in their relevance to the Whorfian kind of hypothesis. For one thing, most of them are extremely restricted in scope. They test a particular kind of discrimination, say, perceptual discrimination, in relation to a limited vocabulary. Obviously the Whorfian kind of hypothesis says much more than that, and I wonder whether, for experiments that are relevant, you do not have to have constructs, both on the cultural side and on the linguistic side, that are far more comprehensive and refer to more phases of the culture than do these limited experiments.

I think there was some feeling yesterday that any type of monistic characterization is just completely implausible. I wonder whether this taking some little experiment and using that as a basis for a very general hypothesis as to the relation of perception and thought to language is not the monistic type of explanation getting in by the back door. I would plead for a more direct approach to the problem, whether it be construction of the Whorfian kind of typologies of different thought-worlds or some other type of construction that at least has a rich content in relation to different cultures and different languages.

FEARING: The other type of experimental or research design in which hypotheses are derived from the linguistic structure regarding nonlinguistic patterns of behavior—these would have to be hypotheses about the way people behave in a community and the observations would have to be conducted independently by several observers—would involve setting up criteria for units of behavior. I use the word "unit" here; I mean patterns that are presumably congruent with what you predicted from a linguistic pattern, whether these kinds of behavior do or do not occur preponderantly.

There are all kinds of difficulties here, but the chief one is to circumscribe the situation in which the behavior occurs. When you say "in a community," that is very hazy and vague. It might have to be restricted a little artificially in some manner, so that the people in the culture can then behave more or less freely, and be observed.

LOUNSBURY: I can conceive of a number of kinds of relationships between linguistic and nonlinguistic cultural material. First is the case where there are linguistic phenomena which we can analyze for their semantic structure. The semantic structure we can then relate to aspects of nonlinguistic behavior. Furthermore, we can find a direct step-by-step mechanical causal relationship between the two. An example is the analysis of kinship systems in those societies which practice consanguineal marriages.

In the second case, we may not be able to find such mechanical cause-and-effect relationships, yet we can define apparent relationships, formulate them, and find statistical correlations. Sticking to kinship, there is much of that nature. Murdock's *Social Structure* (1949) takes a statistical approach.

Then there is a third case, and this is the one which Hoijer mentioned. This is where you can find neither a mechanical causal connection nor statistical correlations between linguistic behavior and nonlinguistic behavior in the sense of intercausality; rather, you are faced with this matter of congruence or consistency. Here there is a research technique, an ethnographic one whereby we concentrate upon activities in a society, describe all that goes into these activities, both linguistic and nonlinguistic, and view the two, not as somehow related or correlated in mutual cause and effect, but simply as different kinds of elements within one and the same system directed toward activities of a certain sort.

These are the three possibilities, but all of them in practice boil down to a combination of old-time philology and ethnology, and they do not look spectacular. I think this sort of thing really gets us much closer to a world view of a people than any amount of "grammaticimancy," if I may use that term.

KAPLAN: I do not mind risking being a little simple-minded with the possibility of a fairly direct approach, perhaps not immediately to the most culturally interesting aspect of the Whorf hypothesis, but connected with it.

It has been quite common in philosophy for some decades to make explicit connections between grammar, especially logical syntax, and the propositions of classical metaphysics. The kind of example that Carnap gave and that was widely discussed in the literature of the period was called "pseudo object sentences" or "pseudo object words," that is, statements that looked as if they were about the world, but which Carnap construed as being in fact grammatical statements. For instance, "A rose is a thing and not an event," he proposed should be rendered, properly speaking, "The word 'rose' is a noun and not a verb."

Now, we talked previously about the fact that an extremely important element in this whole complex of questions concerns the degree of difficulty in, rather than the possibility or impossibility of, dealing with certain subject matters. I am wondering whether one could not devise ways to get at the degree of difficulty that a speaker of a certain language would have in formulating statements which, by our hypothesis of the nature of the world view for the culture, would either be consonant or very little consonant with what is involved in the culture.

If, for instance, someone asserts with respect to the Hopi that they think of time and processes in one way rather than in another, it would not be difficult to formulate explicitly metaphysical statements purportedly about the world or the nature of time or some such thing. One would then want to see with what ease or difficulty the informant or the bilingual person could render these statements in his own language, and one of the possible measures is suggested to me by the kind of procedure that Lenneberg used in his color tests. That is, we could act on the assumption that a uniformity of linguistic rendering corresponded to a high degree of ease, relatively speaking, and that a wide range of variation in the linguistic rendering indicated some difficulty. It is an extremely plausible assumption, it seems to me.

The design would, then, be something like constructing a set of propositions which are intended to fall into two groups: (1) those which embody the kind of metaphysics that, on the basis of a Whorf hypothesis, we would expect a Plato or Aristotle of that culture to formulate, (2) the kind of metaphysics that we would expect, according to his hypothesis, that they would find very strange, implausible, unnatural, distorted, and queer; and then asking groups of speakers of the language to render those statements in their own language, for subsequent analysis. I have no idea in what sort of quantitative, or even impressionistic, way one can tell whether or not two statements in a given language are similar or dissimilar, but that at any rate focuses upon a problem which should be fairly manageable.

HOIJER: I see another difficulty, however, in that there is a certain set of habits of speaking about things in this way which is characteristic only of some cultures and of some of the people who participate in those cultures, and not of others. You would have to deal with inner variants and complexities such as the fact that our own philosophers, for example, are accustomed to making statements of this type and certain other people are not. In a simpler culture, a less large society, you might run into the situation where such statements are not customarily made by anybody, though it is not impossible that they might be made.

HOCKETT: Since we have set up possible tests of Whorf hypotheses, I think it is important to remind ourselves of the difference between a terminology and a theory. I can give a rather neat example.

There used to be in China what was called the doctrine of the "will of heaven." The will of heaven resided in the first instance in the people. If an emperor was good, it was transferred to him, but, as soon as he misbehaved, the will of heaven returned to the people, and they therefore had the right to overthrow the emperor. Now, this sounds like a theory, but, of course, it is simply terminology because there is absolutely no way one can disprove it. It is a terminology in which you can describe what does happen.

I think some of the things that Whorf has to say are not hypotheses, not theories, but are suggestions for a terminology, which he makes because he feels that a particular way of talking about things may, since we are human beings, suggest theories to us. It is not always easy to tell whether a particular set of Whorf's statements is a theory or a terminology, particularly when he speaks of the way in which a human being perhaps manipulates things inside in terms of linguistic forms—in terms, perhaps, of whole categories of linguistic forms rather than of individual morphemes. When he suggests this sort of thing, he is perhaps suggesting that we could talk about some of these matters in terms derived from language rather than in terms like "concept," "idea," and the like, and I do not think this part of what he had to say is a theory at all but a terminological suggestion. It is closely akin to terminological suggestions that Bloomfield was making so emphatically for so many years, but in both cases it is nothing more than that.

The advantage of one terminology over another can be that one terminology can be unproductive of hypotheses that are worth trying to test, whereas another one can be productive of hypotheses that are worth testing.

LENNEBERG: In reply to Singer's call for greater contextual richness, I would like to point out that, although sound psychological experiments will not be rich in context because with richness you get more variables and you finally get so many variables that you cannot control them, I do not think this is detrimental to the general theory. You can have very many delimited experiments which, taken together, will give you some corroboration. Besides, I think this, along with ethnographic data such as Lounsbury mentioned and Hoijer presented, add up to the rich context.

SINGER: I thought Kaplan's proposal was a very interesting one. The sort of thing that Charles Morris has tried, in getting capsule formulations of the seven paths of life and then trying to get cross-cultural responses to them, would be a kind of extension on that, provided you added this variable of degree of difficulty and comprehension and elaboration of any particular path. But there is one crucial difficulty that I wondered how you would get over.

The various philosophic systems have already been formulated, so that when you get your informant you have this dilemma: You want him to indicate his degree of facility of response to a formulation, but if you give him the formulation you have solved most of the problem and, if you do not give it to him, he will never guess what is in your mind.

KAPLAN: I am taking advantage of the important fact that Whorf's papers are written in English. This is why it is a question of ease and difficulty. No one wishes to say that these people cannot formulate it at all, and that, once we have formulated it, we have spoiled the effect we want to study. The point is that there is apparently some difficulty in their handling of one as compared with the other, and one might expect to see that difficulty reflected, for example, in a variability of their own linguistic grammar.

SINGER: You would get something, but I think the fact that it is already formulated is quite an achievement.

FEARING: If I understood Kaplan correctly, his criterion for difficulty was a lack of agreement in the responses, and the criterion for ease was unanimity. Well, if there is great variation, it might mean the opposite from what you imply by "difficulty." It might mean that this is a stimulus rich in its meanings.

KAPLAN: There is another device which has sometimes been spoken of in connection with the theoretical consideration of translation machines, namely, the device of convergent retranslation, or what you hope will be convergent. You start with an English sentence, have it formulated in Navaho, give that to another Navaho speaker for reformulation in English, and perhaps repeat the process, so that you are finally comparing two sentences in English. Here the assumption is quite plausible that in so far as there is ease in grasping and dealing with the idea originally incorporated, your end product should be fairly close to it; you are really getting at a succession of understandings or misunderstandings. Furthermore, you need not be confined to some measurement of closeness of end product to the starting point, but you can also explicitly focus on the kind of distortions that are introduced. If Whorf were right, you would find, in the ideal case, that the distortions by different persons in the translation of different propositions would tend to fall into a pattern.

WRIGHT: It just occurred to me that in preparation for Kaplan's study, which presumably would be a large cross-cultural thing, you would do very well to examine the recorded observations of missionaries throughout the world, in which they report naïvely, at least for China, the kind of things that they could easily accept and the kind of things they could not. This would be, not to prejudge the issue, but to focus the kind of question that you might ask.

KROEBER: It seems to me that the very first things we need if we want to test Whorf are a complete grammar of Hopi—which he did not write or, at any rate, did not publish—a reasonably full lexicon, and a body of accurately translated text. With that material in hand it would be very easy to see which of the statements are validated by the evidence of Hopi, and which are not.

GREENBERG: If possible, I would like one of the basic projects coming out of this meeting to be a full linguistic description of the Hopi language. I hope that the nonlinguists here will realize how very tenuous is our factual basis for evaluating that part of Whorf's theories which has to do specifically with Hopi.

After all, Whorf talked about two things: first, about the Hopi language and certain concurrences we could draw from it and, second, certain general implications of those. Now, of course, we are more interested in the general implications. Still, if we are here centering on the problems of what Whorf did and said, we need, in testing them, some kind of real information about the Hopi language. There are tremendous gaps on the most vital points.

For example, Whorf says that the Hopi do not say "He stayed ten days," but "He left on the eleventh day." No Hopi text is given for that. When I looked in the only source available to me, the glossary to Stephen's *Hopi Journal* (1936), which was annotated by Whorf, I found that numerals after "five" did not seem to have a distinction between cardinal and ordinal forms. Now, I submit that, until we can resolve questions of that kind, we cannot judge anything in regard to the validity of Whorf's theories in so far as they refer to Hopi. We ought to have a complete dictionary, a set of texts, and a grammar of the Hopi language.

HOIJER: While I do not want to change the course of the discussion entirely, it occurred to me that there are very interesting problems in Latin America in connection with the Whorf hypothesis. In so many instances there, we have populations speaking very different languages, who have lived closely together over a long period of time. They have to a certain extent built quite new cultures—amalgams of older and other cultures—and have in some cases exerted a good deal of influence mutually on each others' languages.

MCQUOWN: There is, of course, a large number of cases of languages side by side, of totally different linguistic stocks, subject to several levels of identical influences from above. In Middle America you can start with Toltec and go on to late Aztec, to Aztec influence exerted via Spanish, and to another level where it is straight Spanish influence. I might cite the case of the Xinca language in Guatemala, which is just about extinct. I think the poor Xincas had been kicked around by other people for at least two thousand years, and there is a whole series of layers there. The first layer, interestingly enough, is Mayan. There is very little evidence elsewhere of Mayan linguistic influence on surrounding peoples, but in this particular case there is, so they must have been accepted from the start, and then the subsequent layers are as I have already indicated.

So there are many situations where you could set up a neat problem and attempt to find out the relative influence of the individual linguistic cultures, one on the other, the limiting influences that they exerted, the cultural pressures which overcame them in certain instances, etc.

VOEGELIN: It is remarkable how little change there is between classical Nahuatl and modern Nahuatl so far as the morphemes are concerned. This is the difficulty with the New World languages. Though we do have a time span of a few centuries, there has been no convincing evidence yet that anything happened structurally during this time, and the only thing that remains is to see the differential rate of borrowing in vocabulary and so on.

On the cultural side of Latin America, wherever Spanish influence has hit and despite diversity of native cultures to begin with, the end result has been relatively homogeneous. I do not think you would say the same for North America, and I do not know what you would get in the way of acculturational vocabulary for Latin America.

WRIGHT: I find Indonesian extremely fascinating because it represents an effort to build a modern language by consciously borrowing from a number—I believe it is about five—of existing modern languages, European and otherwise. The building-up of a vocabulary sort of looseleaf style is done by a government commission sitting in a city with an elaborate card file and a certain criterion of frequency. A certain number of frequencies of occurrence permits its temporary filing there, and after it has occurred a few more times it becomes a part of the new Indonesian language. It seems to me that you could have a sort of midwife on a world view here, if somebody examined the kind of borrowings that were being made and tried to find out the basis on which they are made.

ROBERTS: I wonder if we could speculate a little about the kind of collaboration or co-ordination, between people who are doing work in Navaho linguistics and those doing work in Navaho culture, that might shed some light on our mutual interests. For example, we have a series of studies: one of them in Navaho folklore, which is themal in character, one in Navaho music, and another one in Navaho art. It is quite possible that we can achieve co-ordination; it would be a shame not to if there were a fairly obvious way of doing it, maybe no more than the phrasing of some preliminary hypotheses for Navaho and asking people to speculate about them.

HOIJER: I agree with you. We have probably more hope of getting early conclusions in respect to this than any other case, because we have so much material already, and so much is being done. The grammatical material is very complete and will, I hope, be soon written up, and your studies, if I understand you correctly, are rapidly approaching completion.

HOCKETT: Now we are down to cases. We have talked about Hopi, and we have talked about the possibility of similar investigations in the case of Navaho. Why can we not look for a number of cases where perhaps we are reasonably close to the point of being able to work on the whole hypothesis? The Menomini grammar of Leonard Bloomfield is not ready for printing, but last summer I managed to do about 40 per cent of the editing, and in another summer I think I could finish it. I do not happen to know whether ethnographers feel that we have satisfactory information on other aspects of Menomini life, but there is one case where perhaps we are reasonably close to being able to do this. Are there not some others?

HOIJER: Let us go around the table and see what we do have. We will start with Lounsbury and his Iroquois work. That is rapidly approaching completion, too, I think.

LOUNSBURY: Only on Oneida, a language which was documented in Wisconsin where the culture has changed so much. The Oneida do not participate in the typical Iroquois culture today, and the material on the other languages, of New York and Ontario Iroquois, is much less complete.

HOIJER: However, while this is in some respects a serious limitation, it is not wholly so. Many of us are accustomed, I think, as anthropologists, to think that if American Indians no longer participate in the aboriginal culture, we cannot do any culturological studies. Of course, this is not true, as we realize immediately we have said it. The Navaho certainly are not in the aboriginal period, but it is a very live culture and a very live language.

I do not know whether your group in Wisconsin is large enough to be said to constitute or to possess a culture which is distinctive from that of the Americans who live around it, but, if it is, we still can get the kind of data we would need. As a matter of fact, we have better data than the older data on Iroquois, because the latter might not be so pertinent to the case as the present-day cultural activities of the people.

LOUNSBURY: Let me put it this way: The sort of material which is most easy to handle, e.g., texts and so on, is less abundant for Oneida because they lack the wealth of religious ceremonial, political ceremonial, and mythology which is so abundant for the other Iroquois languages, but it will take a little time before an equal amount of linguistic analysis has been done for the other languages.

TAX: Have you speculated on whether there are any linguistic similarities that cover all American Indian languages as opposed to, say, European languages, which correspond to American Indian cultural similarities as opposed to European cultural similarities? Of course, one could refine this down—Middle American versus North American Indians. I think I could point to some broad cultural similarities that differentiate the North American from the Middle American Indians, and I wondered whether one could say the same thing about the language.

Is the language presumed to change together with the cultural changes that go on? What I am asking is whether, in these broader areal and historical and geographic contexts, one could find limitations on the possibility of cultural and linguistic relationships that one could not find if one stuck simply to the one-to-one relations between a particular language and a particular culture.

HOIJER: I think the question of working out typologies, for lack of a better word, of thought-worlds among American Indians or any other groups, and noting certain broad similarities between these that might help to account for the kind of broad cultural similarities that we note in these same areas, is still beyond our capabilities. There do not seem to be any characteristic features of structure which sweep through the entire range of American Indian languages. There are certainly areal features, quite apart from historical relationships of the genetic sort, which might well be isolated, although this is, of course, a problem of a different order.

GREENBERG: There must be a fair number of independent historically unrelated language families in Africa. What is more, one large family, the Hamito-Semitic, is spoken both in the Near East and in Negro Africa, so there is an overlapping even in the language family. Nevertheless, there are certain features, not universally distributed usually, but very widespread, which commonly occur in Africa and do not occur in the Near East, and vice versa. Most of these are semantic details and presumably are the result of very long contact from language to language—the perfect analogues of diffusion which create logical cultural languages. For example, very commonly in Africa, comparison is expressed by a verb meaning "to surpass." To say, "I am larger than you," you also say, "I surpass you in size." The word for "meat" is practically always equated with the word for "animal."

It strikes me that such phenomena characterize areas just as legitimately as the other cultural traits used by ethnologists in setting up cultural areas, but a distinct question is whether such things are causally related in any way with the other features. After all, you might characterize an area as containing moccasins and practicing certain religious ceremonies. That does not mean that they are causally related but only that because the same peoples were constantly in contact, they began to share all kinds of things.

HOCKETT: I took Tax's question to mean still a third thing. Suppose that you manage to get some reasonable formulation of the over-all contours of Menomini life, including practices and language. This, then, is a statement about the Menomini as they are now; or one could interpret the historical records to say how they were in historical times. If we find certain incongruities in the Menomini pattern, that is perhaps a clear indication that certain things are relatively more recent intrusions from some other group than others. If we find certain contours, maybe that has to be hooked up, historically, with the fact that they were at a certain time borrowing certain kinds of words, and other practices, from the Ojibwa. Submitting data to the process of historical analysis will cause the larger contours to emerge.

HOIJER: The time has come to close our discussions. I shall not attempt the difficult task of summarizing our agreements and disagreements. It is clear, however, that all of us have learned a great deal of the problems involved in the Whorf hypothesis and of the difficulties we face in stating these problems and in finding means of solving them. One of these difficulties has been in evidence from the very beginning of our conference: the fact that we must talk about questions involving language in a particular language. If it is true that a language predetermines for its speakers certain modes of observation and interpretation, we are required as a first step to seek some means of breaking through this barrier.

That means, according to Whorf, may be found in contrastive linguistic research, that is, in the process of comparing languages so remote in historical background and cultural setting as to force awareness of our own linguistic and cultural biases. The recognition of these biases does not of course remove them, but it may provide a useful check on both our observations and our interpretations.

REFERENCES CITED IN THE DISCUSSIONS

HARRIS, ZELLIG S.

1951 *Methods in Structural Linguistics*. Chicago, University of Chicago Press.

1952*a* "Discourse Analysis," *Language* **28**:1–30.

1952*b* "Discourse Analysis (A Sample Text)," *Language* **28**:474–94.

HAVIGHURST, ROBERT

Ms. Memorandum on the "Belief in Immanent Justice and Animism among Indian Children of the Southwest and Sioux." Chicago, Committee on Human Development, University of Chicago.

KÖHLER, W.

1937 "Psychological Remarks on Some Questions of Anthropology," *American Journal of Psychology* **50**:271–88.

[LÉVY-BRUHL, LUCIEN]

1949 *Les Carnets de Lucien Lévy-Bruhl*. With a Preface by MAURICE LEENHARDT. ("Bibliothèque de Philosophie Contemporaine.") Paris, Presses Universitaires de France.

MURDOCK, GEORGE PETER

1949 *Social Structure*. New York, Macmillan.

REDFIELD, ROBERT

1953 *The Primitive World and Its Transformations*. Ithaca, Cornell University Press.

SPITZ, R. A.

1946 "The Smiling Response: A Contribution to the Ontogenesis of Social Relations," *Genetic Psychology Monographs* **35**:57–125.

STEPHEN, A. M.

1936 *Hopi Journal*, ed. E. C. PARSONS. New York, Columbia University Press.

WERNER, HEINZ

1948 *Comparative Psychology of Mental Development*. Chicago, Follett.

WHORF, BENJAMIN L.

1952 *Collected Papers on Metalinguistics*. Washington, D.C., Department of State, Foreign Service Institute.

INDEX

INDEX